I0819971

Addison and Europe / Addison et l'Europe

DIE AUFKLÄRUNG IN DER ROMANIA

LUMIÈRES – ILUSTRACIÓN – ILLUMINISMO

Herausgegeben von Klaus-Dieter Ertler

BAND 15

Claire Boulard Jouslin / Klaus-Dieter Ertler (eds.)

Addison and Europe / Addison et l'Europe

PETER LANG

Bibliographic Information published by the Deutsche Nationalbibliothek
The Deutsche Nationalbibliothek lists this publication in the Deutsche Nationalbibliografie; detailed bibliographic data is available in the internet at http://dnb.d-nb.de.

Library of Congress Cataloging-in-Publication Data
A CIP catalog record for this book has been applied for at the Library of Congress.

Printed with the financial support of the University of Paris III – Sorbonne and of the University of Graz. This publication has received financial support from Pr. Anne Marie Miller's grant from the Institut Universitaire de France and from Crea XVIII, Université Sorbonne Nouvelle Paris 3's research group.

Printed by CPI books GmbH, Leck

ISSN 1869-599X
ISBN 978-3-631-81359-1 (Print)
E-ISBN 978-3-631-82010-0 (E-PDF)
E-ISBN 978-3-631-82011-7 (EPUB)
E-ISBN 978-3-631-82012-4 (MOBI)
DOI 10.3726/b17415

Peter Lang – Berlin · Bern · Bruxelles ·
New York · Oxford · Warszawa · Wien

This publication has been peer reviewed.

www.peterlang.com

Acknowledgements / Remerciements

It is our pleasure to acknowledge that this volume has received the financial support of the University of Graz, of the Institut Universitaire de France and of Université Sorbonne-Nouvelle Paris III's research lab Crea XVIII. We are particularly indebted to Pr. Isabelle Bour who heads Crea XVIII and to Pr. Anne-Marie Miller Blaise who generously shared part of her IUF grant to fund this project. We would also like to thank Dr. Tiffane Levick and Anne Tartanson for proofreading some of the articles published in English or French.

La publication de ce volume n'aurait pu se faire sans la contribution financière de l'Université de Graz, du groupe de recherche CREA XVIII de l'université Sorbonne Nouvelle-Paris 3 et de l'Institut Universitaire de France. Que soient ici remerciées les Pr. Isabelle Bour, directrice du CREA XVIII et Anne Marie Miller-Blaise qui a généreusement partager sa bourse d'IUF pour ce projet.

Nous souhaitons enfin remercier Dr. Tiffane Levick et Anne Tartanson pour leurs relectures vigilantes de certains des articles publiés en anglais ou en français.

Contents

List of Contributors

Amélie Junqua
Université de Picardie Jules Verne, Amiens

Endre Szécsényi
University of Aberdeen

Dan Poston
University of Tübingen

Paul Davis
University College London

Klaus-Dieter Ertler
University of Graz

María José Rodríguez Sánchez de León
University of Salamanca

Klara Leszczynska
University of Warsaw

Carmen García Cela
Université de Salamanque

Claire Boulard-Jouslin
University Paris 3 – Sorbonne Nouvelle

Introduction

French readers perusing the June issue of the monthly magazine *Le Nouveau Mercure* in 1719 were informed that "Joseph Addison, the English Secretary of State had passed away yesterday, June 28th, 1719".[1] This announcement, which reminds the readers that 2019 is the tercentenary of Addison's death, is somewhat puzzling to the scholars who have long been taught that Joseph Addison (1672–1719) was one of the few English men of letters to be famous across the Channel in the early eighteenth century.[2] Such a bare piece of news, which highlights Addison's political career and ignores his literary achievement, suggests that Addison's literary reputation was rather parochial and considered negligible by the French intellectual elite. But was it really the case on the continent?

Le Nouveau Mercure's short notice is misleading for several reasons. Firstly, in a periodical whose readership was well-off and well-born, and which devoted a regular section to the English political news and to the carnet mondain, the announcement of Addison's death is confirmation that he was considered a great political figure in France.

Secondly, despite the silence over his literary contribution, the writers and the readers of *Le Nouveau Mercure* were far from being ignorant of Addison's literary career. In 1715, the March issue of the *Nouveau Mercure Galant*[3] had compared at length Addison's tragedy *Cato* with Michel Deschamps's imitation *Caton d'Utique*.[4] It argued that the French play was superior to the original because it respected classical rules of tragedy better than Addison's. The *Nouveau Mercure Galant* thus contradicted the praise that Abel Boyer had lavished in the preface

---

1 "Joseph Addison, ci-devant Sécrétaire d'Etat mourut hier 28". *Le Nouveau Mercure* (Juin 1719), 200. In fact, Addison died on 17 June.

2 Gabriel Bonno, "La Culture et la civilisation britanniques devant l'opinion française de la paix d'Utrecht aux Lettres Philosophiques (1713–1734)". *Transactions of the American Philosophical Society* 38, 1 (1948), 63.

3 *Le Nouveau Mercure* (launched by Buchet in Paris, 1717) was the continuation of *Le Nouveau Mercure Galant* (issued in Paris between 1714 and 1716). Both were continuations of *Le Mercure Galant* (Paris 1670–1714).

4 "Parallèle de deux tragédies nouvelles dont la mort de Caton est le sujet". *Le Nouveau Mercure Galant* (Mars 1715), 62–127.

to his 1713 translation of *Cato* into French.[5] It also launched a controversy over Addison's dramatic merits and the English incapacity to write perfect tragedies, a 'querelle' that was to be prolonged well into the eighteenth century.[6]

Finally, the very short notice and the absence of any obituary might also be a sign of the *Nouveau Mercure*'s chauvinistic bias and subtle revenge upon Addison who had attacked the *Mercure Galant* in *The Spectator*, describing it as the best example of the superficial French modern taste for acrostiches and 'bout rimez'.[7]

In some respect, this anecdote epitomizes the complex relationship Joseph Addison had with the French nation and, as this book aims to show, with some other European countries both in his lifetime and after his death. Indeed, his entire work reflects a critical attitude towards such continental practices as Catholicism and absolutism, which in turn solicited accusations that he was both chauvinistic and openly anti-Catholic.[8]

His childhood and youth may explain some of his opinions. Born in 1672 in a climate of strong anti-Catholicism in England,[9] Addison reached his teenage years when the Edict de Nantes (1685) was repealed, opening an era of anti-Protestant persecution in France as well as fuelling the simmering English hostility to Catholic France. He matriculated at Queen's college in 1687, when the University of Oxford was subject to King James II's romanizing policies. After the Glorious Revolution, he made his Williamite sympathies clear by publishing several Latin poems ('Tityrus et Mopse' [1689]; 'Gratulatio' [1690], 'Pax Gullielmi'

---

5 *Caton. Tragédie par M. Addison*, traduite de l'Anglais par M. Abel Boyer. Amsterdam: Tonson 1713. Abel Boyer chose to translate Addison's *Cato* into French to show the French-reading public that the English excelled in the noblest poetical genre, namely tragedy. *Cf.* "Préface du traducteur".

6 Bonno 1948, 64.

7 *Spectator* no. 60. Ed. Donald F. Bond. Oxford: Clarendon Press 1965, vol. 1, 257. All references to *The Spectator* are from this edition.

8 His *Remarks on Several Parts of Italy* (London: Jacob Tonson 1705) was listed among the forbidden books in the Index by the Vatican in 1729. Several eighteenth-century French biographical dictionaries remark that Addison often made unfair and demeaning comments on French politicians and writers in order to please his English audience. *Cf.* Louis Mayeul Chaudon: *Nouveau Dictionnaire Historique*. Caen: Le Roy 1789, vol. 1, 46. – François-Xavier de Feller: *Dictionnaire historique, ou histoire abrégée de tous les hommes qui se sont fait un nom par le génie*. Augsbourg: Rieger 1781–1784, vol. 1, 36.

9 *Cf.* Peter Smithers: *The Life of Joseph Addison*. Oxford: Clarendon Press 1954. Sur le contexte, *cf.* Tim Harris: *Restoration: Charles II and his Kingdoms, 1660–1685*. London: Penguin 2005. – *Revolution. The great Crisis of the British Monarchy, 1685–1720*. London: Penguin 2006.

[1697]) in which he celebrated William III's victories in Ireland and on the continent over France and over the supporters of the Stuart and Jacobite cause.[10] One may, therefore, legitimately raise the question: Why celebrate Addison by addressing his ambiguous relationship to the continent?

A first answer would be that eighteenth-century Britain was not more isolated from the rest of Europe than today's Brexit Britain. Addison's training as a writer and a politician included many different sorts of contact with continental ideas and aesthetics. His political and religious beliefs and his style of writing were somehow shaped by his classical and modern readings at the Charter House, at Oxford and elsewhere. The sales catalogue of his library shows that the proportion of modern foreign books—especially French fiction, literary criticism and philosophy, although one finds a few Italian and Spanish books in translation—is as high as books by the Ancients. On his shelves, Fontenelle, Pascal, Boileau, Tasso and Guarini shoulder Motteux's translation of the *Quixote*, Paterculus, Cicero and Horace.[11] Such readings could only exercise some influence on his own production. Moreover, Addison completed the Grand Tour in his late 20s and travelled through Holland, France, Italy, Switzerland, Austria and the German states. In those countries, he observed the moors and habits of the people and drew subjects of inspiration from the different economic, religious and political systems. And he translated his observations into his poetry as well as in his various prose writings. We learn through Smither's biography of Addison that he made a number of connections during his travels. He met such distinguished minds as the philosopher Malebranche and the poet Boileau in Paris and Jean Alphonse Turettini, the learned Rector of Geneva's College.[12] Bayle in Holland and Leibniz were also among his network of correspondents. In 1717, his secretaryship for the southern countries further led him to sharpen his knowledge of the countries with which he was to be in diplomatic contact. And he naturally had professional and personal contacts with the French, Portuguese and Spanish ambassadors. We may thus ask how such continental contacts shaped Addison's writings.

---

10 Read also his pamphlet, *The Present State of the War*. London: J. Morphew 1708.

11 *A Catalogue of the valuable Library of the late celebrated Right Honorable Joseph Addison*, sold by Leigh and Sotheby's, London 1799.

12 Addison met and corresponded with Jean Alphonse Turettini and not Samuel Turettini as is erroneously asserted by Smithers 1954, 74. *Cf.* also Karl Brunner: "Joseph Addisons umfassende Interessen". *Anglistische Studien: Festschrift zum 70. Geburstag von Professor Friedrich Wild*. Ed. Karl Brunner/Herbert Koziol/Siegfried Korninger. Wien: Braumüller 1958, 14–26.

To this day, scholarly studies regarding Addison's relationship to the European continent are both scarce and narrow. Quite predictably, early attention has been paid to assess the impact of a classical education on his works and to see how good a classicist he was.[13] The way he digested Ovid, Virgil and Homer's verses in his poetry and his tragedy *Cato* was also focused on.[14] Next, Addison's relationship to France has also triggered some scrutiny. The influences exercised by Molière,[15] Pascal,[16] La Bruyère,[17] Boileau,[18] the French critic Le Bossu[19] as well as Descartes and Malebranche's philosophies[20] have led to several publications. By contrast, research on the way Addison was influenced by the literature and philosophy of modern Italy,[21] Spain,[22] Holland or Germany is quite limited.

---

13 On his mastery of the Latin language, read Thomas B. Macaulay's famous essay on Addison in the *Edinburgh Review* (July 1843), 192. – Lilian D. Bloom: "Addison as Translator: a Problem in Neo-classical Scholarship". *Studies in Philology* 46, 1 (1949), 31–53. – Estelle Haan: *Vergilius Redivivus: Studies in Joseph Addison's Latin Poetry*. Philadelphia: Transactions of the American Philosophical Society 2005. James William Johnson devotes a few pages to Addison's knowledge of the Greek language and culture in his *The Formation of English Neo-Classical Thought*. Princeton: Princeton University Press 1967.

14 As is testified by Charles A. Knight's bibliographical work: *Joseph Addison and Richard Steele, a Reference Guide*. New York: G.K. Hall & Co. 1994.

15 Kathryn E. Wheatley: "Addison's portrait of the neoclassical critic". *The Review of English Studies* 1, 3 (July 1950), 245–247.

16 Ralph Arthur Nablow: "Addison's indebtedness to Pascal in *Spectator*, no. 420". *Studies on Voltaire and the Eighteenth Century* 217 (1983), 183–185.

17 Edward Chauncey Baldwin: "La Bruyère's Influence upon Addison". *PMLA* 19, 4 (1904), 479–495. – Margaret Turner: "The influence of La Bruyère on the *Tatler* and the *Spectator*". *Modern Language Review* 48, 1 (1953), 10–16.

18 Robert L. Montgomery: "Addison and the 'Helps and Ornaments of art' ". *Criticism* 25, 4 (1983), 329–346. – *Cf.* also Alexandre Maurocordato's *La Critique classique en Angleterre de la Restauration à la mort de Joseph Addison: Essai de définition* (*Etudes Anglaises* 18). Paris: Didier 1964.

19 *Cf.* Hugh Thomas Swedenberg: *The Theory of the Epic in England 1650–1800*. Oakland: University of California Press 1944.

20 Hiblert H. Campbell: "Addison's Cartesian' Passage and Nicolas Malebranche". *Philological Quarterly* 46, 3 (1967), 408–412.

21 Richard Thomas: "Trajano Boccalini's influence upon English Literature". *Aberystwyth Studies* 3 (1922), 73–102.

22 To my knowledge, no study on Addison and Spain has been published between W. X. Hendrix: "Quevedo, Guevara, Le Sage, and the *Tatler*". *Modern Philology* 19, 2 (1921), 171–186, and Juan Antonio Garrido Ardila: *The Cervantean Heritage: Reception and*

However, one might suggest that the small number of studies related to Europe's influence on Addison's works is also the result of Addison's own strategy. His bashfulness, his dead-pan humour, his nationalism, his endeavours to define the genre of the moral and literary essay into an intrinsically natural English genre whose elegance and literary superiority, he proclaimed, made it necessary to hide some forms of foreign influence and draw the readers' attention elsewhere. It seems he was successful in this venture since the idea that Addison's style was the epitome of the natural English style and that Addison was the quintessence of Englishness prevailed both in England and in Europe.[23]

One of the aims of this study is therefore to sketch a more balanced portrait of Addison, and to further explore the idea that the English Enlightenment, of which Addison was one distinguished representative, cannot be separated from continental trends. This volume is to help assessing the part played by the various European cultures in Addison's writings and to uncover the way they were used to shape an emerging Englishness and some English patriotic discourse.[24]

Four of the studies included in the present volume give the readers a glimpse of some of the ways Addison was indebted to the European continent and how he interacted with his various contacts there. In her chapter titled "A moment in Amsterdam", Amélie Junqua describes how Addison, still a young man and a budding author, spent his days at the center of the European book trade. It seems Addison made the most of his stay in the Netherlands to acquire new books and to help his London editor, the famous and powerful Jacob Tonson, complete a luxury edition of *Caesar's Commentaries*. Amélie Junqua shows in particular how the book—the result of European collaboration and skills—was puffed up by Addison as the fruit of English intellect and work. Amélie Junqua highlights how Addison reappropriated the book by silencing the help and the debt he owed the European network he had used.

Influence of Cervantes in Britain. London: Modern Humanities Research Association et al. 2009.

23 Read Samuel Johnson's essay on Addison in his *Life of the Most Eminent English Poets* (London: C. Bathurst et al. 1779–1781) and Hugh Blair's *Lectures on Rhetoric and Belles Lettres* (London: A. Strahan et al. 1787) in England. In 1841, in his preface to his schoolbook, *Lectures anglaises cours supérieur Choix de morceaux en prose et en vers extraits des œuvres d'Addison, de Pope...* (Paris: C. Hingray 1841), M. Corréard, professor at the college Charlemagne in Paris explained that Addison's prose writing was so pure that it was the model to be followed when one wished to study English.

24 On the general emergence of Englishness in this period, read the seminal book by Linda Colley: *Britons, Forging the Nation. 1707–1837*. London: Pimlico 1992.

It is another—unexpected and somewhat ironical—debt for someone who was often very harsh on the Congregation of Jesus that Endre Szécsényi brings to light in his article titled "The Jesuit thread in Joseph Addison's aesthetics". Endre Szécsényi's analysis shows that Addison had performed a close reading of the texts published by the two Jesuit fathers, the Frenchman Dominique Bouhours and the Spaniard, Baltazar Gracián. Their philosophy, he argues, was central to Addison's aesthetic theory which he developed in his *Spectator* essays on the Pleasures of the imagination. Addison, he shows, did not only translate and adapt some passages from both authors but he also transferred such notion as the "je ne sais quoi", which Bouhours and Gracián equated with divine grace, from the religious realm to the realm of aesthetic experience. Addison thus created a new transcendental aesthetics whose foundation as well as expression was much inspired by the Jesuit thinkers. Such a study, therefore, enables us to question the nature of Addison's hostility and fascination he held towards the Jesuits, whom he dubbed as traitors to the English nation.[25] It also helps us understand how Addison appropriated a Catholic aesthetics to transform it into an apologetical aesthetics, which became highly popular across eighteenth-century Europe because it transcended religious conflicts.

Dan Poston and Paul Davis for their part revise the portrait of Addison the classicist and the lover of Italian Antiquity. They analyse the mixed and complex feelings Addison expressed towards modern Italy and ancient culture in his epistolary poem "A Letter from Italy", which he wrote while crossing the Alps. In his article "Still on classic ground: Joseph Addison's Italy", Dan Poston explores the poem's ambivalence, showing that while he depicted the modern Italian sceneries in a style and with images borrowed from Virgil's *Georgics*, Addison subtly undermined these Italian beauties to suggest that they were mere illusions. Dan Poston argues that the neo-classical frame of the poem serves as a reminder that classical beauties are shadows of the past which only highlight the solid attraction and the superiority of modern English liberties and of newtonianism over papism and absolutism. Dan Poston thus concurs with Paul Davis who denies Horace Walpole's ironical comment that the poem was the result of a travel through the poets and not through Italy. In his study, "Misguided by a tuneful throng", Paul Davis claims that far from being the source of inspiration for his

25 *Cf. Remarks Upon Several Parts of Italy in the Years 1701, 1702, 1703,* 144 et 473. On Addison's anti-Catholicism, read also Claire Boulard Jouslin's article "Addison, Anti-Catholicism and Politeness". In: *Anti-Catholicism in Britain and Ireland since the Reformation: Practices, Representations and Ideas.* Ed. Claire Gheereart-Grafeuille and Géraldine Vaughan. London: Palgrave, forthcoming.

neo-classical poem, his journey to Italy was the event that prompted his farewell to poetic writing. Paul Davis thus shows that Addison was acutely aware of the discrepancy between the landscapes that had been sung by the Latin poets—in particular the banks of the various Italian rivers—and what he actually observed. Paul Davis concludes that the poem epitomizes the denunciation and the rejection of poetic illusion which Addison defined as a slavish lie; and it proclaims his preference for modern and political Britishness which Addison considered as synonymous with truth. Paul Davis finally points out that the melancholy of the poem proves the choice to be a painful one to the poet since it means to renounce the comfortable shelter of dreamed Italy and of poetic illusion when faced with the harsh contemporary reality. These two studies, therefore, highlight the fact that the trip to Italy was a turning point in Addison's career—Paul Davis calls it 'the crossing of the Rubicon'—for it paved the way to his political engagement on the one hand and on the other hand, it enabled him to find his best literary voice: prose writing celebrating British modernity.

Last of these four studies, Klaus-Dieter Ertler's "Addison, reader of Bayle" illustrates how Addison digested parts of new books and modern fiction to write his *Spectator* essays and to instruct his readers. In this case, drawing from Smithers's observation that Addison was often seen working with Bayle's *Dictionnaire historique et critique* (1697) on his table, Klaus-Dieter Ertler patiently identified a high number of short fictions originally published in Bayle's dictionary and adapted or rewritten by Addison in some of the *Spectator* essays. As a result, Klaus-Dieter Ertler highlights the formal porosity and proximity existing between the genres of the encyclopedic entry and of the essay periodical as well as the intellectual links that united Bayle and Addison. He also emphasises Addison's ability to make encyclopedic knowledge a form of entertainment.

Klaus-Dieter Ertler's article brings Addison's Grand Tour to an end—Addison considered visiting Bayle in Holland before returning to England—and closes this first part about Europe's influence over Addison. It also opens the second great chapter of this volume seeking to measure the scope of Addison's legacy in Europe. For Klaus-Dieter Ertler's analysis of the migration of Bayle's short fictions from the *Dictionnaire* to the *Spectator* and finally to the highly popular French translation of the *Spectator*, *Le Spectateur ou le Socrate moderne* (1714–1726), proves that Addison was far from being a mere borrower. His rewriting, his fictional and didactic techniques turned his essays into a literary model which was widely circulated across Europe. Klaus-Dieter Ertler brings here some further evidence that it would be nonsensical to celebrate the tercentenary of Addison's death without paying attention to the European impact of his prose writing and more specifically of his spectatorial essays. Thus, his study confirms that examining continental essay periodicals is also a roundabout way of assessing Addison's influence in Europe and of paying tribute to the English writer.

Indeed, today's historiography shows that the link between the *Spectator* and Europe is actively scrutinized. At the forefront of this research is the University of Graz's database project whose aim is to identify and to transcribe all the translations, imitations and adaptations of the *Spectator* in Europe.[26] The database has already records of a significant network of French, Spanish, Portuguese and Italian periodicals and provides free access to useful material to scholars. It completes the pioneering studies by Walter Oberkampf,[27] Wolfgang Martens,[28] Fritz Rau on the German and European *Spectators*,[29] and those by Jean Sgard, Alain Gilot and Alexis Lévrier on the French *Spectators*,[30] which had already triggered new research in such countries as Spain or Italy. All of this research thus provides an invaluable map of the geographical, linguistic as well as literary

26 The project is headed by Klaus-Dieter Ertler from the University of Graz and is accessible with the following link: *Moralische Wochenschriften-GAMS*, <http://gams.uni-graz.at/archive/get/context:mws/sdef:Context/get?locale=fr>.

27 Walter Oberkampf: *Die zeitungskundliche Bedeutung der moralischen Wochenschriften. Ihr Wesen und ihre Bedeutung*. Dresden: Risse-Verlag 1934.

28 Wolfgang Martens: *Die Botschaft der Tugend. Die Aufklärung im Spiegel der deutschen Moralischen Wochenschriften*. Stuttgart: Metzler 1968.

29 Fritz Rau: *Zur Verbreitung and Nachahmung des* Tatler *und* Spectator. Heidelberg: Carl Winter 1980.

30 Alexis Lévrier: *Les Journaux de Marivaux et le monde des "spectateurs"*. Paris: Presses Universitaires de Paris Sorbonne 2007. Read as well Stephen Botein/J. R. Censor/H. Ritvo: "The Periodical Press in Eighteenth-Century English and French Society. A Cross-Cultural Approach". *Comparative Studies in Society and History* 32, 1 (1981), 464-490. - Alain Gilot: "Le journaliste masqué; personnages et formes personnelles". In: *Le Journalisme d'Ancien Régime*. Ed. Pierre Retat. Lyon: Presses universitaires de Lyon 1982. – Claire Boulard: "The *Spectator*'s curtailed legacy": The influences of the French and the English eighteenth-century presses on each other ». In: *Better in France? The Circulation of Ideas across the Channel in the Eighteenth Century*. Ed. Frédéric Ogée. Lewisburg, PA: Bucknell University Press 2000. – Klaus-Dieter Ertler/Alexis Lévrier/Michaela Fischer (eds.): *Regards sur les spectateurs, Periodical Essay, Feuilles volantes, Moralische Wochenschriften, Fogli moralistici, Prensa moral*. Frankfurt am Main: Peter Lang 2012. – Klaus-Dieter Ertler: "Le système narratif des 'spectateurs' et leur réception en Espagne: quelques vecteurs discursifs dans le *Pensador* de José Clavijo y Fajardo". *El Argonauta español: Pratiques journalistiques aux premiers temps de la presse espagnole (XVIIIe-début du XIXe siècles)* 11 (2014). – <https://journals.openedition.org/argonauta/2002>. – Maud Le Guellec: *Presse et culture dans l'Espagne des Lumières*. Madrid: Casa Velázquez 2016.

influence of the journal. In its way, the second part of this volume constitutes a modest attempt to the understanding of this large European spectatorial and Addisonian jigsaw.

Starting with Spain, María Rodríguez Sánchez de León reminds the readers that although Addison's aesthetic theory outlined in the essays on the pleasures of the imagination first reached Spain through the French translation *Le Spectateur ou le Socrate moderne*, it became popular only in the early nineteenth century, once Munarriz, the famous translator and Member of the Royal Academy of the Fine Arts of San Fernando, translated Hugh Blair's critical essays *Lectures on Rhetoric and Belles Lettres* in 1798. In her study "Varying life: the idea of fiction in the Spanish version of Joseph Addison's *The Pleasures of the Imagination*", she explains, however, that in a country where classic Aristotelian ideas were still prevailing, Addison's theory of the imagination brought a real artistic Esthetic revolution.

While some research has been done proving that the *Spectator* was influential in Russia,[31] it seems that so far the impact of the *Spectator* in Poland has only been timidly admitted. Klara Leszczynska breaks with this trend and argues in her article "How Mr. Spectator became the father of the Polish essay" that in a country that was historically much impregnated by French culture, the essay periodical press that was launched by the enlightened bishop prince Ignaci Krasicki (1735–1801) was rooted more in the Addisonian essay tradition than in the one derived from Montaigne's *Essays*. Klara Lesczcynska shows that Addison's influence was not restricted to Krasicki's most famous paper, *Monitor* (1763–1768).[32] It is also to be felt in Krasicki's last work, *Uwagi*, a collection of essays which was published posthumously and which contained moral and patriotic remarks, short pieces of fictions and letters aiming at reforming and entertaining Polish readers. Klara Leszczynska thus explores a middle path between the conclusions of the great critic Zdzisław Libera who considered that *Uwagi* was inspired by Montaigne and Hume[33] and the more recent analysis expressed

31 Carole Chapin: "Spectateurs, traductions, et périodiques satiriques: la réception des feuilles moralistes en Russie au XVIIIe siècle". In: Ertler/Lévrier/Fischer 2012, 249–268.

32 Richard Butterwick: *Poland's last King and English Culture: Stanislaw August Poniatowski, 1732–1798*. Oxford: Clarendon Press 1998. – Zofia Sinko: "La discussion sur le théâtre dans le 'Monitor' polonais et le 'Spectator' anglais". In: *Le théâtre dans l'Europe des lumières: programmes pratiques, échanges*. Eds. Mieszyslaw Klimovicz/ Alesander Wit Labuda. Warsaw: Wydawnictwo Uniwersytetu Wroclawskiego 1985, 191–208.

33 Zdzisław Libera: "Krasicki myśliciel. Refleksje nad 'Uwagami". In: Ignacy Krasicki: *Uwagi*. Wstęp i opracowanie. Warszawa: Czytelnik 1997, 6 ss.

by Jan Tomkowski, whose anthology of Polish essays anchors *Uwagi* in Fénelon's tradition and shrugs off the legacy of the English Enlightenment.[34]

Carmen García Cela's article, "Scènes de lecture", focuses on a French imitator of the *Spectator*: *La Spectatrice* (1728–1729), supposedly written by a lady. It explores how the periodical appropriates what Alain Bony pointed as Addison's original and central strategy in the *Spectator*[35]: to empower the readers with the capacity to see, imagine and eventually to reason and correctly interpret the journal. Carmen Garcia, however, notes that *La Spectatrice* is fundamentally different from its model in that it does not make room for its female readers. She thus highlights the limits of the influence of the English periodical and points to the inner contradiction of *La Spectatrice*, whose female editor with her proto-feminist tones displays a feminine perspective that should, one expects, put the female readers at the heart of the periodical, but that in reality does not.

Finally, Claire Boulard Jouslin seeks to measure Addison's popularity through the way the translations of the *Spectator* and *Guardian* were received in Switzerland. In her chapter "Addison in Lausanne", she analyses the minutes of the weekly conferences that were organized in Lausanne by the Société du Comte de la Lippe (1742–1747) for the instruction of the young German Count of Lippe Detmold. She highlights the pedagogical, moral and political use the Protestant preceptors made of the French translations of the *Spectator* and the *Guardian* in this club in order to teach moral principles and political virtue that would turn their aristocratic ward into an enlightened ruler. Claire Boulard Jouslin, therefore, shows that the *Spectator* whose original aim was to popularize philosophy and literature could become in translation, an elite book, a part of a princely education manual. She also points out that mid-eighteenth-century continental readers already attributed the authorship of the most elevated essays of the *Spectator* and *Guardian* to Joseph Addison and not to Richard Steele. Such attribution reveals that Addison was not merely perceived by the German and Swiss elite as a popular moralist whose elegant and entertaining pen published ephemeral flyingsheets, but as a serious pedagogue and politician whose moderate philosophy and principles could prove

34 Jan Tomkowski: *Polski esej literacki. Antologia*. Warszawa: Zakład Narodowy im. Ossolińskich 2017. I am grateful to Dimitri Garncarszyck for his bibliographical help.

35 Alain Bony: *Joseph Addison et la création littéraire: essai périodique et modernité*. Thèse de doctorat. Paris III, 1979 [Lyon: Ceran, 1985].

useful to a future sovereign. Claire Boulard Jouslin thus refines the portrait of Addison and shows that in the Protestant European states, both Addison and his periodical writings were considered as major proponents of the European Enlightenment.

Claire Boulard-Jouslin *Paris, Fall 2019*

Avant-propos

En juin 1719, le magazine mensuel *Le Nouveau Mercure* informait ses lecteurs français que « Joseph Addison, ci-devant Secrétaire d'Etat mourut hier 28 ».[1] Si cette annonce nous rappelle opportunément que voici trois siècles qu'Addison a disparu, elle ne laisse pas d'étonner. Son laconisme et l'allusion à la seule fonction politique d'Addison ne permettent pas au lecteur non averti de deviner que c'est l'un des plus brillants hommes de lettres anglais de sa génération qui vient de rendre l'âme.[2] Comment interpréter cet encart nécrologique?

En réalité, l'annonce confirme à la fois qu'Addison était renommé et que sa disparition méritait d'être signalée en France et que d'autre part, sa célébrité était diversement appréciée. En effet, sa tragédie *Cato* traduite en français dès sa sortie en 1713 avait été au centre d'une controverse sur les mérites comparés des dramaturges modernes anglais et français et sur leur capacité à écrire des tragédies néoclassiques.[3] La pièce d'Addison, comparée au *Caton d'Utique* de Michel Deschamps[4] soulevait la question de la supériorité culturelle des deux nations et initiait une querelle sur la rivalité littéraire franco-anglaise à laquelle le *Nouveau Mercure Galant*[5] avait eu part – contre Addison – et qui allait dominer la première moitié du XVIIIe siècle.[6]

L'absence d'hommage littéraire dans *Le Nouveau Mercure* pouvait donc être la vengeance mesquine du magazine envers Addison qui considérait *Le Mercure*

---

1 *Le Nouveau Mercure* (Juin 1719), 200. Joseph Addison mourut en réalité le 17 juin.

2 Gabriel Bonno : « La Culture et la civilisation britanniques devant l'opinion française de la paix d'Utrecht aux Lettres Philosophiques (1713–1734) ». *Transactions of the American Philosophical Society* 38, 1 (1948), 63.

3 *Caton, Tragédie par M. Addison*, traduite de l'Anglais par M. Abel Boyer. Amsterdam: Tonson 1713. Abel Boyer explique dans la préface de sa traduction, qu'il avait choisi la pièce d'Addison afin de montrer au public français que les anglais excellaient dans le genre poétique le plus prestigieux qu'était la tragédie.

4 « Parallèle de deux tragédies nouvelles dont la mort de Caton est le sujet ». *Le Nouveau Mercure Galant* (Mars 1715), 62–127.

5 *Le Nouveau Mercure Galant* (Paris 1714–1716) et le *Nouveau Mercure* (Paris 1717–1721) étaient des continuations du *Mercure Galant* (Paris 1670–1714).

6 Bonno 1948, 64.

Galant comme la meilleure illustration du goût français pour les bouts rimés, des morceaux littéraires qu'il jugeait superficiels et anecdotiques.[7]

A bien des égards, cette annonce particulière reflète la relation complexe que Joseph Addison (1672–1719) entretint de manière plus large avec l'Europe de son vivant et au-delà de la tombe. Son œuvre témoigne d'un regard critique envers certaines pratiques continentales – le catholicisme et l'absolutisme par exemple – qui teintèrent ses productions d'un chauvinisme et d'un anticatholicisme qui lui furent reprochés.[8]

Son enfance et sa jeunesse permettent d'expliquer partiellement ses positions. Né en 1672 de parents anglicans et lui-même voué à l'origine au ministère anglican, il grandit dans un climat protestant très hostile aux catholiques, marqué par la révocation de l'Edit de Nantes et l'intolérance religieuse de Louis XIV en France et par la politique pro-catholique et absolutiste de Jacques II en Angleterre.[9] Aussi, défenseur whig de la révolution de 1688 qui fit de l'anglicanisme la religion d'état et qui transforma l'Angleterre en monarchie parlementaire, il mit très vite sa plume au service de Guillaume III et n'eut de cesse dans sa poésie et sa prose de justifier les libertés anglaises et la politique militariste de son roi sur le continent.[10]

Pourquoi alors, en cette année de tricentenaire de la disparition d'Addison, célébrer l'homme par le biais de son rapport ambigu au continent européen, plutôt que par celui de son anglicité ?

Aussi nationaliste a-t'il pu être, Addison ne s'est pas formé, aussi bien comme homme de plume que comme homme politique sans avoir été en contact avec le continent de multiples façons. D'une part, voyageur ayant effectué un tour d'Europe, il a parcouru la Hollande, la France, l'Italie, la Suisse, l'Autriche

7 *Spectator* n° 60. Ed. Donald F. Bond. Oxford : Clarendon Press 1965, vol. 1, 257. Toutes les références proviennent de cette édition du *Spectator*.

8 Son anticatholicisme valut à son ouvrage *Remarks on several Parts of Italy &c, in the years 1701, 1702, 1703* (London : Jacob Tonson 1705) d'être mis à l'Index par le Vatican en 1729. Les dictionnaires français de personnages illustres le décrivent dans les notices qu'ils consacrent à Addison, comme partial. *Cf.* Louis Mayeul Chaudon: *Nouveau Dictionnaire Historique*. Caen: Le Roy 1789, vol. 1, 46. – François-Xavier de Feller: *Dictionnaire historique, ou histoire abrégée de tous les hommes qui se sont fait un nom par le génie*. Augsbourg: Rieger 1781–1784, vol. 1, 36.

9 *Cf.* Peter Smithers : *The Life of Joseph Addison*. Oxford: Clarendon Press 1954. – Sur le contexte, *cf.* Tim Harris : *Restoration : Charles II and his Kingdoms, 1660–1685*. London: Penguin 2005. – *Revolution. The great Crisis of the British Monarchy, 1685–1720*. London: Penguin 2006.

10 *Cf.* son pamphlet, *The Present State of the War*. London : J. Morphew 1708.

et l'Allemagne, autant de pays où il a puisé des sources de méditations et de réflexion sur les paysages, l'art, sur les pratiques et croyances religieuses, sur les effets du climat, sur les systèmes économiques et politiques, ou encore sur les rapports entre les sexes dont il fait part dans sa poésie, dans les *Remarks on Several Parts of Italy* (1705), dans ses essais périodiques, dans son essai sur les médailles. Il y fait également des rencontres et entretient par la suite un réseau de correspondants qui incluait des philosophes tels Leibniz en Allemagne et Malebranche en France, des savants comme Bayle en Hollande ou comme le recteur du collège de Genève, Jean Alphonse Turettini en Suisse.[11] Par la suite, sa fonction de Secrétaire d'état au sud (en 1717) l'oblige encore à approfondir sa connaissance politique, culturelle et économique des pays qui sont sous sa responsabilité diplomatique et bien sûr d'être en contact épistolaire mais aussi personnel avec les ambassadeurs d'Espagne, du Portugal, de France.

D'autre part, la diversité et la créativité culturelles du continent ne pouvaient manquer d'exercer très tôt une véritable attraction et une influence durable sur le brillant intellectuel qu'était Addison. Son érudition classique acquise à Oxford, mais également, ses convictions religieuses et politiques, son écriture enfin se sont forgées aussi bien grâce à l'Europe continentale que contre celle-ci. Grand lecteur, sa bibliothèque montre qu'il s'est nourri autant de culture antique que des productions littéraires, scientifiques, esthétiques et religieuses européennes modernes. Fontenelle, Pascal, Boileau, Le Tasse et Guarini cotôyaient sur ses étagères, les traductions de *Don Quichotte* (par Pierre Antoine Motteux), Paterculus autant que Horace et Cicéron.[12] Comment ces différents contacts avec les cultures continentales ont ils façonné l'écriture d'Addison?

La question doit être posée car les études sur le rapport entre Addison et le continent sont à la fois limitées, lacunaires et déséquilibrées. De manière prévisible, c'est l'impact d'une éducation classique sur son œuvre qui a fait l'objet d'un intérêt académique ancien. Parfois controversés d'ailleurs,[13] sa maîtrise et

---

11 *Cf.* la biographie de Smithers 1954, 74. Smithers confond cependant Samuel et Jean Alphonse Turettini. *Cf.* aussi Karl Brunner : « Joseph Addisons umfassende Interessen ». *Anglistische Studien : Festschrift zum 70. Geburstag von Professor Friedrich Wild.* Ed. Karl Brunner/Herbert Koziol/Siegfried Korninger. Wien : Braumüller 1958, 14–26.

12 *A Catalogue of the valuable Library of the way Addison has digested Ovid, the late celebrated Right Honorable Joseph Addison*, vendu par Leigh and Sotheby's. London 1799.

13 Sur la maîtrise du latin, lire l'essai « The Life and Writings of Addison » de Thomas B. Macaulay dans *Edinburgh Review* (July 1843), 192. – Lilian D. Bloom: « Addison as Translator : a Problem in Neo-classical Scholarship ». *Studies in Philology* 46, 1 (1949), 31–53. Pour une étude plus récente, lire Estelle Haan : *Vergilius Redivivus : Studies in Joseph Addison's Latin Poetry*. Philadelphia: Transactions of the American Philosophical

son traitement de la culture antique, la manière dont Addison a su faire son miel de ses lectures d'Ovide, Virgile et Homère[14] dans ses poésies ou dans sa tragédie *Cato* ont été analysés de bonne heure. Parallèlement, c'est le rapport d'Addison à la France qui a suscité le plus d'intérêt, dont témoignent des travaux ponctuels sur l'influence qu'ont pu exercer sur sa production certains grands auteurs comme Molière,[15] Pascal,[16] La Bruyère.[17] On trouve également des tentatives d'exploration de l'influence de la critique française de Le Bossu[18] sur son analyse de la poésie épique ou de Boileau sur son esthétique.[19] Des traces du Cartésianisme et de la philosophie de Malebranche ont aussi été analysées.[20] Rares en revanche sont les études sur les rapports qu'Addison entretenaient avec les littératures et philosophies italiennes,[21] espagnoles,[22] néerlandaises et allemandes.

Plus généralement le faible nombre d'études consacrées à l'influence des cultures européennes sur l'œuvre d'Addison et la concentration relative sur les

---

Society 2005. Sur la connaissance du grec et de la culture héllénistique d'Addison, James William Johnson consacre quelques pages dans *The Formation of English Neo-Classical Thought*. Princeton : Princeton University Press 1967.

14 Voir par exemple la liste des publications sur Virgile et Ovide que dresse Charles A. Knight dans sa bibliographie *Joseph Addison and Richard Steele, a Reference Guide*. New York : G.K. Hall & Co. 1994.

15 Kathryn E. Wheatley : « Addison's portrait of the neoclassical critic ». *The Review of English Studies* 1, 3 (July 1950), 245–247.

16 Ralph Arthur Nablow : « Addison's indebtedness to Pascal in *Spectator* n° 420 ». *Studies on Voltaire and the Eighteenth Century* 217 (1983), 183–185.

17 Edward Chauncey Baldwin : « La Bruyère's Influence upon Addison ». *PMLA* 19, 4 (1904), 479–495. – Margaret Turner : « The influence of La Bruyère on the *Tatler* and the *Spectator* ». *Modern Language Review* 48, 1 (1953), 10–16.

18 Voir Hugh Thomas Swedenberg : *The Theory of the Epic in England 1650–1800*. Oakland: University of California Press 1944.

19 Robert L. Montgomery : « Addison and the 'Helps and Ornaments of art'. *Criticism* 25, 4 (1983), 329–346. Voir aussi des passages chez Alexandre Maurocordato : *La Critique classique en Angleterre de la Restauration à la mort de Joseph Addison : Essai de définition. Etudes Anglaises* 18. Paris : Didier 1964.

20 *Cf.* par exemple l'article de Hiblert H. Campbell : « Addison's Cartesian' Passage and Nicolas Malebranche ». *Philological Quarterly* 46, 3 (1967), 408–412.

21 Voir Richard Thomas : « Trajano Boccalini's influence upon English Literature ». *Aberystwyth Studies* 3 (1922), 73–102.

22 Il ne semble pas y avoir eu d'étude entre celle de W. X. Hendrix : « Quevedo, Guevara, Le Sage, and the *Tatler* ». *Modern Philology* 19, 2 (1921), 171–186 et Juan Antonio Garrido Ardila : *The Cervantean Heritage: Reception and Influence of Cervantes in Britain*. London: Modern Humanities Research Association et al. 2009.

origines françaises de son écriture, pourraient être également la conséquence d'une stratégie addisonienne. Sa retenue, son humour pince-sans-rire, son nationalisme, son écriture dite naturelle, le genre même de l'essai moral et critique étaient autant d'éléments qu'il revendiquait comme constitutif d'une identité britannique dont il proclamait la supériorité et qu'il prônait comme modèle. Faire oublier les origines continentales de certains de ces travaux était alors nécessaire. Il semble qu'il ait partiellement réussi puisque Addison est encore chanté comme le chantre de l'anglicité.[23]

Il va sans dire que les contributions rassemblées ici, issues d'une journée d'études qui eut lieu à l'Université Sorbonne-Nouvelle Paris 3 et qui fut organisée conjointement avec l'Université de Graz ne fournissent pas un tableau exhaustif des relations d'Addison au continent européen. Modestement, un des buts de cette étude est d'explorer plus avant l'écriture addisonienne et cette idée que les lumières anglaises étaient indissociables des courants d'idées et des pratiques continentales et de réévaluer l'apport des cultures européennes dans l'élaboration d'une anglicité et d'un patriotisme qui s'affirmaient.[24] Il s'agit aussi de brosser un portrait plus nuancé de ce « True born Englishman » qu'Addison semblait incarner et de mettre en lumière certains des fils de trame européens et (quasi) invisibles de la toile addisonienne.

A cet effet, quatre articles nous offrent un aperçu des dettes addisoniennes et de la manière dont il a réagi aux divers contacts qu'il a pu avoir avec le continent.

Dans son étude intitulée « A moment in Amsterdam » Amélie Junqua lève une partie du voile sur la manière dont Addison, encore jeune et auréolé d'une gloire littéraire naissante, use du continent pour mieux l'ignorer ensuite dans certaines de ses publications. Elle montre notamment qu'il avait mis à profit son séjour

23 L'idée est relayée par Samuel Johnson dans son essai sur Addison (*Life of the Most Eminent English Poets*, London: C. Bathurst et al. 1779–1781) et par Hugh Blair (*Lectures on Rhetoric and Belles Lettres*, London: A. Strahan et al. 1783–85) en Angleterre. En 1841, dans sa préface au manuel de langue, *Lectures anglaises cours supérieur. Choix de morceaux en prose et en vers extraits des œuvres d'Addison, de Pope…* (Paris : C. Hingray 1841, 11), M. Corréard, professeur au collège Charlemagne à Paris explique : « […] moins heureux comme poète que comme prosateur, il a fait pour la langue anglaise ce qu'il a vainement tenté pour la scène dramatique : il l'a purifiée, régularisée. Addison, principal rédacteur de ces ouvrages périodiques dont nous venons de parler, se fait remarquer par la pureté de son goût, son élégance, sa correction, son atticisme. C'est un modèle qu'il faut recommander aux jeunes gens qui se livrent à l'étude de la langue anglaise ».

24 Voir l'ouvrage de Linda Colley sur la construction de l'anglicité à cette époque: *Britons, Forging the Nation 1707–1837*. London : Pimlico 1992.

aux Pays-Bas – haut lieu du commerce, de l'édition et des échanges intellectuels – pour acheter des livres introuvables à Londres, mais aussi pour aider son éditeur Jacob Tonson à publier une luxueuse édition de *Caesar's Commentaries.* Amélie Junqua met ainsi en lumière le travail d'occultation de tout le réseau européen de contacts qu'Addison avait sollicités dans cette tâche et qu'il omet de mentionner lorsqu'il fait la publicité de l'ouvrage dans le *Spectator.*

C'est également une reconnaissance de dette à laquelle Endre Szécsényi procède dans un article original intitulé: « *The Jesuit thread in Joseph Addison's aesthetics* ». Endre Szécsényi met en effet en évidence la bonne connaissance qu'Addison avait des textes des pères Jésuites français et espagnol Dominique Bouhours et Baltasar Gracián – qu'Addison cite en passant – et qui occupent une place centrale dans la théorie esthétique qu'il expose dans les essais sur les plaisirs de l'Imagination du *Spectator.* Endré Szécsényi montre notamment qu'Addison transfère la notion de 'Je ne sais quoi', à l'origine synonyme pour Gracián et Bouhours de grâce divine, et l'adapte au domaine de l'expérience esthétique, créant ainsi une esthétique de la transcendance en des termes qui reprennent ceux des deux Jésuites. Une telle analyse permet ainsi de nuancer l'hostilité qu'Addison nourrissait envers les Jésuites qu'il décrivait comme naturellement traitres à la nation anglaise dans ses *Remarks on several Parts of Italy.*[25] Elle révèle enfin la manière dont Addison construit, à partir d'une esthétique catholique, une forme d'apologétique esthétique, qui parce qu'elle transcende les conflits religieux, connut un vif succès en Europe au XVIIIe siècle.

Dan Poston et Paul Davis quant eux, analysent toute la complexité des sentiments qu'Addison nourrit envers la culture antique et l'Italie contemporaine qui affleurait déjà dans le poème épistolaire « A Letter from Italy » qu'il rédigea en visitant l'Italie et qu'il adressa à son mécenne Charles Montagu. Dans son étude intitulée « Still on classic ground : Joseph Addison's Italy », Dan Poston explore l'ambivalence du poème. Ce dernier en effet tout à la fois dépeint les paysages italiens contemporains en imitant et adaptant des extraits des *Géorgiques* de Virgile, suggère que ces beautés antiques sont illusoires et révolues et, *in fine* se réfère au cadre néoclassique afin de célébrer la supériorité des libertés anglaises et du newtonianisme sur le 'papisme' et l'absolutisme. Il rejoint ainsi Paul Davis qui récuse l'idée ironique d'Horace Walpole que ce poème serait le fruit d'un

25 Voir notamment ses remarques hostiles aux Jésuites du collège de Lorette dans *Remarks Upon Several Parts of Italy in the Years 1701, 1702, 1703*, 144 et 473. Voir aussi l'article de Claire Boulard Jouslin : « Addison, Anti-Catholicism and Politeness », à paraître dans *Anti-Catholicism in Britain and Ireland since the Reformation: Practices, Representations and Ideas.* Ed. Claire Gheereart-Grafeuille et Géraldine Vaughan, London : Palgrave.

voyage chez les poètes antiques plus que d'un réel voyage en Italie. Dans son article « Misguided by a tuneful throng », Paul Davis explique que le voyage d'Italie fut non pas la source de sa verve poétique néoclassique, mais au contraire l'événement qui l'incita à faire ses adieux à l'écriture poétique. Montrant qu'Addison était conscient de la césure entre le paysage chanté par les poètes latins – en particulier les rivières et fleuves italiens – et la réalité historique du XVIIIe siècle, Paul Davis voit dans le poème la dénonciation et le rejet de l'illusion poétique définie comme un mensonge servile et l'annonce du choix de la modernité britannique qui serait politique et synonyme de vérité. Il souligne néanmoins la mélancolie du poète face à ce renoncement à une Italie rêvée et plus généralement à la poésie comme refuge contre des réalités inconfortables. Ainsi, ces deux articles mettent en lumière que le voyage d'Italie fut un tournant – Paul Davis le nomme le passage du Rubicon – dans la carrière littéraire d'Addison car il permit à ce dernier de trouver sa voie politique et en dernière instance sa voix littéraire – celle de l'écriture en prose célébrant la modernité britannique.

Enfin, l'étude de Klaus-Dieter Ertler sur « Addison, lecteur de Bayle » fournit un exemple précis de la façon dont Addison s'appuyait dans les essais du *Spectator* sur des ouvrages récents et porteurs d'une pensée novatrice tels que le *Dictionnaire historique et critique* (1697) de Bayle pour instruire son public. Après un travail de recherche patient et minutieux, Klaus-Dieter Ertler a recensé un grand nombre des micro-récits du dictionnaire qui ont été adaptés et réécrits par Addison pour les besoins du *Spectator*. Il met ainsi en lumière la porosité formelle entre le genre de l'essai périodique et celui de l'article encyclopédique continental ainsi que les liens intellectuels qui unissaient Bayle et Addison. Et il souligne la capacité d'Addison à transformer un savoir encyclopédique en un savoir attrayant.

Par ailleurs, l'étude de Klaus-Dieter Ertler permet à la fois de clore le Grand Tour addisonien – Bayle, rappelons-le, vivait en Hollande et Addison envisageait de lui rendre visite avant de retourner en Angleterre – et les influences que l'Europe a pu exercer sur l'écrivain et d'ouvrir le deuxième chapitre de cet ouvrage consacré à mesurer l'ampleur et l'impact de l'héritage d'Addison en Europe par le biais de l'essai périodique. Car, comme le montre l'analyse des migrations intertextuelles de micro-fictions du dictionnaire de Bayle vers le *Spectator* et vers sa traduction française *Le Spectateur ou le Socrate moderne*, les procédés fictionnels et didactiques employés par Addison ont diffusé un modèle d'écriture brève et fictionnelle qui, adaptée, imitée ou traduite, influença l'Europe entière. Célébrer le tricentenaire de la disparition d'Addison sans prêter attention à l'héritage européen qu'il a laissé par le biais de l'essai périodique et de l'essai spectatorial en particulier serait un non-sens puisque c'est le genre de l'essai périodique qui, par son originalité et son élégance, a assuré à Addison une gloire durable sur le continent.

L'historiographie montre que le lien entre l'essai périodique spectatorial et l'Europe suscite un regain d'intérêt. Il fait à l'heure actuelle l'objet d'une recherche de longue haleine qui consiste à recenser en une base de données dirigée par Klaus-Dieter Ertler, les traductions et imitations du *Spectator* en Europe et à esquisser une géographie de l'influence du *Spectator*. D'ores et déjà elle fournit un aperçu de la richesse de cet héritage journalistique en Italie, en France, en Espagne, au Portugal et met à la disposition des chercheurs un nombre important de textes.[26] Les travaux pionniers de Walter Oberkampf,[27] Wolfgang Martens[28] et Fritz Rau,[29] prolongés par ceux de Jean Sgard et Alexis Lévrier sur les spectateurs français,[30] ont ainsi stimulé une recherche qui s'étend progressivement à tous les pays d'Europe. Ces études nous permettent

---

26 Voir la base de données: *Moralische Wochenschriften-GAMS*, <http://gams.uni-graz.at/ archive/get/context:mws/sdef:Context/get?locale=fr>.

27 Walter Oberkampf: *Die zeitungskundliche Bedeutung der moralischen Wochenschriften. Ihr Wesen und ihre Bedeutung*. Dresden: Risse-Verlag 1934.

28 Wolfgang Martens: *Die Botschaft der Tugend. Die Aufklärung im Spiegel der deutschen Moralischen Wochenschriften*. Stuttgart: Metzler 1968.

29 L'ouvrage de Fritz Rau : *Zur Verbreitung and Nachahmung des* Tatler *und* Spectator. Heidelberg : Carl Winter 1980, est consacré à la fois aux Spectateurs allemands et européens.

30 Alexis Lévrier : *Les Journaux de Marivaux et le monde des "spectateurs"*. Paris : Presses Universitaires de Paris Sorbonne, 2007. – *Cf.* aussi Stephen Botein/J. R. Censor/H. Ritvo : « The Periodical Press in Eighteenth-Century English and French Society. A Cross-Cultural Approach ». *Comparative Studies in Society and History* 32, 1 (1981), 464–490, et Alain Gilot: « Le journaliste masqué; personnages et formes personnelles ». In: Pierre Retat (ed.): *Le Journalisme d'Ancien Régime*. Lyon : Presses universitaires de Lyon 1982. – Claire Boulard : « The *Spectator*'s curtailed legacy: The influences of the French and the English eighteenth-century presses on each other ». In: Frédéric Ogée (ed.): *Better in France ? The Circulation of Ideas across the Channel in the Eighteenth Century*. Lewisburg, PA: Bucknell University Press 2000. – Klaus-Dieter Ertler/Alexis Lévrier/Michaela Fischer (eds.) : *Regards sur les spectateurs. Periodical Essay, Feuilles volantes, Moralische Wochenschriften, Fogli moralistici, Prensa moral*. Francfort : Peter Lang 2012. – Klaus-Dieter Ertler : « Le système narratif des 'spectateurs' et leur réception en Espagne : quelques vecteurs discursifs dans le *Pensador* de José Clavijo y Fajardo ». *El Argonauta español : Pratiques journalistiques aux premiers temps de la presse espagnole (XVIII*e*-début du XIX*e *siècles)* 11 (2014), <https://journals.openedition.org/argonauta/2002>. – Maud Le Guellec : *Presse et culture dans l'Espagne des Lumières*. Madrid : Casa Velázquez 2016.

de mieux cerner l'étendue géographique, formelle et intellectuelle de l'influence du périodique et de son créateur. Le présent volume tente, dans ce deuxième chapitre d'apporter quelques pièces supplémentaires du puzzle européen que constitue l'influence addisonienne et spectatoriale.

Commençons tout d'abord par l'Espagne. María Rodríguez Sánchez de León rappelle que si les idées esthétiques qu'Addison expose dans les essais sur les plaisirs de l'imagination pénètrent d'abord en Espagne grâce à la traduction française du *Spectator*, *Le Spectateur ou le Socrate moderne* (1714–1726), elles connaissent le succès tardivement au tournant du XIXe siècle, suite à la traduction en espagnol des essais critiques de Hugh Blair, *Lectures on Rhetoric and Belles Lettres* en 1798 par Munarriz, traducteur et membre de l'Académie royale des Beaux Arts de San Fernando. La théorie de l'imagination d'Addison n'en constitue pas moins dans une Espagne où l'aristotélisme est encore très ancré une réelle révolution esthétique qui va bouleverser les modes de production artistique.

Si l'on savait que la géographie spectatoriale s'étendait jusqu'en Russie,[31] son influence sur la Pologne semblait moins probante. Klara Leszczynska, dans son article « How Mr. Spectator became the father of the Polish essay » confirme que dans ce pays historiquement très influencé par la culture française, la presse d'essai qui s'y développe notamment grâce à Ignaci Krasicki (1735–1801), prince-évêque et grande figure des lumières polonaises, puise ses sujets et surtout sa forme davantage dans l'essai addisonien que dans celui de Montaigne. Klara Lesczcynska montre que l'influence d'Addison n'est pas confinée au plus célèbre des périodiques de Krasicki, *Monitor* (1763–1768) qui a déjà fait l'objet de quelques analyses,[32] mais est aussi perceptible dans les essais du dernier opus de Krasicki, *Uwagi*, un recueil d'essais publié de manière posthume: lettres, fictions, considérations morales et patriotiques sont livrés aux lecteurs afin de les réformer et montrent que Krasicki a su adapter la formule spectatoriale au contexte polonais. Klara Leszczynska explore ainsi une voie médiane entre

31 Voir Carole Chapin : « Spectateurs, traductions, et « périodiques satiriques » : la réception des feuilles moralistes en Russie au XVIIIe siècle ». In : Ertler/Lévrier/Fischer 2012, 249–268.

32 Voir Richard Butterwick : *Poland's last King and English Culture : Stanislaw August Poniatowski, 1732-1798*. Oxford : Clarendon Press 1998. – Zofia Sinko : « La discussion sur le théâtre dans le 'Monitor' polonais et le 'Spectator' anglais ». In : *Le théâtre dans l'Europe des lumières : programmes pratiques, échanges*. Eds. Mieszyslaw Klimovicz/ Alesander Wit Labuda. Warsaw : Wydawnictwo Uniwersytetu Wroclawskiego 1985, 191–208.

celle du très respecté critique Zdzisław Libera qui considérait les *Uwagi* comme inspiré par Montaigne et Hume, entre autres essayistes anglais[33] et celle plus récente de Jan Tomkowski, dont l'anthologie d'essais polonais situe les *Uwagi* dans un sillage fénelonien et peine à reconnaître l'apport des lumières anglaises.[34]

L'article de Carmen García Cela intitulé « Scènes de lecture » est quant à lui, consacré à un avatar français et féminin du *Spectator*, *La Spectatrice* (1728–1729). L'auteur anonyme adopte les mêmes stratégies réformatrices et esthétiques que le *Spectator*, dont notamment celle qui consiste à placer le lecteur en capacité de voir et d'imaginer, et donc de donner un sens aux essais et au périodique.[35] Carmen García Cela note cependant une différence majeure entre les deux périodiques: *La Spectatrice* ne fait aucune place aux lectrices. Elle souligne ainsi à la fois les limites de l'influence du périodique anglais, qui, lui s'adressait aux lectrices, et la contradiction du périodique français au ton parfois proto-féministe, qui bien qu'annonçant une figure éditoriale féminine et donc, implicitement, une vision féminine qui placerait les lectrices au centre de son système, les met en réalité de côté.

On peut mesurer le succès et la popularité d'Addison non seulement à la variété des imitations et des adaptations mais également à la réception des traductions et à leurs usages. Dans son article « Addison in Lausanne », Claire Boulard Jouslin analyse les compte-rendus des conférences hebdomadaires de la Société du Comte de la Lippe (1742–1747), destinées à parfaire à Lausanne, l'instruction et l'éducation du jeune Comte allemand de Lippe-Detmold. Elle met en lumière l'usage pédagogique international et politique que les précepteurs protestants faisaient des traductions françaises du *Spectator* et du *Guardian* dans le monde germanique. Ils usaient en effet, entre autres textes, de ces deux périodiques pour inculquer au jeune Comte les principes de droiture et de vertu qui feraient de lui un prince éclairé. Cette étude montre donc que d'ouvrage populaire, le *Spectator* faisait partie intégrante d'un manuel du prince, ouvrage de l'élite par excellence. Elle souligne ensuite que dans l'esprit des lecteurs continentaux du milieu du XVIIIe siècle, c'est la figure d'Addison et non celle de Richard Steele

33 Zdzisław Libera : « Krasicki myśliciel. Refleksje nad 'Uwagami' ». In : Ignacy Krasicki : *Uwagi*. Wstęp i opracowanie. Warszawa : Czytelnik 1997, 6 ss.

34 Jan Tomkowski : *Polski esej literacki. Antologia*. Warszawa : Zakład Narodowy im. Ossolińskich 2017. Tous mes remerciements vont à Dimitri Garncarszyck pour son aide bibliographique.

35 *Cf.* Alain Bony : *Joseph Addison et la création littéraire : essai périodique et modernité*. Thèse de doctorat. Paris III, 1979 [Lyon : Ceran, 1985], qui y voit là une des caractéristiques de l'écriture addisonienne.

qui était intimement associée aux essais du *Spectator* et du *Guardian*. Cet usage pédagogique des deux journaux prouve donc que l'élite allemande et suisse percevait Addison non pas seulement comme un moraliste populaire à la plume élégante et divertissante mais comme un politique dont la philosophie modérée pouvait devenir précieuse à un futur souverain.

Claire Boulard Jouslin affine ainsi le portrait d'Addison en Europe. Son étude montre comment dans les états protestants, l'écrivain – dont les essais périodiques sont aujourd'hui sortis du canon littéraire – mais aussi l'homme politique étaient bel et bien considérés comme des figures incontournables des lumières européennes.

Claire Boulard-Jouslin *Paris, Automne 2019*

Europe's influence on Addison's writings/ L'influence de l'Europe sur l'écriture addisonienne

Amélie Junqua

(Université de Picardie Jules Verne, Amiens)

A moment in Amsterdam—Joseph Addison and Jacob Tonson in 1703

At the close of his Grand Tour (1699–1703) through France, Italy, and Switzerland, Joseph Addison reached Amsterdam and set up a meeting with the bookseller Jacob Tonson in Amsterdam. The relationship between Joseph Addison and Jacob Tonson appears to have been mutually beneficial, and pragmatically symbiotic. Even if it appeared devoid of any warmth or feeling, it was undoubtedly functional, as can be attested by the network of Whig literati to which Tonson introduced Addison at the start of the latter's career and the string of lucrative publications Addison later provided Tonson. This sojourn in Amsterdam is seldom commented on by the critics, mostly due to the scarcity of material—Tonson left no records of his transactions there, and what has survived is mostly anecdotal. Yet, we argue that this moment in Amsterdam was the auspicious start of Addison's political and literary career.

In the centre of the European booktrade, Addison's and Tonson's interests and preoccupations converged—searching for paper, subscribers and intellectual excellence. This short collaboration in Holland was the start of a swift ascent to literary fame in Britain, later relayed throughout Europe thanks to the networks of intellectuals Addison had been in contact with. Jacob Tonson (the elder), topping bookseller, publisher and printer, like other top-range members of the profession (the scholarly Estienne family or William Bowyer the Younger, who were well-versed in classical languages), was far more educated than the average bookseller. His sharp sense of business and keen perception of talent made him a prominent figure in the intricately intertwined realms of poetry and propaganda. Tonson presided over the Kit-Kat Club, where poetry and political strategies were discussed in equal measure. He had knowledge of several languages, including French, which he must have spoken better, in the course of his negotiations with Parisian and Dutch booksellers, than the shy Addison. Seventeen years older than Addison, affluent and influential, Jacob Tonson held visible sway. An arbiter of literary tastes who published many of the now canonical literature of the eighteenth century and held the copyrights for the works of Milton and Shakespeare, he was aware of their worth and instrumental in making them popular again. It is very probable, judging from the mutually beneficial relationship he had with Addison, that he asked the latter to write in the *Spectator* to help advertise his publication projects. The most salient examples of this are the *Spectator*'s entire week devoted to Milton's *Paradise*, though Milton was already popular,[1] and the puff for his *Caesar's Commentaries*, also in a *Spectator* essay, that will be analysed below.

In 1703, Addison cultivated Tonson, as can be observed in the tone of his letters. Tonson had already published his early poems in Latin and English in the popular *Miscellanies*, and Addison was preparing another translation from Ovid for him. In 1703, a meeting was set up in Amsterdam in the course of which Adddison somewhat tactlessly declined an offer Tonson had been charged to relay from the Duke of Somerset, to tutor his son during his Grand Tour. Addison was just finishing his own Tour and probably wished to go home rather than hit the road again. And his father had died while he was on his travels. Perhaps to make amends for the embarrassment he caused Tonson by turning down this offer, Addison studiously assisted Tonson in his quest for engravings and subscribers in preparation of a luxury edition of *Caesar's Commentaries*.

The main source of information we may rely on to establish any fact is contained in the few letters Addison sent from the Continent, incomplete as they are. The biographers, for lack of anything else, focus on his stay in France and Italy, and gloss over this period of his life, before earnestly focusing on his first publications in London. Yet, because this small number of letters have only been summarised or quickly quoted, they are found to reveal a little more information when checked against other primary sources, such as Addison's library sale catalogue. Tonson, on the other hand, left no accounting records of his transactions in Amsterdam, and only mentions Addison in his correspondence concerning the aforementioned failed business transaction.

The locations mentioned in the letters allow us to map Addison's progress and meanderings. In January 1703, he wrote from Dresden and, three months later, from Hamburg. He stayed in Leyden in May, then went to Rotterdam, then Amsterdam where the dates of the remaining letters reveal he resided for two months. The rest of his sojourn is a strange, monthly alternation of locations, from the Hague to Amsterdam. One of the last letters mentions that he had awaited a packed boat in Delft, from where, however, no letter was sent. Judging

1 "It is clear that Addison did not need to sell Milton to the eighteenth-century reading public. His essays were only a contribution to a reputation already become traditional" (Geduld 1969, 127).

from his correspondence, what did Addison do in Holland, apart from drinking? What did he write there and is there a perceivable influence of his environment on the works he produced there?

Addison is recorded to have associated with other British travellers, and to have visited Frederick Ruysch, the Dutch botanist and anatomist.

> Charles Perrot was evidently a travelling companion of Addison for several weeks, for on May 17, the two signed their names in the *Album Amicorum* of Frederick Ruysch of Amsterdam. With them at that date were Edmund Chishull and George Dashwood. The *Album* may now be seen in the Universiteitsbibliotheek. (Graham 1941, 38, note 1)

What Addison there thought of Ruysch's macabre and whimsical embalming jars or his spirited anatomical displays[2] may perhaps be found in the essay he wrote upon virtuosi in *Tatler* 216.

> It is indeed wonderful to consider, that there should be a Sort of learned Men who are wholly employed in gathering together the Refuse of Nature, if I may call it so, and hoarding up in their Chests and Cabinets such Creatures as others industriously avoid the Sight of (Bond 1987, III, 133).

Addison meeting and engaging in conversation with the antiquary and clergyman Edmund Chishull is another felicitous coincidence of his stay in Amsterdam. Their common interest in numismatics and Roman ruins, and the similarity of Chishull's career with that of Addison's father (both being employed in foreign lands as chaplains, Lancelot Addison in Tangiers, and Chishull in Smyrna)[3] must have provided him with rich, scholarly exchanges. But at the same time that Addison was engaged in intellectual enquiries he was also, by his own avowal, drinking quite profusely.

> Dear Sir
> My hand at present begins to grow steddy enough for a Letter so that the properest use I can put it to is to thank the honest Gentleman that set it a shaking. (Letter 33 to John Wyche, Leyden, May 1703; Graham 1941, 39)

A letter to a rather dissipated College friend, and many others to acquaintances, record the drinking of healths, toasts, and sundry other alcoholic salutations that indicate Addison drank and networked in equal measure. These two undoubtedly pleasant activities, as well as the fact that there appeared to be no pressing obligation for him to fulfil in England—where the debts he had left in Oxford,

---

2 See the illustrative plates of his *Thesaurus Animalium Primus* (1710, 42), for peculiar examples of tasteful morbidity.

3 See his life by William Gibson in *ODNB*.

rather than an employment, awaited him—can explain why Addison loitered in Holland. Two letters mention that his father, Dr. Lancelot Addison, had died on April 20, 1703, while he was travelling between Hamburg and Leyden. Yet, Addison did not rush back to England on that account. If he could not be present at the burial and subsequent settling of the estate, Addison did contribute to the ordering of his father's affairs by writing a conciliatory letter to Dr. John Hough, Bishop of Lichfield (Graham 1941, 45), with whom Lancelot had had some disagreement before his death. He wrote from Rotterdam in May 1703, waiting for the "Packet-boat, At my coming to Rotterdam I found there was none at present on this side the water: so that I intend to stay at Delf till one arrives" (Letter 36. To John Colbatch, Rotterdam, May 1703, Graham 1941, 42). However, the last letter sent from the continent is dated from September, at the Hague, and the subsequent surviving letter, written from London, was sent as late as March 1704.

> Il est hors de doute que la ville d'Amsterdam a gardé une prépondérance absolue dans la librairaie néerlandaise pendant les décennies autour de 1700 et que les autres villes néerlandaises ont produit proportionnellement beaucoup moins de livres [...]. Après Amsterdam suivent respectivement La Haye, Leyde, Utrecht et Rotterdam comme les plus importantes parmi les centres typographiques des Provinces-Unies. (Bots 1992, 58–59)

In this nexus of paper merchants, printers and booksellers, intellectuals, spies, wealthy travellers and courtiers, Addison repeatedly visited its most active cities. It is, therefore, likely that he found the time to read and acquire books, and to add the final touch to his *Remarks* that were to be published in 1705 by Tonson. If his relative idleness and more certain dissipation in Holland,[4] and the subsequent two-year period he spent in London are taken into account, it may be safely assumed that over this period (from 1703 to 1705) he was working on the first four acts of his tragedy, *Cato*.

In London, Addison remained almost two years without employment, in mediocre lodgings. The *Campaign*, hastily published in 1704 to coincide with Marlborough's return, brought him some renown and only later, in 1705, with the Whigs in power, the post of Under-Secretary of State, accompanying Lord Halifax on a diplomatic mission to Hanover, Germany. Although he must have

4 "At my first arrival I receivd the melancholy news of my Fathers Death and ever since have bin engaged in so much Noise and Company that it was impossible for me to think of Rhiming in it, unless I had bin possest with such a Muse as Dr Blackmore that coud make a couple of Heroic poemes in a Hackney-coach and a Coffy-house" (Letter 42; Graham 1941, 47).

been able occasionally to contribute to Steele's first journalistic endeavours in 1709, thanks to the lighter format of the essay, his then secretaryship to the new Lord Lieutenant of Ireland, Lord Wharton, is unlikely to have allowed him enough scope and leisure to write his far bulkier tragedy. Ergo, though performed in 1713, the better part of *Cato* may well have been written before 1705. Tonson (according to Joseph Spence, 35) is said to have professed to have seen the first four acts of *Cato* upon Addison's return from his travels in 1703.

> Addison wrote the four first acts of his Cato abroad; at least, they were written, when I met him, accidentally on his return, at Rotterdam—*Tonson*. (Spence 1858, I, 35)

And here arises an interesting quandary: if Spence's report is incorrect (the meeting was planned, not accidental, and arranged to take place in Amsterdam rather than Rotterdam), can this still be trusted? If it can, we have some indication of what both men talked about when they met. They talked shop, that is, literature, with Tonson describing his projected edition of *Caesar's Commentaries* and Addison showing Tonson his latest productions.

What did Addison take from this short, though extended, stay in Holland ? Some remarks Addison made about a popular form of theatre in Amsterdam were sent in the last letter he wrote from there to John Wyche, on September 1703 (Graham 1941, 48), and later recycled in *Tatler* 20. We know from the 1799 sale catalogue of his library as well as from Spence's anecdotes that Addison possessed and extensively used a 1702 French edition of Pierre Bayle's *Dictionnaire Historique*, published in Amsterdam. Addison also owned Tonson's 1710 translated edition.

> 654 Bayle Dictionnaire Historique, 3 tom. *Amst.* 1702 [...]
> 434 Marolles Tableau du Temple des Muses *Par.* 1655 [...]
> 436 Bayle's Historical and Critical Dictionary, 4 vol. 1710. (*Catalogue* 1799, 11, 17)

Interestingly, even though the volumes auctioned in 1799 were mostly, but not entirely, bought by Addison, it is very probable that Marolles' *Tableau du Temple des Muses* as well as the 1702 French *Dictionnaire* were brought back to England together.

In May 1703, Addison wrote to Tonson from Leyden, to arrange a meeting in Amsterdam on the following day. At the start of the letter, Addison communicated the most pressing piece of news, that is, a reference to Marolles' book of prints, a work which Tonson might have been eager to purchase from a local bookseller.

> Sir,
> I have shown your letter to Mr. Conningham. He will speak to the bookseller about ye Tableau des Muses, but can't possibly meet at Leiden so soon as you mention, expecting

a letter by every post from England. (Letter 34 to Jacob Tonson, Leyden, May 1703; Graham 1941, 39)

One may wonder why Addison acquired a book Tonson was initially looking for. According to a 1862 *Manuel du Libraire*, the first, original edition contained a rather risqué print depicting Salmacis and Hermaphrodite that was later removed and replaced in the subsequent editions.[5]

Bloemaert, Cornelis II: *Salmacis et Hermaphrodite*. 1655.
Buy permission Roger Viollet ©]

5 "Édition originale, recherchée des amateurs, à cause de 60 figures gravées par Bloëmert, d'après Diepenbeke, dont elle est ornée […]. Dans la plupart des exempl. de ce livre, on a remplacé l'estampe de *Salmacis et Hermaphrodite*, grav. par Bloëmert, laquelle était trop libre, par une autre estampe sur le même sujet, gravée par *Poilly*" (Brunet 1862, III, 1443).

Was Tonson looking for this particular plate? Had he been commissioned to buy this singular piece of erotica? In a natural setting replete with less-than-subtle symbols (the rivulet flowing at the base of the erect tree trunk), an already decidedly androgynous nymph, Salmacis, robustly collars a reluctant Hermaphrodite as she is about to be merged with him by the gods. If Tonson did find an original, first edition with this particular plate, why did Addison keep it in his library? One may wonder what other curiosities and influences Addison carried back to London in 1704.

Many aspects of his reflections that were later published in the *Spectator* could have been inspired by his travels, his observations and readings there and then, but were later carefully "nationalised", that is, edited so as not to retain the appearance of foreignness, thus promoting a staunchly English, Protestant and Whig ideology. However pleasant or influential Malebranche's disquisitions seemed to him when he visited him in Paris, however profound Fontenelle's influence may have been in the didactic strategy of Mr. Spectator, Addison screened these influences and instead quoted John Locke.

Thus, notwithstanding the conscious reworking of European influence in his prose and the dearth of material, it may be safely claimed that this brief meeting in Amsterdam represented the start of Addison's career—his ascent of "Jacob's ladder" as satirised by William Wycherley in a letter to Pope.[6]

As has already been suggested, the rungs of the ladder were politics and literature. In Amsterdam, Tonson enlisted Addison in his literary endeavours, and perhaps in more secret schemes. Mr. Conningham, mentioned in Addison's letter in reference to Marolles' book, appears to have worked as a minor British spy, according to Walter Graham, and later came to work under Addison's orders while a "resident at Venice, 1715–17" (Graham, 39). Judging from the lack of any introduction prefixed to his name in Addison's letter, Conningham was a common acquaintance of both Tonson and Addison. Tonson's biographer, Kathleen Lynch, records that

> As early as 1703 a political mission was read into Tonson's journey to Holland in that year. (Lynch 1971, 60)

Tonson could indeed use his frequent travels to the Continent to gather information on behalf of the Whig faction.

6 Letter 21, May 1709 (Roscoe 1847, VI, 59–60).

> In 1713, when Tonson went to the Continent on business connected with his trade, he was also entrusted with a political mission for the Kit-Cats […]. By November, Tonson was in Paris, investigating [Matthew] Prior's apparent involvement in Jacobite plots. (Lynch 1971, 82)

Whether there was a political motivation in his 1703 trip, and whether Addison helped him, we have no means to make any fresh claims, but can only express suspicions. Jacob Tonson's other occupation, that is, literature, provides us with far more elements, and some in particular, of a considerable size.

Tonson's edition of *Caesar's Commentaries* required the whitest paper, unavailable in England due to the still relatively primitive production of paper there as opposed to the French and Dutch manufactures. Addison must have conferred at length with Tonson concerning this venture, as he was able to describe the future edition in great details, in terms that are not unrelated to Addison's own *Remarks*. Indeed, a similar educational or antiquarian emphasis on comparing classical literature with surviving cultural artefacts can be noticed.

Moreover, Addison actively employed himself in the quest for engravings and subscribers.

> As I dined with my Ld Cutts t'other day, I talk't of your Caesar, and let him know y^{t} two German generals had subscribed. He ask't me who had ye taking of the subscriptions, and told me he believ'd he could assist you if they were not full […]. (Letter 34 to Jacob Tonson, Leyden, May 1703; Graham 1941, 40)

In another letter written to Leibniz on behalf of Tonson, Addison described the book as a precise rendition of the original Latin text with as many contemporary illustrations as could be found at the time—engravings of coins, frescoes and sculptures—so as to elevate the aesthetic value of the book and enable the reader to grasp some of the reality of the classical text. Far more surprising, though, was Addison's request to Leibniz. He begged him to write a note for the edition comparing a buffalo owned by the king of Prussia with Caesar's description of an Auroch or Urus.

> […] I have lately receiv'd a letter from a friend of mine that is now upon an Edition of Caesars Commentarys and desires me to make you acquainted with his Design. He has heard that the King of Prussia has one of those Buffalos that Julius Caesar calls an Urus and gives so particular a description of. He intends to spare no cost in the Edition of this Book which will probably be the noblest Volume that ever came from the English press. *He would therefore be very glad to get a Drawing of this Beast if possible which he would have engraved at Amsterdam*, where they are now at work on several other prints that are to have a place in the same Book. He intends to enrich his Edition with Palladio's Cutts of Caesars Battles, Machines and Encampments, with all the ancient Medals Statues and Bas reliefs that have any relation to his Authour, and with prints of any modern pictures

> that have been taken from the Commentaries and are esteem'd by the best Masters. One of the greatest ornaments of his Book however would be any observations of M[r] Leibnitz. *If therefore you think it worth your while to compare the Animal with the description that Caesar had made of it, and to see whether it has all the Qualities that there attributed or any other that there omitted* I am sure it woud be a very great Obligation not only to the Undertakers of this work but to the learned world in general. (Letter to Gottfried Wilhelm Leibniz, Hague July the 10th 1703, Graham 1941, 43–44, my emphasis)

In the way he described the as yet unpublished book, Addison stressed that this was not merely a luxury venture, but also an intellectual quest for exact knowledge and beauty. Yet, the incongruity of asking Leibniz, of all people, to examine a buffalo obviously escapes Addison, and might have inclined Leibniz to turn down the request.

However, it appears that Tonson's buffalo did ultimately manage to step into his edition. Walter Graham mentions the existence of a picture of "the Urus in which Addison was interested" that "covers two full pages (between 134 and 135 in vol. 1) and was engraved by C. Huijberts" (Graham 44). The drawing of the beast, therefore, might have been made possible through the intercession of the philosopher.

C. Huijberts, Auroch plate, courtesy of Bauman Rare Books©

One may, at first sight, wonder why a Latin text needed a double page entirely filled by a formidable, black bovine. If one, however, reflects on the commercial acumen Tonson demonstrated in the course of his long and illustrious career, then the grandiloquent illustration, and all of the other splendid engravings of paintings and bas-reliefs, make more sense. They were inserted into the text to attract a wider range of customers. Publisher John Murray's expostulation to one of his authors reflects precisely the same commercial imperative: "What signifies a learned and ingenious Book to me where there are not learned and ingenious men enough to buy?" (Zachs 1998, 72).

In 1712, when the *Commentaries* were finally published on the Dutch paper bought in 1703, Addison inserted a puff for the book in the *Spectator*. The sale catalogue of his library shows that he did own a copy, in its largest, and most expensive, format.

> 825. Caearis Commentaria, a Clarke, *large paper* 1712. (*Catalogue* 1799, 21)

ESTC records only one surviving copy of the large paper edition (held at the Huntington Library in San Marino). It is an elephant folio with uncut margins and is a remarkable 51.3 cms in height. Posterity has now established that Tonson accurately perceived how his edition of *Caesar's Commentaries* would captivate its audience. The very few, and smaller, remaining copies that have been advertised on Sotheby's, Abebooks and Bauman Rare Books websites were consequently sold for a price varying from £3,500 to $13,500. Ironically, what makes a copy dearer or cheaper today is precisely the presence or absence of the Urus on pages 134 and 135, since, as was often the case, the striking double page engraving was detached to be framed and used in a separate capacity for interior decoration. Among bibliophiles, the engraving that Addison was instrumental in bringing about is well known, and simply called "the bison".

Tonson's publication appeared on April 7 and this *Spectator* essay on May 1. The *Commentaries* had also already been advertised as "this day published" in the preceding *Spectator* essay—it was both economical and commercially sound for Tonson to advertise his publication twice in a newspaper he himself printed.

> The several Presses which are now in *England*, and the great Encouragement which has been given to Learning for some Years last past, has made *our own Nation* as glorious upon this Account, as for its late Triumphs and Conquests. The new edition which is given us of *Caesar*'s Commentaries has already been taken *notice of in Foreign* Gazettes, and is a Work that does Honour to *the* English *Press*. It is no wonder that an Edition should be so correct, which has passed through the Hands of one of the most Accurate, Learned and Judicious Writers this Age has produced. The Beauty of the Paper, of the Character, and of the several Cuts with which this noble Work is Illustrated, makes it

> the finest Book that I have ever seen; and is a true Instance of *the* English *Genius*, which, though it does not come the first into any Art, generally carries it to greater heights than any other Country in the World. I am particularly glad that this Author comes *from a* British *Printing-House* in so great a Magnificence, as he is the first who has given us any tolerable Account of our Country. (*Spectator* 367, Bond 1965, III, 381–382, my emphasis)

Since Addison himself contributed, however indirectly, to the fulfilment of the edition, this puff could be read as a sincere encomium. Yet, the highlighted passages clearly show that a strategy of re-appropriation is afoot. No mention is made of the Prussian, showstopping buffalo, of the provenance of the paper, of the Dutch engravers responsible for the illustrations, of the Italian works these illustrations copy,[7] nor is the name of Leibniz brought to the light (if he ever did examine that buffalo). The entirety of the cultural prestige attributed to the book becomes national, that is, eminently and visibly British, although it objectively represents a European collaborative production.

Thus, this particular edition, even more than his continental correspondence, exemplifies Addison's representation or rewriting of his travels. By rewriting, we mean a strategic re-appropriation and screening of European influences, making it difficult for us to pick apart what he might have brought back from Holland. Wine, certainly, literati and aristocratic networks, some prints, some books, and Tonson's esteem, along with the whitest Dutch paper.

References

ADDISON, Joseph: *The Letters of Joseph Addison*. Walter Graham (ed.). Oxford: Clarendon Press 1941.

ADDISON, Joseph/Richard Steele et al.: *The Tatler*. Donald F. Bond (ed.). Oxford: Clarendon Press 1987. 3 vols.

ADDISON, Joseph/Richard Steele et al.: *The Spectator*. Donald F. Bond (ed.). Oxford: Clarendon Press 1965. 5 vols.

ADDISON, Joseph: *A Catalogue of the Valuable Library, of the Late Celebrated Right Hon. Joseph Addison*. London: Leigh and Sotheby 1799.

BELLINGRADT, Daniel: "Trading Paper in Early Modern Europe". *Jaarboek voor Nederlandse boekgeschiedenis* 21 (2014), 117–131.

BOTS, Hans: "Le rôle des périodiques néerlandais pour la diffusion du livre (1684–1747)". In: Christiane Berkvens-Stevelinck (ed.): *Le Magasin*

7 Nine of its illustrative plates are engraved copies of Andrea Mantegna's paintings for the Gonzaga palace in Mantua, Italy, *The Triumphs of Caesar* (1484–1492).

de L'Univers: The Dutch Republic as the Centre of the European Book Trade: Papers Presented at the International Colloquium Held at Wassenaar, 5–7 July 1990. Leyden: E. J. Brill 1992, 49–70.

BRUNET, Jacques-Charles: *Manuel du Libraire*. Paris: Firmin Didot Frères 1862. 3 vols.

CAESAR, Caius Julius: *Quae Extant*. Samuel Clarke (ed.). London: Jacob Tonson 1712.

GEDULD, Harry M.: *Prince of Publishers: A Study of the Work and Career of Jacob Tonson*. Bloomington: Indiana University Press 1969.

GIBBS, G.C.: "The role of the Dutch Republic as the intellectual entrepôt of Europe in the seventeenth and eighteenth centuries". *BMGN—Low Countries Historical Review* 86/3 (1971), 323–349.

https://www.baumanrarebooks.com/rare-books/gaius-julius-caesar/c-julii-caesaris-que-extant/ 86428.aspxn (last visited January 29, 2019).

https://books.google.fr/books/about/A_Catalogue_of_the_Valuable_Library_of_t.html?id=LVAVAAAAQAAJ&redir_esc=y (last visited January 29, 2019).

LYNCH, Kathleen M.: *Jacob Tonson, Kit-Cat Publisher*. Knoxville: The University of Tennessee Press 1971.

MAROLLES, Michel de: *Tableau du Temple des Muses, tirez du cabinet de feu M. Favereau, et gravez en tailles donc par les meilleurs maistres pour représenter les vertus et les vices sur les plus illustres fables de l'antiquité avec les descriptions, remarques, et annotations*. Paris: Antoine de Sommaville 1655.

POPE, Alexander: *The Works of Alexander Pope, Esq.* William Roscoe (ed.). London: Long-man, Brown and Co. 1847.

RUYSCH, Frederik: *Thesaurus Animalium Primus*. Amsterdam: Joannem Wolters 1710.

SPENCE, Joseph: *Anecdotes, Observations and Characters of Books and Men Collected from the Conversation of Mr Pope and Other Eminent Persons of His Time*. London: John Russel Smith 1858.

ZACHS, Bill: *The First John Murray and the Late Eighteenth-Century Book Trade*. London: Oxford University Press for the British Academy 1998.

Endre Szécsényi

(University of Aberdeen)

The Jesuit thread in Joseph Addison's aesthetics

In my chapter,[1] I will claim that Joseph Addison, one of the pioneers of modern aesthetic thinking, exploited and utilized certain conceptions and ideas which had been elaborated by seventeenth-century Jesuit authors, while he wrote his seminal moral essays on a new type of experience that we can retrospectively call aesthetic. I will discuss some characteristic features of the Addisonian aesthetic experience which were anticipated and pre-modelled in the writings of Baltasar Gracián and Dominique Bouhours whom Addison explicitly mentions in different contexts of *The Spectator*. When I try to reconstruct the Jesuit thread in Addison's "aesthetic" thinking, I would like to suggest a stronger thesis than to say that authors—like Gracián, Bouhours, René Rapin and others—who were Addison's inspirational sources in the elaboration of his aesthetics and literary criticism, happened to be eminent Jesuits. To be sure, Addison was deeply imbedded in the Protestant, Latitudinarian theological and devotional tradition, by no means he was a crypto-Jesuit;[2] still, it seems to me, he introduced the modern "aesthetic" experience as a form of everyday spiritual exercises which originally, at least in this Christian version, were initiated and elaborated by St. Ignatius of Loyola, then developed by his fellow-Jesuits. And we know, for example, from Louis Martz's seminal book that Continental Jesuit meditations, books of prayers and guides of Christian life were highly popular and saw numerous English editions (some of them were adaptations to Protestant views) throughout the seventeenth century. Besides Ignatius, Luis de Granada (a Dominican friar inspired by Ignatius) and Gaspar Loarte, mostly St. Francis de Sales, had an enormous impact on English poetry and devotional literature

1 I wish to express my thanks to the Research Institute of Irish and Scottish Studies of the University of Aberdeen for the financial support which made it possible for me to participate in the conference *Addison et l'Europe* held at the Université Sorbonne Nouvelle-Paris 3 on 7–8 December 2018.

2 At the same time, his explicit anti-Catholicism—like John Locke's or Richard Steele's—was rather of political than theological nature (Bloom-Bloom 1971, 146).

(Martz 1954, 5 ff; Davies 1975, 82–85). Both these Jesuit texts[3] and the English literature influenced by them could make a stimulating environment for Addison when he invented a new language for the emerging "aesthetic" experience.

The scholarly tradition to which I would connect my article is the historiography of modern aesthetics in which Gracián's concept of *gusto* and Bouhours' language of *délicatesse* have had an eminent part at least since Benedetto Croce's narrative first published in 1902 (Croce 1908, 214–226).[4] While the most recent historical narratives written by Timothy M. Costelloe or Paul Guyer appreciate Addison's contribution to modern aesthetics (Costelloe 2013, 37–49; Guyer 2014, I, 63–73), they omit the seventeenth-century chapter of the story. Hopefully, this chapter will be able to show that some significant aspects of the emerging modern aesthetic remain unnoticed, if we accept these recent approaches.

In his *Spectator* essays, Addison refers to Gracián first as a Machiavellian thinker who gave a strange, but still intriguing, political-practical advice of why we should avoid unlucky people and not aid them: "notwithstanding the Baseness of the Precept to an honest Mind, may have something useful in it for those who push their Interest in the World" (Addison 1965, III, 42).[5] This embarrassingly "immoral" aspect of Gracián's thinking was obvious to Addison and to many of the contemporary readers.[6] Second, Gracián is the subject of the first sentence of Addison's essay No. 409 on taste which is the introductory piece to his *The Pleasures of the Imagination* series (*The Spectator*, Nos. 411–421): "Gratian very often recommends the *fine Taste*, as the utmost Perfection of an accomplished

3 Certainly, Ignatian and Salesian spirituality was only one ingredient of the broader Catholic devotion including the Carmelites (Sts Teresa of Avila and John of the Cross), the cult of the Rosary and that of the Sacred Heart (Davies 1975, 485–489) which directly or indirectly influenced on the seventeenth- and early eighteenth-century British religious life.

4 In respect of Gracián, Croce relies exclusively on Karl Borinski's book of 1886: *Die Poetik der Renaissance und die Anfänge der litterarischen Kritik in Deutschland*, while, in his influential historical narrative written in 1923, Alfred Baeumler refers only to another Borinski's book, *Baltasar Gracian und die Hofliteratur in Deutchland* of 1894 (Baeumler 1967, Pt. I, ch. 1).

5 Probably, Addison thought of, for example, the aphorism no. 64 of Gracián's *Oráculo manual*: "thou'll do better to let another be Discontented, than to become so thy Self, and that without Remedy" (Gracián 1705, #64).

6 Norbert Elias provides a concise comparison between Machiavelli and Gracián, in which he remarks: despite the differences between their viewpoints, "the conduct recommended by both Machiavelli and Gratian appears to middle-class people as more or less 'immoral' " (Elias 2000, 545–546, no. 6).

Man" (Addison 1965, III, 527). This allusion to the Spaniard[7] can be understood as Addison's effort to connect the social world and the delicate social practices created by and around good taste to his newly discovered realm of "a polite imagination" and its "gentle exercise".

In No. 62, Addison calls Bouhours "the most penetrating of all the *French* Criticks", who represents the finest Neo-Classic taste by convincingly claiming "that it is impossible for any Thought to be beautiful which is not just, and has not its Foundation in the Nature of things: That the Basis of all Wit is Truth; and that no Thought can be valuable, of which good Sense is not the Ground-work" (Addison 1965, I, 268). Here, presumably, Addison thinks of *La Manière de bien penser dans les ouvrages d'esprit* of 1687; there was also an English translation of it by "a Person of Quality" under the title *The Art of Criticism* (Bouhours 1705); later John Oldmixon adapted it to English literature (Bouhours 1728). For our purpose, however, his *Les Entretiens d'Ariste et d'Eugène* of 1671 is more important (Bouhours 2003); though this popular book, which contains six conversations—amongst them are somc "aesthetically" relevant ones as "La mer", "Le bel esprit" and "Le je ne sais quoi"—has never been translated into English, the original French was perfectly fine for Addison. The availability of English and/or French translations, however, is an issue in the case of Gracián, since, in all probability, neither the original Spanish works, nor their seventeenth- and early eighteenth-century Italian and German translations were accessible for Addison and most of his British contemporaries.

As far as I know, the first scholar who discussed briefly the possible intellectual relationship between Gracián and Addison in regard of the emerging aesthetic was Clarence DeWitt Thorpe more than eighty years ago (Thorpe 1937, 1126–1127; 1940, 61–64). He focused on the category of "novelty"—from amongst the famous Addisonian tripartite "aesthetic" division of "*Greatness, Novelty*, or *Beauty*" (Addison 1965, III, 540)—but this seemingly fertile hint has not been exploited later in scholarship.[8] Following in Thorpe's track, I presume

7 There is no consensus in the scholarship about the particular work which could have been in Addison's mind here. In my opinion, most probably, it was the *Oráculo manual* of 1647 (Gracián 1685; 1705).

8 Moreover, "novelty" itself has faded, having been overshadowed by the beautiful and the sublime, since at least the middle of the eighteenth century (especially after the publication of Edmund Burke's *Philosophical Enquiry into the Origin of Our Ideas of the Sublime and the Beautiful* in 1757). In recent decades, there were at least some interesting scholarly attempts to rehabilitate "novelty", to show its significance in Addison and in the history of modern aesthetics—without mentioning Gracián, though (Cf., Dix 1986; Paulson 1996, 48–75; Black 2001).

that Addison could read all of Gracián's three works which had been translated into French or English by the first decade of the eighteenth century: the *Oráculo manual y arte de prudencia* of 1647,[9] which enjoyed great popularity in its time (it was later rediscovered and translated by Arthur Schopenhauer in the nineteenth century); *El Héroe* of 1637,[10] which can be regarded as the predecessor to the first in many respects[11]; and, finally, the first volume of his allegorical pilgrimage, *El Criticón* of 1651 (Gracián 1681; 1696). By using only translations, Addison and his British contemporaries were obliged to read and understand these texts through the interpreters' glasses, and in the context of their sometimes extensive commentaries (and not in the broader context of the *Siglo De Oro* literature or even of Gracián's whole *oeuvre*). Thus, especially the major French translator, Abraham-Nicolas Amelot de La Houssaie stepped forward as a kind of co-author[12]; who, indeed, inventively transformed Gracián's terms into a delicate Bouhoursian language.

In what follows, I am going to present the volatile and delicate quality of *despejo* or *je ne sais quoi* as the general model of the Addisonian "aesthetic"

9 *L'Homme de cour*, first published in 1684, was Abraham-Nicolas Amelot de La Houssaie's influential translation with commentaries (Gracián 1685); the English edition which came to light in 1685, then in 1694, and an improved version in 1702 (Gracián 1705) was a translation of Houssaie's French by Mr. Savage (the edition of 1702 already contains Houssaie's annotations, too).

10 *L'Héros* by Sr. Gervaise was published in 1645 (Gracián 1645), while *The Heroe* by John Skeffington in 1652 (Gracián 1652). I also consulted two modern editions translated and introduced by Christopher Mauer (Gracián 1992; 1996, 1–55).

11 Further French and English translations of *El Héroe* and *Oráculo manual*—and also those of other important works like *El Politico* of 1640 and *El Discreto* of 1645—were available from the 1720s onwards, that is, these came to light after Addison's death (the first Latin version of *Oráculo manual* was published only in 1734). Beside *El Criticón* (Gracián 1681; 1696), the only exception is the 1693 French translation by Houssaie of *El Comulgatorio* of 1655, which could have been in the hands of Addison, but Gracián's Ignatian spiritual meditations were hardly known (Gracián 1693); despite the fact that Houssaie's (and thus Savage's) preface to *Oráculo manual* conveys a brief survey of Gracián's *oeuvre* including his seventh book, *El Comulgador* as the only piece which was published under the author's own name during his lifetime. At the same time, some chapters and passages (or their resumés) of *El Discreto* (and, of course, of *El Héroe*), furthermore some references to *El Politico* and to the two versions of *Agudeza y arte de ingenio* of 1642 and 1648 could be found in Houssaie's annotations to *L'Homme de cour.*

12 From the 1720s onwards, Joseph de Courbeville, another Jesuit, became the number one French translator of Gracián's works.

experience; second, I am going to briefly outline a possible historical connection between a chapter of *El Criticón* and the position of Addisonian "aesthetic" spectator.

Neither *El Héroe*, nor *Oráculo manual* were merely pragmatical sometimes almost cynical guides for courtiers swarming in the "Nurseries of Vanity *[palacios de la vanidad]*" (Gracián 1705, #11), from which they could learn how to survive and how to raise their own reputation in an extremely competitive and hostile social environment. Such was the absolutistic royal court, in which a courtier had to face that he was always visible: "Even then when he is alone, he acts as if he were in the presence of all Men, because he knows that all Things must come to be known" (Gracián 1705, #297). The claim of permanent self-defence led to the recommendation of different Machiavellian techniques,[13] as Addison also noticed in his above-mentioned remark. It was, however, only one aspect of Gracián's social world, and he discussed some other significant subjects, like human perfection, good taste and those volatile and fine qualities which were the unprecedented cultural outcomes of the common social "practice", the gentle and prudent interaction, of *discretos* or *honnêtes gens*. Beside the palaces of vanity, there were also the "Theatres of Heroism", that is, the "Academ[ies] of Prudence and good Behaviour" (Gracián 1705, #11), or in Houssaie's words: "[les] académie[s] de prudence et de politesse". These were the dedicated places where real perfection could be gained via conversations with wise and good men in a manner which combined learning with sociable pleasure, understanding with taste. The "Theatres of Heroism" were tokens of the existence (even if it was undoubtedly faint) of a higher order, these places could demonstrate that the claim of adding *Cielo* to *mundo*[14] is not a nonsense. Gracián paints a rather dark picture of his age, but he recommends nonetheless to "Let a Prudent Man suit himself to the present Times whether in relation to Body, or Mind although the Past may even seem better to him" (Gracián 1705, #120). The "Rule" of living is to adopt oneself to one's time:

> We must not speak after the old Fashion; our Relish must accommodate it self to the New *[no se ha de discurrir a lo viejo, y se ha de gustar a lo moderno]*. [...] Let a Wise Man *[discreto]* then Live as he can, if he cannot as he would. Let him be content with

---

13 For "Man's Life is a perpetual Conflict with Man himself. An expert Person uses for Weapons the stratagems of Intention" (Gracián 1705, #13).

14 "In Heaven All Is Pleasure *[contento]*; in Hell All Pain *[pesar]*. The World being in middle, has a Share of both. [...] This World *[mundo]* is a Cypher: Alone it is Nothing; when join'd with Heaven *[Cielo]*, it is worth a great deal" (Gracián 1705, #211).

> what Fortune hath lent him, as if it were better than what she hath denied him. (Gracián 1705, #120)

This modern *gusto* was the major instrument of the adaptation to time, at the same time, it made possible for the courtiers to experience certain gentle qualities which were the most valuable moments in their lives. These qualities were expressed around the term *gracia* whose inherent polysemy (cf. Covarrubias Orozco 1674, 37) Gracián exploited, and on which he established a connection between different—celestial and worldly—spheres.[15] In Chapter 12 of *El Héroe* titled "The Love of People *[gracia de las gentes]*", he prefers modern graces to ancient ones:

> And to say truth, the Grace of God, and of the king, and of the people, are 3 graces of more beauty than those other 3 that were feigned by antiquity. *[Y verdad, que la (gracia) de Dios, del Rey, y de las gentes, son tres gracias mas bellas, que las que se singieron los antiguos]* They hold hand in hand, and are so streightly enterlaced that if any of them fayl; let it be able to shew a good cause.[16] (Gracián 1652, 99–100)

The three modern graces are ordered in a hierarchy (they belong to different spheres) but they all express or connect somehow to the winning of the attention and attraction. God's *gracia* is his *grace*, the king's is *mercy*, and the people's *gracia* is the kind of love, applause or favour that comes under taste, which, in turn, always complements utility. In each instance when Gracián uses the word *gracia*, he means something that reaches and captures us—more exactly, our will *(voluntad)*—immediately, without having to pass through the roundabout ways of reason (such as reflection, deliberation or calculation), even though this is not contrary to reason in the end.

Norbert Elias claims that "the emphasis [is] on the 'how' rather than the 'what' of any procedure" in courtly society. "What we think of as 'external', as 'formalism', is nothing other than an expression of the primacy of the relationship of all things and events to the status or power of the *person* involved in relation to others" (Elias 1983, 109). "Manner" or "manière" is stressed, indeed, in

15 This kind of connection is far from being new: "*Charis* [*gratia* in Latin] refers to the attractive 'charm' of the beautiful, but it also means 'grace'. '*Charis* is poured out upon your lips,' sings the nuptial psalm (44.3). We believe that what is beautiful in this world—being spirit as it makes its appearance—possesses a total dimension that also calls for moral decision" (Balthasar 1982, 34). Here Hans Urs von Balthasar speaks about the transition from the sphere of nature to that of grace, from philosophy to theology. Gracián, however, drags "the social" into this relationship which is, as far as I know. not customary.

16 The last clause in the French translation: "que ce soit par ordre" (Gracián 1645, 84).

Gracián's writings, too. In his comment attached to aphorism no. 14,[17] Houssaie cites lengthily from chapter 3 of *El Discreto*: "Truth has Force; Reason, Authority; and Justice Power: But they are still without Lustre, if the graceful Manner be wanting; when with it, every thing is let off to the greater Advantage". "Lustre" is one of his volatile values which are difficult to grasp, to teach, or even to imitate the practice in which those appear; they do not fit well in the traditional discursive framework: neither in logic, nor even in rhetoric. They are partly gifts from heaven, partly results or achievements of social interactions.

Among these new elusive values, there is Gracián's *despejo* (rendered by Houssaie—and later also by Courbeville—as the *je ne sais quoi*)[18] which seems especially significant in the mirror of its reception in the history of aesthetics. Gracián discussed it in chapter 13 of *El Héroe* and in maxim no. 127 of the *Oráculo manual.* It is all about the *hows* and the *manners*: it "is the Life of great Qualities, the Breath of Words, the Soul of Actions, and the Lustre of Beauties. Other Perfections are the Ornament of Nature; the Inexpressible *Somewhat,* is that of Perfections themselves". To a certain extent, this notion goes back to Baldassare Castiglione's *sprezzatura*—a kind of ease or a certain nonchalance in everything that a courtier does—but assumes a greater role and significance in Gracián. "Without it all Beauty is dead, all Gracefulness Ungraceful [*toda gracia, desgracia*]". This "Secret Charm, or the Inexpressible Somewhat [*despejo*]" is worthier than anything else: "It hath the pre-eminence over Valour, Discretion, Prudence, nay, and Majesty it Self" (Gracián 1705, #127). The *despejo* is useful in prudential and political matters, too, but, at the same time, it "transcends" (*transcendental*) all worldly merits; thus, it may create a new kind of link between the terrestrial and the celestial. This transcendental concern was clearly understood by Houssaie who, in his explanation to no. 127, called *despejo* "tres-métafysique" in itself (Gracián 1685, 158), translated—almost the whole chapter 13 of *El Héroe* into French to present here, and completed this commentary with some of Bouhours' passages from the fifth dialogue "Le je ne sais quoi" of the *Entretiens d'Ariste et d'Eugène.*

---

17 "The Substance is not enough, unless it be cloathed with its Circumstances. [...] The *How* does much in all things. A free and easy Manner charms the Minds of Men, and makes the compleat Ornament of Life" (Gracián 1705, #14).

18 The phrase or term *je ne sais quoi* was quite fashionable and widely spread from the second half of the seventeenth century until the middle of the eighteenth century, and Jesuits like Gracián, Bouhours and later Feijoó y Montenegro made the most significant contributions to its language.

Notably, this dialogue ends with the explicit and infamous identification of the *je ne sais quoi* with divine grace.[19] The *je ne sais quoi* is an experience which directly touches the heart (without any contribution of the understanding or reason), that is, its irresistible emotional effect determines our will but without limiting our freedom, it makes us feel Christian mysteries as well, like the immortality of our soul and the existence of an afterlife:

> [L]e je ne sais quoi est de la grâce aussi bien que de la nature & de l'art. […] [L]a grâce elle-même, cette divine grâce, qui a fait tant de bruit dans les écoles, & qui fait des effets si admirables dans les âmes; cette grâce si forte & si douce tout ensemble, qui triomphe de la dureté du cœur, sans blesser la liberté du franc-arbitre, qui s'assujettit la nature en s'y accommodant; qui se rend maîtresse de la volonté, en la laissant maîtresse d'elle-même; cette grâce […] qu'est-ce autre chose qu'un je ne sais quoi surnaturel, qu'on ne peut ni expliquer, ni comprendre? (Bouhours 2003, 294)

A traditionally negative theological commonplace is being re-formulated here in a proto-aesthetic language. Nevertheless, both the transcendental connotations and the direct irresistible impact on the human will are worth emphasising.

In the characterization of the pleasures of the imagination (i.e., the aesthetic experience) of *The Spectator* No. 411, Addison clearly refers us to the seventeenth-century vocabulary of the *je ne sais quoi*:

> It is but opening the Eye, and the Scene enters. The Colours paint themselves on the Fancy, with very little Attention of Thought or Application of Mind in the Beholder. We are struck, *we know not how*, with the Symmetry[20] of any thing we see, and immediately assent to the Beauty of an Object, *without enquiring into the particular Causes and Occasions of it.*
>
> A Man of a Polite Imagination is let into a great many Pleasures, that the Vulgar are not capable of receiving. […] It gives him, indeed, a kind of Property in every thing he sees, and makes the most rude uncultivated Parts of Nature administer to his Pleasures: So that *he looks upon the World,* as it were *in another Light*, and discovers in it a *Multitude of Charms,* that conceal themselves from the generality of Mankind. (Addison 1965, III, 538—my emphases, E. Sz.)

---

19 It launched a vehement debate between Jesuit and Jansenist authors right after the publication of *Entretiens* (cf. Scholar 2005, 64–69).

20 In this place, "symmetry" can mean something like the irregular symmetry of "l'agrément" (another version of the *je ne sais quoi*) in François de La Rochefoucauld's maxim no. 240: "On peut dire de l'agrément séparé de la beauté, que c'est une symétrie dont on ne sait point les règles, et un rapport secret des traits ensemble, et des traits avec les couleurs et avec l'air de la personne" (La Rochefoucauld 2007).

Thus, aesthetic experience is characterised as an extraordinarily strong or charming emotional reaction whose cause always remains unknown to us, exactly as Ariste would say: "Il est bien plus aisé de le sentir que de le connaître [...]. Ce ne serait plus un je ne sais quoi, si l'on savait ce que c'est; sa nature est d'être incomprehensible et inexplicable" (Bouhours 2003, 280).[21] In the next essay, Addison considers "those Pleasures of the Imagination, which arise from the actual View and Survey of outward Objects: And these, I think, all proceed from the Sight of what is *Great*, *Uncommon*, or *Beautiful*" (Addison 1965, III, 540). This far-reaching aesthetic triad covers "all" of the possible types of the "aesthetic" experience, but they appear very rarely in their pure forms, most often we encounter some mixture of them. Their combination, however, strengthens the effect. The paradigmatic example of this intensifying synthesis of the three qualities is the perception of a broad natural landscape—a location which is associated with walking in nature. All these three aesthetic qualities are conceived on the model of the secret charm or the *je ne sais quoi* which has irresistible emotional effects, and whose cause remains always unknown. This is why Addison deals with their final causes in No. 413, their providential functions in the divine order of the Creation, instead of their efficient causes.[22]

When Addison explicitly discusses the experience of beauty, he applies the language of the *je ne sais quoi*, which offers him an alternative to the classical conception of beauty:

> [T]there is nothing that makes its way more directly to the Soul than *Beauty*, which immediately diffuses a secret Satisfaction and Complacency thro' the Imagination, and gives a Finishing to anything that is Great or Uncommon. The very first Discovery of it strikes the Mind with an inward Joy, and spreads a Chearfulness and Delight through all its Faculties. (Addison 1965, III, 542)

21 At the end of this passage, Bouhours explicitly refers to Gracián's *El Héroe*, and its phrase concerning *despejo*: 'un parentesco de los corançones'.

22 Recently, following Jerome Stolnitz's paper of 1963, Eduard Ghiță analysed this argumentation on the basis of Addison's explicit reference to and terms borrowed from John Locke's *Essay concerning Human Understanding*, claiming that Addison relies on Locke's epistemological scepticism about the "necessary connection" between the primary qualities in the body and the sensations produced by them in us (cf. Ghiță 2017, 101–103). Though Locke had a great impact on Addison's discourse in this place, indeed, our reflected ignorance concerning the efficient causes of our sensations does not necessarily trigger irresistible and striking emotional response in us: the *je ne sais quoi* experience must be a very special case of this epistemological problem, and I doubt that the Lockean language is suitable to properly grasp it.

He distinguishes two kinds of beauty: the first belongs to “every different Species of sensible Creatures” and eventually consists in the erotic/sexual attractions between males and females, or it is associated with the warmth and violence of sensual love. The other, calmer kind is best represented with the “secret Delights” in colours which was—beside the irresistible and inexplicable nature of love—another seventeenth-century commonplace for the perception and enjoyment of the *je ne sais quoi*. The recurrent adjective “secret” simultaneously means the intimate nature of these feelings (i.e., these pleasures arise in our mind without external signs or gestures in the body) and our inevitable ignorance of their efficient causes. In the whole Addisonian explanation of the effects of beauty, we can read only a half sentence on the symmetry, proportion and arrangement of parts as the source of this quality, which is only a fleeting reference to the traditionally obligatory sources of beauty.[23] Both the erotic attraction and the secret delight of bright colours[24] are much more significant in this experience. They constitute its paradigmatic model. And the “Finishing” character of beauty may remind us of Gracián's *despejo*, as we have seen above.

In the case of the two other categories, greatness (sublime) and novelty, Addison uses a Bouhoursian vocabulary, too. In *The Spectator* No. 489, reflecting on the *Greatness* of Imagination series (in the form of a reader's letter), Addison discusses how “Sea or Ocean” affects the imagination:

> I cannot see the Heavings of this prodigious Bulk of Waters, even in a Calm, without a very pleasing Astonishment; but when it is worked up in a Tempest, so that the Horison on every side is nothing but foaming Billows and floating Mountains, it is impossible to describe the agreeable Horrour that rises from such a Prospect. A troubled Ocean, to a Man who sails upon it, is, I think, the biggest Object that he can see in Motion, and consequently gives his Imagination one of the highest Kinds of Pleasure that can arise from Greatness. (Addison 1965, IV, 233–234)

It is hard not to notice its likeness to Bouhours' description of the emotional effects of the troubled ocean in terms of the *je ne sais quoi* in the first dialogue “La mer” of his *Entretiens*:

> Il me semble que la mer n'est jamais aussi belle que dans sa colère, lorsqu'elle s'enfle, qu'elle s'agite, qu'elle mugit d'une manière effroyable, & qu'il se fait une espèce de guerre entre les vents & les flots. Ces vagues qui s'entrechoquent avec tant d'impétuosité; ces

---

23 Symmetry, order, proportion are not really emphatic even in the artistic examples of beauty, we can only find some faint allusions like the to “well-ordered Garden” of Virgil's *Aeneid* (Addison 1965, III, 564).

24 For the complex role of colours in Addison's thinking, read Junqua 2011.

> montagnes d'eau & d'écume qui s'élèvent & qui s'abaissent tout d'un coup; ce bruit, ce désordre, ce fracas, tout cela inspire je ne sais quelle horreur accompagné de Plaisir, & fait un spectacle également terrible & agréable. (Bouhours 2003, 56–57)

David B. Morris rightly emphasizes that in this essay (No. 489) Addison "is comparing two ways of knowing the Deity: through rational analysis and imaginative perception". It displays "the importance and validity of imaginative experience in strengthening faith. Simply by opening his eyes to the sublimity of nature, a reasonable being can achieve a new power of religious conviction, one made accessible by the imagination, rendered persuasive by the feelings, and ultimately confirmed by the understanding" (Morris 1972, 137). This imaginative experience, like the *je ne sais quoi*, offers a direct link between the sensory or even the sensual and the transcendental, between the instinctive-emotional and the spiritual, while omitting or by-passing the rational approaches though not in a contradictory way.

Both the proto-aesthetic experience of the sublime[25] and novelty were interwoven with that of the *je ne sais quoi*. The novelty, as Thorpe has already suggested, was perhaps the most significant in the aesthetic triad (Thorpe 1937). This category sank into oblivion from the middle of the eighteenth century partially because it was exclusively interpreted as a relative quality, an enjoyment of some uncommon occurrence in the mainstream of the ordinary things and events. "Every thing that is *new* or *uncommon* raises a Pleasure in the Imagination, because it fills the Soul with an agreeable Surprize, gratifies its Curiosity, and gives it an Idea of which it was not before possest" (Addison 1965, III, 541). However, the surprise flies by, the novel quickly runs into the stream of the known and the ordinary. Yet, "novelty" was something more than this, as it was clear in Bouhours' characterization of the prospect of the ever-changing sea which is more interesting and emotionally more effective for the spectator than that of the Sun, the traditionally highest and noblest visible object of the Creation:

> Cette immense étendue d'eau ; ce flux et ce reflux ; le bruit, la couleur, les figures différentes de ces flots qui se poussent régulièrement les uns les autres, ont je ne sais quoi de si surprenant & de si étrange, que je ne sache rien qui en approche. [...] [La mer] paraît toujours nouvelle, parce qu'elle n'est jamais en un même état. (Bouhours 2003, 55)

25 In his *Sublime Poussin*, Louis Marin discusses the common structure of "the presentation of the unrepresentable" behind both the sublime and the *je ne sais quoi*, though "the sublime stems from the 'je ne sais quoi,' but the 'je ne sais quoi' cannot be reduced to the sublime" (Marin 1999, 209–223, 210).

In the Imagination papers, Addison's illuminating example of "novelty" is not the sea, but another natural scene:

> Groves, Fields, and Meadows [...] in the Opening of the Spring, when they are all new and fresh, with their first Gloss upon them, and not yet too much accustomed and familiar to the Eye. [...] [W]here the Scene is perpetually shifting, and entertaining the Sight every Moment with something that is new. (Addison 1965, III, 542)

The inexhaustibility and ever-changing feature of the experience can strongly remind us of Bouhours' sea. And it also preserves that transcendental connotation which the *je ne sais quoi* inherently possesses. To show it, I do not refer to the oft-cited teleological (and providential) explanation of the pleasures of the imagination from the next essay (No. 413), that is, in the case of novelty, to the benevolent Creator who "has annexed a secret Pleasure to the Idea of any thing that is new and uncommon" to encourage and stimulate scientific discoveries of "the Wonders of his Creation" (Addison 1965, III, 545). Because it is an external and subsequent explanation of the possibility of a special human experience in which we encounter this quality; we need, instead, some inner devotional content as a constituent of the experience. This, at the same time, leads us to the second point of this chapter.

In the closure of the last piece of his Cheerfulness papers (No. 393), Addison emphatically points to the example of a Spring-time walk in nature, to show a broad way (available to everybody) of how the "vernal Delight" offered by this experience can be improved "into a Christian virtue", that is, the religious-devotional significance is not a posterior addendum, but the inevitable part of the experience:

> When we find our selves inspired with this pleasing Instinct, this secret Satisfaction and Complacency, arising from the Beauties of the Creation, let us consider to whom we stand indebted for all these Entertainment of Sense, and who it is that thus opens his Hand and fills the World with Good. [...] The Chearfulness of Heart which springs up in us from the Survey of Nature's Works is an admirable Preparation for Gratitude. [...] A grateful Reflection on the Supreme Cause who produces it, sanctifies it in the Soul, and gives it its proper Value. Such an habitual Disposition of Mind consecrates every Field and Wood, turns an ordinary Walk into a Morning or Evening Sacrifice, and will improve those transient Gleams of Joy [...] into an inviolable and perpetual State of Bliss and Happiness. (Addison 1965, III, 475–476)

Both the "secret Satisfaction and Complacency" and the "transient Gleams of Joy" seem to be the versions of the *je ne sais quoi* and, as such, the proper "material" or indispensable "agent" of the improvement of that "habitual Disposition of Mind" which we can retrospectively call one of the first formulations of the modern aesthetic consciousness. The aesthetic, due to the context of the *je ne sais quoi*, is inevitably a spiritual experience,[26] it has to do with the eternal bliss and happiness available to all of us in this world. This "habitual Disposition of Mind" establishes and maintains a new—dynamic and so to speak "interactive"[27]—relationship between the sensual and the transcendental, between "vernal Delight" and heavenly "Bliss and Happiness".[28]

Addison did suggest that the outcome of this "religious Practice" he finally recommended to everybody was something different from, and perhaps *beyond* "a rational Admiration in the Soul" which could be reached by natural philosophy or a (Protestant) occasional meditation[29]: the latter "quickens [the] Taste of the Creation" as "a perpetual Feast", "considers the several Ends of Providence which are served by them, and the wonders of Divine Wisdom which appear in them", yet its "rational Admiration" remains always "little inferiour to Devotion" (Addison 1965, III, 475). Moreover, in the mirror of his essay of No. 465 on the different methods of strengthening religious faith, it seems that Addison posited the "aesthetico"-devotional exercise—"an habitual Adoration of the Supreme Being, as well in constant Acts of Mental Worship, as in outward Forms"—higher even than the fervent practice of morality, saying that the former is a "more Persuasive" method.[30]

Gracián showed the possibility of tasting the divine in the social-political environment, while Addison exhibits something very similar in an "aesthetic" mode of perception of nature (inspired in many respects by Bouhours). His

26 Or, as Brian Michael Norton comments on this essay: "To appreciate the world's aesthetic splendours [...] is for Addison an inherently spiritual, even reverential act" (Norton 2015, 129).

27 Cheerfulness is not only passively delighted here, for example, by some "lively picture", "gay embroidery", "elegant symmetry" of nature (Barrow 1700, 87) instead, it actively "consecrates every Field and Wood".

28 The "grateful Reflection on the Supreme Cause" as the producer of natural beauties does not presuppose the intellectual or scientific position of a physico-theologian or a naturalist, one does not need to know anything about the discoveries of the modern natural sciences to remember this traditional truth of the Revelation.

29 For a relevant interpretation of this essay from the perspective of Robert Boyle's occasional meditations, see Mayhew 2004, 84.

30 "The Devout Man does not only believe, but feels there is a Deity. He has actual Sensations of him; his Experience concurs with Reason [thus this experience cannot become dangerous enthusiasm]; he sees him more and more in all his Intercourses with him, and even in this Life almost loses his Faith in Conviction" (Addison 1965, IV, 143).

spectator of a polite imagination is *ab ovo* a sociable man of "fine Taste" who can relish the heavenly joy of an ordinary experience like the view of a sunset, a neighbouring meadow, a spring garden, a couple of laced birds, a shiny colour, and so on. Already the natural imagination can find enjoyment "in the Murmur of Brooks, and the Melody of Birds, in the Shade of Groves and Woods, or in the Embroidery of Fields and Meadows" (Addison 1965, III, 475), while its exercised, "polite" version can approach to the height of the spiritual senses.

To support this insight, finally, I am briefly discussing a possible historical link between Gracián's *El Criticón* and Addison's conceptions of his aesthetic triad and, more importantly, of the "innocent pleasure" of the imagination.[31] In the second piece of his Cheerfulness-series (No. 387), Addison uses the metaphor of *theatrum mundi* which became more and more popular from the late sixteenth century onward: "the whole Universe is a kind of Theatre filled with Objects that either raise in us Pleasure, Amusement or Admiration" (Addison 1965, III, 453). The title of the second chapter of Gracián's allegorical pilgrimage happens to be "The Grand Theatre of the Universe". Here we can read about Andrenio who had been slumbering in a cave of a mountain on the island of Saint Helena, and who then was freed and awakened by an enormous earthquake. This was the first time in his life when Andrenio could set his eyes on the world outside and he was astonished and shocked by the view of the "grand Theatre of Heaven and Earth".[32] Critilo, his collocutor, the allegorical representative of the *mundo civil*, reflects on Andrenio's natural state of mind as follows:

> O! How much I envy thee […] this unknown happiness of thine, the only priviledge of the first Man *[l'unique privilege du premier homme]*, and you, the Faculty of seeing

31 Elsewhere I elaborated it in detail (cf. Szécsényi 2017). This historical relationship between Gracián and Addison was first discussed by Thorpe (cf. Thorpe 1937).

32 There is an interesting prototype of Andrenio's cave and his first reactions to the world outside the cave. In his essay No. 465, Addison referred to Aristotle's lost treatise via Cicero's *De natura deorum*: "should a Man live under Ground, and there converse with Works of Art and Mechanism, and should afterwards be brought up into the open Day, and see the several Glories of the Heav'n and Earth, he would immediately pronounce them the Works of such a Being as we define God to be" (Addison 1965, IV, 144). When men from beneath the earth would first see "the earth and the seas and the sky", they would realize "the size and beauty" of these natural prospects, and (mostly) they would come to know their fixed eternal order as the clear proof of the existence of gods (cf. Cicero 1967, 215). There is a significant difference, however, between this sober and basically intellectual reaction which establishes a natural theology and Andrenio's astonishment and emotional-instinctive response which results in a proto-aesthetic attunement to the created world.

> all at once, and that with Observation, the Greatness, Beauty, Harmony, Stability, and Variety *[la grandeur, la beauté, les accords, la fermeté & la varieté]* of this created Fabrick. (Gracián 1681, 16; 1696, 18)

This can be the direct source of Addison's aesthetic triad, on the one hand, and, on the other, it can be the explanation of the "innocence" of his "aesthetic" pleasures which are strictly differentiated from both the joys of the intellect and the "sensual Delights" in the Imagination series (cf. Addison 1965, III, 539)—a tellingly similar division can be found in No. 201 concerning "the pleasures of devotion as distinct from those of reason and sense" (Morris 1972, 132). I think that the Addisonian "innocence" has nothing to do with the concept of disinterestedness. Moreover, it is not simply the heir of the "innocent delight" by means of which the seventeenth- and early eighteenth-century physico-theologians or naturalists described the emotional response to the scientific recognition of the design and order in the Creation.[33] Rather, it has to do with Andrenio's regard of the first man: in his eyes, the whole creation, the grand theatre of the universe always unveils itself as beautiful, uncommon or great, or, in other words, the whole Creation looks like a Spring landscape with its ever renewing energy and wonderful variety and inexhaustibility (which is the substantive meaning of "novelty"). Andrenio's example shows that it is possible, and it is highly beneficial for us to see the world where we walk every day with another eye, and (as only the French translation phrases it) "goûter [...] le plaisir de chaque chose" which we have not been able to perceive at all earlier (Gracián 1696, 19)—like Addison's "man of a polite imagination" who "looks upon the World, as it were in another Light, and discovers in it a Multitude of Charms, that conceal themselves from the generality of Mankind".

Andrenio's viewpoint, since it is that of "the first Man", is a spiritually distinguished one. Addison seems to transform this original regard of "the first Man" into the privilege of an "aesthetic" faculty of a man of a polite imagination or of the "aesthetico"-devotional mental disposition of a cheerful man. Thus, we, by means of the proper and regular exercises of these natural human capacities, are able to reconstruct the position of the first man. Modern aesthetic experience was conceived as a spiritual experience, not simply as a mental-hygienic one or a preparation for moral improvement: it basically fostered and maintained

33 For example, Lisa Zeitz claims that "Addison's psychology of aesthetic perception grows out of a *shared aesthetic argument* in physico-theological thought. *The Spectator*'s observations on human responses to nature [...] are in part inspired by a similarly 'affective' and 'aesthetic' component in some of the period's popular 'design arguments' for the existence of God" (Zeitz 1992, 493).

an ever-renewing and incessant wonder at the Creation exemplified either as *theatrum mundi*, or a Spring-time meadow, or the ever-changing ocean. This is why Addison warmly recommends us to extend the realm of our pleasures of the imagination. His "aesthetic" spectator will be able to feel fully and deeply the '*Great, Uncommon*, or *Beautiful*' in his "innocent pleasures", and to re-taste the freedom and dignity of the first man.

References

ADDISON, Joseph & Others: *The Spectator*. Donald F. Bond (ed.). 5 vols. Oxford: Clarendon Press 1965.

BAEUMLER, Alfred: *Das Irrationalitätsproblem in der Aesthetik und Logik des 18. Jahrhunderts bis zur* Kritik der Urteilskraft. Darmstadt: Wissenschaftliche Buchgesellschaft 1967.

BALTHASAR, Hans Urs von: *The Glory of the Lord: A Theological Aesthetics. Vol. I: Seeing the Form*. Erasmo Leiva-Merikakis (trans.). Edinburgh: T. & T. Clark 1982.

BARROW, Isaac: *The Works of the Learned Isaac Barrow, D.D. The Second Volume Containing Sermons and Expositions upon All the Articles in the Apostles Creed*. The Second Edition, Corrected. London: J. Heptinstall 1700.

BLACK, Scott: "Addison's Aesthetics of Novelty". *Studies in Eighteenth Century Culture* 30 (2001), 269–288.

BLOOM, Edward A./Lillian D. Bloom: *Joseph Addison's Sociable Animal. In the Market Place, on the Hustings, in the Pulpit*. Providence: Brown University Press 1971.

BOUHOURS, Dominique: *The Art of Criticism: or the Method of Making a Right Judgment upon Subjects of Wit and Learning*, trans. a Person of Quality. London: D. Brown & A. Roper 1705.

BOUHOURS, Dominique: *The Arts of Logick and Rhetorick*. John Oldmixon (trans.). London: John Clark and Richard Hett, etc. 1728.

BOUHOURS, Dominique: *Les entretiens d'Ariste et d'Eugène*. Bernard Beugnot et Gilles Declercq (ed.). Paris: Honoré Champion 2003.

CICERO: *De natura deorum. Academica*. H. Rackham (trans.). (The Loeb Classical Library XIX) Cambridge, MA: Harvard University Press 1967.

COVARRUBIAS OROZCO, Sebastián de: *Del origen y prinzipio de la lengua castellana, o Romance que oy se vsa en España*. Madrid: Melchor Sánchez 1674.

DIX, Robin: "Addison and the Concept of 'Novelty' as a Basic Aesthetic Category". *The British Journal of Aesthetics* 26 (1986), 383–390.

COSTELLOE, Timothy M.: *The British Aesthetic Tradition. From Shaftesbury to Wittgenstein*. Cambridge: Cambridge University Press 2013.

CROCE, Benedetto: *Estetica come scienza dell'espressione e linguistica generale. Teoria e Storia*. Terza edizione riveduta. Bari: Gius Laterza & figli. 1908.

DAVIES, Horton: *Worship and Theology in England. Vol. II: From Andrewes to Baxter and Fox, 1603–1690*. Princeton, NJ: Princeton University Press 1975.

ELIAS, Norbert: *The Court Society*. Edmund Jephcott (trans.). Oxford: Blackwell 1983.

ELIAS, Norbert: *The Civilizing Process. Sociogenetic and Psychogenetic Investigations*. Revised Edition, Edmund Jephcott (trans.). Malden, MA: Blackwell 2000.

GHIȚĂ, Eduard: Theological Underpinnings of Joseph Addison's Aesthetics. *Journal of Early Modern Studies* 6, 2 (2017), 95–117.

GRACIÁN, Baltasar: *L'Héros de Laurens Gracian gentil-homme arragonois*, trad. Sr. Gervaise médecin ordinaire du Roy. Paris: Pierre Chevalier 1645.

GRACIÁN, Baltasar: *The Heroe, of Lorenzo, or the Way to Eminence and Perfection*. Sir John Skeffington (trans.). London: John Martin and James Allestrye 1652.

GRACIÁN, Baltasar: *The Critick, Written Originally in Spanish by Lorenzo Gracian One of the Best Wits in Spain*. Paul Rycaut (trans.). Esq. London: Henry Brome 1681.

GRACIÁN, Baltasar: *L'Homme de cour de Baltasar Gracian*. Troisième edition revûë & corigée, trad. & comm. Amelot de la Houssaie. Paris: Veuve-Martin & Jean Boudot 1685.

GRACIÁN, Baltasar: *Modèle d'une sainte et parfaite communion*, trad. Nicolas-Abraham Amelot de la Houssaye. Paris: Jean Boudot 1693.

GRACIÁN, Baltasar: *L'Homme detrompé, ou Le Criticon de Baltazar Gracián*, trad. Guillaume de Maunory. Paris: Jacques Collombat 1696.

GRACIÁN, Baltasar: *The Art of Prudence: or a Companion for a Man of Sense*. The Second, Corrected Edition, Mr. Savage (trans.). London: Jonah Bowyer 1705.

GRACIÁN, Baltasar: *The Art of Worldly Wisdom, a Pocket Oracle*. Christopher Maurer (trans. & intro). New York: Doubleday/Currency 1992.

GRACIÁN, Baltasar: *A Pocket Mirror for Heroes*. Christopher Maurer (trans. & intro). New York: Doubleday/Currency 1996.

GUYER, Paul: *A History of Modern Aesthetics*. 3 vols. Cambridge: Cambridge University Press 2014.

JUNQUA, Amélie: "Joseph Addison and the contemplation of colours: aesthetic attraction and control in the periodical essays". In: Peter Wagner and

Frédéric Ogée (eds.): *Taste and the Senses in the Eighteenth Century.* Trier: Wissenschaftlicher Verlag Trier 2011, 27–34.

LA ROCHEFOUCAULD, François de: *Collected Maxims and Other Reflections. New Translations with Parallel French Text.* Oxford: Oxford University Press 2007.

MARIN, Louis: *Sublime Poussin.*Catherine Porter (trans.). Stanford: Stanford University Press 1999.

MARTZ, Louis: *The Poetry of Meditation. A Study in English Religious Literature of the Seventeenth Century.* New Haven: Yale University Press 1954.

MAYHEW, Robert J.: *Landscape, Literature and English Religious Culture, 1660–1800.* Basingstoke: Palgrave Macmillan 2004.

MORRIS, David B.: *The Religious Sublime: Christian Poetry and Critical Tradition in 18th-Century England.* Lexington: The University Press of Kentucky 1972.

NORTON, Brian Michael: "*The Spectator* and Everyday Aesthetics". *Lumen: Selected Proceedings from the Canadian Society for Eighteenth-Century Studies* 34 (2015), 123–136.

PAULSON, Ronald: *The Beautiful, Novel, and Strange: Aesthetics and Heterodoxy.* Baltimore: The Johns Hopkins University Press 1996.

SCHOLAR, Richard: *The* Je-Ne-Sais-Quoi *in Early Modern Europe. Encounters with a Certain Something.* Oxford: Oxford University Press 2005.

SZÉCSÉNYI, Endre: "The Regard of the First Man: On Joseph Addison's Aesthetic Categories". *History of European Ideas* 43, 6 (2017), 582–597.

THORPE, Clarence DeWitt: "Addison and Some of His Predecessors on 'Novelty' ". *Publications of the Modern Language Association of America* 52, 4 (1937), 1114–1129.

THORPE, Clarence DeWitt: *The Aesthetic Theory of Thomas Hobbes, with Special Reference to His Contribution to the Psychological Approach in English Literary Criticism.* Ann Arbor: The University of Michigan Press 1940.

ZEITZ, Lisa M.: "Addison's 'Imagination' Papers and the Design Argument". *English Studies: A Journal of English Language and Literature* 73, 6 (1992), 493–502.

Dan Poston

(University of Tübingen)

Still on classic ground: Joseph Addison's Italy

"A Letter from Italy to the Right Honourable Charles Lord Halifax in the Year 1701" is an epistolary poem written in strict heroic verse from Addison to one of his most important patrons. In this chapter, I would like to suggest and very briefly outline three readings of the poem that express Addison's surprising ambivalence towards Italy and the classical tradition. The first reading of the poem starts from the poet's political positioning and ends with Addison's patriotic pledge of allegiance to his Whig benefactors and their imperial ambitions for Britain. The second reading takes Addison more seriously as a poet, as such, a competitor to Virgil; in the wake of Milton, he ultimately casts his lot with the distant, melancholic Saturn of modernity over Virgil's classical, patriotic dream of Italy as the golden-age seat of a returned, agricultural Saturn. A third reading, then, partially integrates the previous two readings by arguing that both the Whiggish political imperial confidence and the new role of the poet in modernity vis-à-vis classicism found a common ground in the cold Saturnalia of Newton's proven overturning of ancient cosmography.

Just after the emphasized new century's year, 1701, of the poem's title, a Latin epigraph from Book II of Virgil's *Georgics* announces one of the main pleasurable tensions that run through the work: the oscillating optics between Virgil's *Georgics* and Addison's marked attempt at imitation and adaptation. Whereas Virgil's homodiegetic poet sustains a passionate enthusiasm for his Italy's enchanting vistas throughout his poem, Addison's poet's revelry is both disrupted and overly heightened by the memory of his classical reading and by thoughts of faraway home. His Italian journey sensually enwraps him, impressing him with a lived experience of literature's confirmation. He declares in the most famous line of the poem: "And still I seem to tread on classic ground".[1]

The interpretation of the poem hinges, in this chapter's analysis, on three different valences of the insistent or contradictory word "still" in this line. "Still", in Addison's sly usage, can denote, first, persistence through time: the neoclassical

---

1 All citations from "A Letter from Italy" are taken from Bohn's 1903 edition of Addison's works.

speaker is "still" treading like Virgil through a classical Italy that seems to remain present. "Still", in this first valence, problematizes the illusion that "seem" would, on the other hand, suggest: the persistence of classical ground troubles the idea of modernity being a new time. Classical authority overwhelms. The poet is simply still Virgil, come again to report that Italy is unchanged, inspiring of no truly necessary new verses, though waiting perhaps for truly great and modern actions.

The second valence of "still", however, would tend to simultaneously extend and slightly contradict the first. The alienation or exile of the modern subject is complete enough that the classical ground in fact recedes into a past dream. In this valence, "still" would denote the modern writer and reader's self-aware, physically and emotionally unmoved state: the writer and reader are now "still", though *seeming* to be subject to intense, literary visions and the intoxicating memory of former walks. Virgil—the creative, passionate, classical poet—was lying. The true poet, composing the poem after leaving the landscapes he describes, sits in a room and calculatingly fills up blank pages, the real classical landscape from a melancholic, modern point of view.

The third valence, then, would integrate the first two, suggesting a new landscape requiring new action and new poetry. "Still" *seeming* "to tread on classic ground" can denote what Virgil did not know he was doing and what the modern poet cannot escape doing in spite of his knowledge. "Classic ground", in this valence, is not merely a golden literary illusion nor merely a country artificially frozen in time: it is the optical illusionary stage of life on a rock called Earth, now known to be hurtling through vast, contingent space. Even though the writer *seems* to rove significantly in the classical landscape, he knows his true position is "still" and gravitationally fixed compared to the recently revealed, tremendous scales of time and space. Addison's speaker can be understood to query: If things are not what they seem, why do they *still* seem to be so, in Italy or in our time? The answer he eventually provides reveals much about the young Addison's ambitions for himself and his Whig sponsors, for his nation as an imperial vanguard of liberated reason, and for his young century as a clearing, Saturnine age.

The third valence of "still", having to do with the revelations of astronomy, may seem unlikely to a casual reader of the poem, but one of the purposes of this chapter is to emphasize how the shadow of Newton's modern cosmography haunted Addison's poetics and the general project of the Enlightenment very closely.[2] Biographically, Addison was connected to Newton, his scientific hero,

2 For an exploration of Newton's heavy impact on Addison and his contemporaries, see Nicolson 2015.

directly through Lord Halifax, Charles Montagu, the addressee of "A Letter from Italy". Montagu had arranged for Addison to receive a royal grant for the purposes of traveling and bettering his mind in anticipation of his future service to the state. The patron was himself a neoclassical poet known for his panegyrics to Charles II and William III, but by the turn of the century he was generally much better known as one of the chief English ministers of state. His rise to power as a leader in the first Whig Junto had inspired such jealousy and hostility that by the time Addison composed the 1701 epistle to him, he stood impeached by Parliament and had entered a temporary, semi-retirement from political office. It was a crucial time to collect letters of loyalty in order to gauge a potential comeback and remember who to reward if that comeback were to succeed (*cf.* Smithers 1968, 43, 53, 63, 70–74).

Montagu likely saw in Addison a potential Augustan poet-politician protégé in his own mold, though the younger poet came from clergy and not from the nobility. Addison had made a name as a classical scholar and Latin translator in Dryden and Jacob Tonson's high orbits. This achievement would have impressed Montagu, who had founded a Philosophical Club at Cambridge with Newton and whose championing of the great recoinage (overseen by Newton) may have turned Addison on to the pleasure of studying old Roman coins (*cf.* Smithers 1968, 53; Hall 1996, 324). Addison owed to Montagu not only the royal travel grant for his European Grand Tour and a clue about numismatics but also the unusual dispensation that allowed him to keep his Oxford fellowship without having to take clerical orders, an obligation that would have confined him to a more provincial fate. Addison's poem, then, probably must be read as a cheering thank-you note and expression of support for a troubled benefactor and potential future employer.

What one might expect, one finds. On its surface, the poem has its poet reveling in a golden landscape he has read much about. He imitates Virgil, making Montagu the new Maecenas to whom he addresses an enthusiastic *Laudes Italiae*. Reading quickly, perhaps only the transition to the poem's conclusion would give one pause in this interpretation, since Addison concludes with an anti-Italian, jingoistic celebration of British war on the continent in the name of Liberty. Virgil's *Laudes Italiae* becomes Addison's *Laudes Brittaniae*.

Including the epigraph, Virgil is named three times in the poem, so it is clear that Addison wanted his imitation and adaptation to be noticed. Indeed, Virgil and Montagu are always mentioned in close proximity, with Addison positioning the two together as the great poets whom he can only meekly imitate. Yet, there is something not entirely deferential to both his supposed poetic heroes in the final section of the poem, when he confesses having to restrain his muse from launching more fully into the epic mode.[3] He explicitly demures to his elder and better, but his display of martial rage clearly positions him to take the role of public panegyrist from Montagu, should the next great military victory come—as it would with Marlborough's triumph at Blenheim in 1704 and Addison's acclamatory poem, *The Campaign*.

The same passage likewise challenges the tonal authority of Virgil's original. *Georgics* was itself an imitation of Hesiod's *Works and Days*, a cautionary celebration of the agricultural life as a cure for self-exiles from a poisoned political world. Virgil was careful to celebrate Augustus' imperial military exploits, but the emphasis of his praise was on peace. Ceasar Augustus, through his triumphant wars, kept violence and invaders far away from Rome so that Maecenas—Augustus' close advisor and sometimes deputy—could cultivate his famous garden and the flowering of poets. For the georgic Virgil, Maecenas was to be extolled for his decision to remain an Equestrian and keep his distance from the noisy theatre of the Senate. The poets' role, in such a political configuration, was to connect the hard work of domestic renewal—plowing the land, grafting the seeds, year after year of unremitting, ever-changing labor and harvest—to the inspiring pastoral energies of his more naïve, wandering youth. He was to preach a second, hand-wrought coming of the mild, golden age of Saturn in a land rich with natural bounty and agricultural potential.

Since Montagu—a city Whig—was not likely to turn pacifist and spend the rest of his life enjoying the countryside, Addison would have likely found himself caught politically between patron and classical model. His solution was to split the elder Virgil's careful synthesis and moderation of epic and pastoral partially back into their component parts. If Virgil's georgic mode was somewhere around 80 percent pastoral grafted onto 20 percent epic, Addison's poem remarkably preserves the same rough ratio, with the grafted modes divided from each other into two separate parts. The longer first part has the 29-year-old poet seductively playing the enthusiastic reveler in the sunny Italian fields and brambles of immortal verses; he catalogs rivers, he praises plants and the climate, he marvels in Rome's picturesque decayed beauty and has his breath taken away by

3 As I mention later in this article, Johnson criticized this passage of the poem for mixing its metaphors, making the muse into a horse and the horse into a thing that launches, like a boat (*cf.* Johnson 2006, 24). If one grants the young Addison a level of subtlety that Johnson would deny him, it could be that the criticized metaphorical slippages are intentional: Addison is ironically criticizing his poetic wish to put the horse in front of the boat, to make the poet the general of a war effort yet to be launched by his patrons back on the home island.

a landscape dotted with Renaissance art and churches. Dear Boss, it's more wonderful than I ever could have imagined, thanks for making it possible for me to be here, I wish I could express it all as well as you would.

The second, shorter part of the postcard would read: but the people aren't as happy as back home, can't wait to get back there and back to our important work! Addison, after all, was also a politico and an ambitious man. The second, shorter part of the poem becomes Addison's paean to militant, British Liberty. He appeases the ghost of Virgil by digging up the famous scene in Hades from the epic *Aeneid* in which Aeneas's father, Anchises, prophecies for his still-living son his coming victory in Italy. Virgil had Anchises exalting Rome's fate among nations at first as a negative artistic capacity:

> Others shall beat out the breathing bronze to softer lines, I believe it well; shall draw living lineaments from the marble; the cause shall be more eloquent on their lips; their pencil shall portray the pathways of heaven, and tell the stars in their arising: be thy charge, O Roman, to rule the nations in thine empire; this shall be thine art, to ordain the law of peace, to be merciful to the conquered and beat the haughty down. (Virgil 1934, Book VI, 126)

Addison's unmarked paraphrasing of the Virgil passage is fairly direct, with an important omission (or two) and a crucial replacement:

> Others with towering piles may please the sight,
> And in their proud, aspiring domes delight;
> A nicer touch to the stretched canvas give,
> Or teach their animated rocks to live:
> 'Tis Britain's care to watch o'er Europe's fate,
> And hold in balance each contending state,
> To threaten bold, presumptuous kings with war,
> And answer her afflicted neighbours' prayer. (ll. 141–148)

Running just underneath the classical imitation of "A Letter from Italy" is a careful, mathematical calculus of the sort that might have pleased Montagu and his intimate friend Newton, who together were laying the foundations for the modern British imperial financial system. Addison took Virgil's passage, added Britain where conquering Rome had been, and subtracted two negatives: he would not go so far as to take away from mighty Britain its supremacy in either literature or cosmography. The former might have offended his poetic patron. The latter might have offended his patron's scientist friend, a more complex matter to which I will return.

The first reading of the poem, thus, might be described as Addison's performance of juvenalia. Still treading on classic ground, the young poet was overwhelmed by the superior skill of his patron, the enduring mastery of Virgil, and the lived immersion in the Roman muses' homeland, Italy. His poetic skills did not match the exhilarating travel experience, which was only marred by the decadence of the Italian people, who he believed had fallen into servile tyranny when compared with the denizens of his colder but freedom-loving country of origin. Perhaps, then, the hail of Virgil with which he opened the letter to Montagu—the calling out to the Land of Saturn—could be neoclassically transmuted into a hail Britannia, via Saturn's well-known dual aspect. If Saturn was not to rule again on Earth over a golden, agricultural age, if modernity was an age of Jove and his terrible son Mars, then perhaps the new Land of Saturn was—in keeping with the Greco-Roman god's second, later aspect—a colder, severer, righteously vengeful, rational island-nation on the fringes of the classical world.[4]

Virgil's glowing references to agricultural Saturn feature strongly in his *Georgics*. Outside of the opening epigraph, Addison does not mention the god, or any deity except a pregnant Liberty, in his "Letter from Italy". But given the overall closeness with which he was reading and adapting Virgil, such a conscious, slyly ironic twist for his more coterie audience of wise classical readers like Montagu would have been in keeping with his other neoclassical performances. The late December Saturnalia, celebrating the gap between reaping and sowing, was associated with the overturning of class distinctions and masters waiting on slaves at table in imitation of an egalitarian life under a generous, divine king (*cf.* Frazer 307–08). Roman Saturn, like the more ancient Greek god Kronus that was absorbed into his worship, was an ambivalent god who in his exile after his earthly rule dwelled "at the uttermost end of land and sea" (Klibansky 1979, 134–5). The English tradition had long associated him with punishment, destruction, cold maladies, but also "a system of counting by weight and measure"; he was the inventer of coin-minting (*Ibid.*, 193–194). The Neoplatonist tradition with which Addison would have been familiar exalted him as the symbol of intellect, as opposed to Zeus, the soul. Kiblansky, Panofsky, and Saxl wrote that "The myth of his devouring his children could be interpreted so as to mean that the intellect, until it brings forth the soul, retains its offspring within itself" (*Ibid.*, 153). Saturn, the god of the spleen and melancholy, resonated with Addison's age in

4 Drawing parallels between Virgil's prophecies of a second golden age and English politics was a common trope in Addison's literary-political milieu, so his play with the trope may have carried very specific nuances, given the tensions around partisan politics, war, and the royal succession at the time. Joseph Hone notes that Jacobite Tories, at least, associated the Virgilian return of "Saturn's Days" with a new Stuart restoration under Anne (*cf.* Hone 2017, 76–80).

this respect. John Milton—Addison's poetic hero—had celebrated Melancholy in his poem "Il Penseroso" as having a positive and spiritual value.[5] Certainly for the surviving veterans of the Commonwealth during the Restoration, melancholy had been "superior to the jovial enjoyment of life", a dark, regal, and even heroic figure in contrast to how she had been portrayed in much of the continental tradition. Her

> ...saintly visage is too bright
> To hit the sense of human sight;
> And therefore to our weaker view,
> Ore laid with black staid Wisdoms hue.
> (quoted in Klibansky 1979, 230)

Removed from the terrestrial plane, melancholy is absorbed in other visions: the heavens are in her eyes.

If we read "A Letter from Italy" keeping in mind the figure of the still poet—a spleeny, saturnine, melancholic traveler, shut with his books and articles away from the over-golden landscapes outside—a second reading of the poem emerges. Here the poet with "ravished eyes" is surrounded by a geography in which every feature has already been sung and transformed into "heavenly numbers" (ll. 9, 16). Like Lucretius' ambitious adventurer or Ovid's young Hermaphrodite, "Fir'd with a thousand raptures" (25), he enthusiastically recatalogs all the flowing rivers of classical verse, at first undaunted by the discrepancies between the observations of his time and those "immortalized in song": "misguided by the tuneful throng" (31–32), he discovers that some classical rivers have disappeared, gone silent, or now run dry. The famous Tiber is now "destitute of strength" (39), more a memorial to itself than a river. "So high the deathless muse exalts her theme" (43)—the poet begins to reflect and draws the conclusion that martial heroism and verse itself drive the hyperbolic representation of nature; nature itself fails to inspire him to create "Unnumbered beauties" (53).

5 Addison declares Milton, excelling all classical poets, to be the quintessential master of imaginative poetry at the end of *Spectator* 417. He then gives Milton "First Place" among English poets in *Spectator* 562 (*cf.* Addison and Steele 1987). It can be that the contrast Addison drew between a tyrannized Italy and a liberated England was suggested by his reading of Milton. In *Areopagitica* (1644), Milton had reported that learned men he met in Italy (during the same trip in which he visited the jailed Galileo) had bemoaned the "servile state into which learning amongst them was brought" by the tyranny of religious censorship. Milton's Italian interlocutors counted him "happy to be born in such a place of philosophic freedom as they supposed England was" (Milton 2011, 363).

The coldness of this more revealed experience of the classics—allegorized as the withering of Italian plants "transplanted and preserved with care" (57) in the Northern clime of England—provokes in him a regressive desire to be covered by the classical landscape again, in the green retreats where "western gales eternally reside" and "the whole year in gay confusion lies" (65, 68). For a moment, the youthful traveler does not want to get back to timely work. His ambition, however, symbolized by supposedly immortal Rome, revives again in the interiority of his mind. Again, the revival is troubled: "Rome's exalted beauties … Magnificent in piles of ruine lye" (71–72). The Colisseum, symbolizing both his mind's interiority and the womb of classical nations, takes on the ghostly, upraiding function of theatre, spurring the poet and the nations with vigorous passions pulled up from the blood or the river-strewn Hades of history.

But the progeny are base and degenerate. The poet is still "still", even as "to new scenes [his] wandering muse retires/And the dumb show of breathing rocks admires" (83–84). Exiled from living Roman history, the poet notes the effort of constructing immortality out of silent and still stones. Continuing chronologically, with Etruscan pastoralism and Roman theatre behind him, the poet feels lost amongst the "soft variety" (100) show of the Renaissance. He declares that "Fain would [he] Raphael's godlike art rehearse" (93), though Charybdis-like "the pleasing airs [his] ravished soul confound/With circling notes and labyrinths of sound" (101–102).

Italy's history reviewed as landscape, the thought forms itself: the blessings of Italy, of warm youth, of the motherly classical ground of Earth are wasted while "proud oppression in her vallies reigns,/And tyranny usurps her happy plains /… the poor inhabitant beholds in vain/The reddening orange and the swelling grain:/Joyless he sees the growing oils and wines" (111–115). Suffocated by sensuous classicism, he starves and dies for thirst.

Addison's poet, liberated, then extols Liberty, the goddess that "Britannia's isle adores" (127) and his homeland, where the people do not envy the warmer land that "lies/In ten degrees of more indulgent skies" (135–6). The skies are clearer above cold Britain, the rocks and mountains happy although barren. Here comes the epic call for Britain to take up Rome's role as a continental imperialist and mighty, emancipating law-giver between contending states. But Britain stands here also as a figure of the modern, critical poet's saturnine sovereignty as severe balancer of traditions, passions, histories, and cosmographies. The liberty of modernity was enough to make an ugly landscape beautiful: "poverty", the poet declares to his goddess, "looks cheerful in thy sight" (124). The drumbeat of Liberty stirs the poet again towards movement. As Johnson noted with critical disapproval in his commentary on this part of the poem, Addison's muse, indeed, seems to have become primarily a vehicle—that is, a horse—launched towards liberation.

In contrast, near the end of Book II of his *Georgics*, Virgil declares himself a priest to the Muses "whose great love" has smitten him (Virgil 1934b, 321). His main prayer is to them for cosmological revelation – to understand and see where and how the stars move, the earthquakes, the seas wax and wane, and the days and nights alternate. Confined by his human heart's need for warmth, he settles for the gold of Italy's nature.

The third valence of "still" then opens. Italy and most of the world still looked rather the same as when Virgil's muses enchanted the land with their secret, unrevealed knowledge of the mysterious heavens. This was the classic ground on which Addison and we still mostly walk and imagine and live our lives. Addison and his generation, however, had not the muses but rather Newton, their Warden of the Mint, to thank for granting to them the wish of cosmological revelation that Virgil had expressed in vain.[6] Addison and his compatriots were left "still" seeming to tread on what was the same classic ground as Virgil but what was now known by them to indeed only *seem* to be that. The ground was, in fact, an utterly contingent surface of an alien planet hurtling at vast speed through infinite, acentric space and time. Newton was, to Addison, "the Miracle of the present Age" because of his demonstrated ability to map, weigh, and measure the cosmos (Addison and Steele 1987, no. 543, 442). What modern telescopes had revealed and what Newton had proven mathematically was that the Earth's star was lost in an unnumbered host of such suns to what were likely just as many worlds. Consequently, Addison imagined that if our particular sun and its planets were "utterly extinguished and annihilated, they would not be missed more than a grain of Sand upon the Sea-Shore" (*Ibid.*, no. 565, 529–530).

Back on Earth, in Italy, the same landscapes, the human theatre and womb of ghosts still crowded and towered around Addison and his compatriots in ruins and rocks, but the enchantment that Virgil pulled from the covering sky was gone, was revealed to be the illusion of passionate, earthbound verse, so many

6 The modern cosmography of Copernicus, Bruno, Kepler, Galileo, and Descartes shaped seventeenth- and eighteenth-century debates and understandings of the universe. But Newton's mathematical proofs and systemization through gravitational theory decisively settled educated consensus on that cosmography in Addison's time (*cf.* Russell 1972, 227). Hans Blumenberg stressed that Newton's work restaged Earth and the entire time of material existence as a rather odd event, at best a useful laboratory from which to try to grasp greater understanding (*cf.* Blumenberg 1972, 74).

numbers but few that gave the truth and cold clarity of the intellect liberated from the local, tyrannical illusion of gravity.
The ambivalence of the poem is expressed in what Howard Erskine-Hill called the eighteenth century's twofold vision, its two optics (Erskine-Hill 1997)—one a modernity that was still classical, one a neoclassicism in the service of modern, emancipated truth. Italy was the site of this optical-illusional oscillation for Addison, the young poet. His later masterworks—his essay "On the Pleasures of the Imagination" and his tragedy *Cato*—would synthesize a more integrated, balanced approach to the problem of classical humanistic aesthetics confronted by stark Newtonian world-remaking. The later Addison would posit the cultivated pleasure of viewing art and nature as more philosophically equal to understanding and expose Cato in his zeal for truth as a mis-reader, blind to the need for simple human persistence. Jupiter, the thunderer, whom Newton identified on commemorative medals with the generals William III and Marlborough (*cf.* Hone 2016, 126–129), may have been training zealous soldiers through the younger Addison's verse. But it was already Saturn, his withdrawn, melancholic father, leaving earth to merge into the dark places of the cosmos, who lent that same verse: the silent cold rivers and the touch of minted gold.

References

ADDISON, Joseph: *The Works of Joseph Addison*. Vol. 1. Henry G. Bohn (ed.). London: George Bell and Sons 1903.

ADDISON, Joseph/Richard Steele: *The Spectator*. Vol. 4. Donald F. Bond (ed.). Oxford: Oxford University Press 1987.

BLUMENBERG, Hans: "Die Kopernikanische Konsequenz für den Zeitbegriff". In: Jerzy Dobrzycki (ed.): *The Reception of Copernicus' Heliocentric Theory*. Dordrecht-Holland: D. Reidel 1972, 57–77.

ERSKINE-HILL, Howard: "Twofold Vision in Eighteenth-Century Writing". *ELH* 64, 4 (December 1997), 903–924.

FRAZER, James George: The Golden Bough. Vol. VI. *The Scapegoat*. London: Macmillan 1913.

HALL, A. Rupert: Isaac Newton: Adventurer in Thought. Cambridge: Cambridge University Press 1996.

HONE, Joseph: "Isaac Newton and the Medals for Queen Anne". *Huntington Library Quarterly* 79, 1 (Spring 2016), 119–148.

HONE, Joseph: Literature and Party Politics at the Accession of Queen Anne. Oxford: Oxford University Press 2017.

JOHNSON, Samuel: "Addison". In: Roger Londsdale (ed.): *The Lives of the Poets*. Vol. 3. Oxford: Oxford University Press 2006.

KLIBANSKY, Raymond/Erwin Panofsky/Fritz Saxl: *Saturn and Melancholy*. Nendeln: Kraus Reprint 1979.

MILTON, John: *Milton's Selected Poetry and Prose*. Jason Philip Rosenblatt (ed.). New York: W. W. Norton & Co 2011.

NICOLSON, Marjorie Hope: *Newton Demands the Muse: Newton's Opticks and the 18th Century Poets*. Princeton: Princeton University Press 2015.

RUSSELL, John L: "The Copernican System in Great Britain". In: Jerzy Dobrzycki (ed.): *The Reception of Copernicus' Heliocentric Theory*. Dordrecht-Holland: D. Reidel 1972, 189–239.

SMITHERS, Peter: *The Life of Joseph Addison*. Second Edition. Oxford: Clarendon Press 1968.

VIRGIL: "The Aeneid". In: J. W. Mackail (trans.): *Virgil's Works*. New York: Modern Library 1934a.

VIRGIL: "The Georgics". In: J. W. Mackail (trans.): *Virgil's Works*. New York: Modern Library 1934b.

Paul Davis

(University College London)

"Misguided by the tuneful throng": Addison at the Rubicon

It was in a letter to the poet Richard West, sent in October 1740, that Horace Walpole delivered his famous *bon mot* about Addison having "travelled through the poets, and not through Italy; for all his ideas are borrowed from the descriptions, and not from the reality" (Lewis et al. 1937–1983, xiii. 231), which has been the favourite point of departure for discussions of Addison's travel writing ever since. Walpole was referring to the 150 or so quotations of verse, classical and post-classical, with which Addison interlarded his *Remarks on Italy* (1705), and despite the best efforts of commentators to explain the cultural and pedagogic rationale underlying that practice, it has proved impossible to dislodge the image of Addison the bookish classicist travelling round Italy with his copy of Virgil held up in front of his eyes, blocking out the landscape.[1] This chapter challenges that view, using material turned up during my ongoing editorial work on Addison's poems to offer a fresh account of the relationship between literature and 'reality' in his Italian travel writings—the *Remarks* and particularly its verse counterpart, the 'Letter from Italy' (1702).[2]

The 'Letter from Italy' is every bit as packed with references to the Roman poets as the *Remarks*, even if those references are less explicit, taking the indirect forms of echo and allusion more often than outright quotation. Of course, I'm not the first person to attempt to defend the poem against Walpole's witticism, and there's an obvious way of doing this—namely, by pointing out that

1 See, for instance, Redford 1996, 33: "Addison's approach 'through the poets' ... compels the reader to turn himself into a collator, experiencing landscape through literature, and validating present experience through constant comparison with the records of the past".

2 My edition of Addison's *Poems and Translations* will make up the first two volumes of the five-volume set of *The Non-Periodical Works of Joseph Addison* (Oxford University Press), under my general editorship, which also comprises two volumes of Addison's *Miscellaneous Prose Writings*, edited by Henry Power (Exeter), and a volume of *Dramatic Works*, edited by David Francis Taylor (Oxford).

Walpole's 'pre-romantic' assumptions about travel writing are at odds with the generic coding of the 'Letter'. Walpole assumed that the travel-writer's primary task was one of impartial description, whereas the 'Letter' belongs within a tradition of georgic verse, running from John Denham's *Coopers Hill* (1644) to Pope's *Windsor Forest* (1713), in which cities and landscapes are not simply described but interpreted in terms of history and culture, for frankly didactic purposes. Addison's serial allusions to Virgil in the 'Letter'—particularly to the so-called 'Laudes Italiae' ('Praises of Italy') in Book II of the *Georgics*, and Anchises's speech to Aeneas in *Aeneid* VI, prophesying the future achievements of Roman *imperium* by contrast with those of Greek art and civilisation—combine to inculcate a vision of Britain as the successor of Augustan Rome.

In the 'Laudes Italiae', Virgil contrasted the innocent fecundity of Italy with the monster-breeding prodigality of the East. Now, in the 'Letter', Italy, oppressed by the Pope and the invading French, has become an eastern tyranny, while Britain, despite its dismal climate, inherits Italy's mantle as the land of fruitfulness. The fruit in question being not oranges or lemons but 'Liberty', as emerges in the climactic passage of the poem, so beloved of Whiggish readers, a virtual translation of Anchises's famous comparison of Rome and Greece during his exchange with Aeneas in the underworld:

> Others with Towring Piles may please the sight,
> And in their proud aspiring Domes delight;
> A nicer Touch to the stretcht Canvas give,
> Or teach their animated Rocks to live:
> 'Tis Britain's Care to watch o'er Europe's Fate,
> And hold in Balance each contending State.
> To threaten bold presumptuous Kings with War,
> And answer her afflicted Neighbour's Pray'r. (Addison 1704, 10)

"Others ... may" there translates the subjunctive phrase "Excudent alii" ("Others may mould"), which begins Anchises's sentence. In Virgil, that sentence lasts seven lines; writing in couplets, Addison could not keep exactly to that odd number, and so rounded it out to eight. Among the arts Virgil's Anchises concedes the Greeks primacy in is that of "pleading their causes" ("orabunt causas melius"), by which Virgil meant rhetoric, perhaps hinting at sophistry. But Addison wasn't prepared to allow that the British, inventors of constitutional monarchy, yielded to anyone in their respect for law. So he substituted the more suspect arts of painting and especially baroque architecture (with "proud aspiring Domes" evoking the Popish grandiosity of the Vatican). Similarly, in re-applying to British military power, Anchises's celebrated formula for Roman *imperium*—"Parcere subjectis et debellare superbos" ("to spare the defeated, and wage war on the proud")—Addison removed any taint of bellicosity by reversing the order of Anchises's clauses, ensuring the final emphasis would fall on Britain's compassion for her "afflicted Neighbour"—that is, Italy.

That sort of reading, illustrating Addison's dynamic use of Virgil in the 'Letter', offers some defence against Walpole's sneer. But it basically amounts to the critical equivalent of a block or parry. What I want to do here is meet Walpole's challenge head-on, in the hope of turning it to more positive critical effect. Rather than batting aside his distinction between 'poetry' and 'reality' as naive or anachronistic, I will argue that Addison himself had pressing anxieties on this score at the time he wrote the 'Letter', and that those anxieties lie near the heart of his achievement in the poem. In seeking to make this case, I will particularly be concerned with a section of the poem rather less well known than its Virgilian exordium about Britain as the land of Liberty, indeed largely bypassed by commentators—the long section near the beginning, comprising the third, fourth, fifth, and sixth verse paragraphs (ll. 17–50), which deals with the rivers in and around Rome. When I say "particularly concerned", I mean it in the full sense of the phrase—this close focus will eventually bring into view some more substantial and far-reaching questions about Addison's personal and literary development during his travels in Italy, a crucial turning-point in his life and career.

In one sense, the rivers section of the 'Letter' provides further grist to Walpole's mill. For Addison certainly saw these rivers through the eyes of poets. Again and again, the epithets and circumstantial details attached to rivers in the 'Letter' can be traced back to passages in Virgil and Horace, Lucan and Martial, Claudian and Silius Italicus—passages that, in many cases, Addison also quoted when discussing the relevant rivers in the *Remarks on Italy*. Thus, for instance, when the "Mincio" is said by Addison to "draw his watry Store/Through the long windings of a fruitful Shore" (Addison 1704, 3), the phrase "long windings" translates "tardis ... flexibus" from Virgil's account of the Mincius in Book III of the *Georgics* ("tardis ingens ubi flexibus errat/Mincius"). Or again, when Addison describes seeing "hoary *Albula*'s infected Tide/O're the warm Bed of smoaking Sulphur glide" (Addison 1704, 3), his phrasing splices together two descriptions of the "Albula" (an old name for part of the Tiber) in Martial's *Epigrams* (1.12 and 4.4), both of them cited in the parallel discussion in the *Remarks*, whilst also drawing on some lines from an obscure panegyric by Claudian, quoted elsewhere in the *Remarks*, about a different sulphurous river—the Nar. Even the one case where Addison appears to break with poetic precedent is probably deceptive. The Tiber itself he calls "gentle" (Addison 1704, 4), whereas the Virgilian norm was "swift" or "rapid". That earned him a ticking-off from his nineteenth-century American editor G. W. Greene, who said it was 'not a proper expression' (D. R. Johnson 1976, 36, n. 5). But the chances are that Addison was remembering Ovid's typically contrarian description of the Tiber, in Book VI of the *Fasti*, as "placidus".

Those accounts of particular rivers come in the third, fourth, and sixth paragraphs. But the section pivots on the fifth paragraph, where Addison reports that he went to visit the sites of certain other unnamed rivers he had read about in the works of the Roman poets, only to find they no longer existed in reality:

> Sometimes misguided by the tuneful Throng,
> I look for Streams immortaliz'd in Song,
> That lost in Silence and Oblivion lye,
> (Dumb are their Fountains and their Channels dry)
> Yet run for ever by the Muses skill,
> And in the smooth Description murmur still. (Addison 1704, 3)

So far as I know, the only commentator to have paid attention to this passage is D. R. Johnson, in an under-valued article on "Addison in Italy", published in *Modern Language Studies* in 1976. Like me, Johnson was concerned to defend the 'Letter from Italy' against Walpole, and he rightly noted that the passage shows Addison emphasising the very "discrepancy ... between literature and reality" Walpole mocked him for ignoring. However, Johnson didn't pursue that line of thought, quickly assimilating the passage instead to what he considered the central theme of the 'Letter'—the "general decay in Nature" between ancient and modern times (D. R. Johnson 1976, 34). Moreover, he stressed the Virgilian character of that theme, suggesting the reason Addison drew out "conflicts between the literary accounts of ... streams and rivers ... and the historical reality presenting itself to the observer in 1701" was to "demonstrate the fulfillment" of Virgil's 'prophecy' in Book I of the *Georgics*, that 'all below, whether by Nature's curse/Or fate's decree, degen'rate still to worse" (D. R. Johnson 1976, 35, citing Dryden's translation). That is, in effect, to reaffirm the primacy of the poetic over the real for Addison—to re-admit by the back-door the Walpolean construction of him as a sheltered classical scholar, peering out at modern Italy through a Virgilian lens.

Yet, Addison's reference to himself as "misguided by the tuneful Throng" problematises that image. I'm going to dwell on this phrase in detail, an intensive focus that can be justified by noting its symptomatic status in Addison's writings about Italy as a whole. We've already seen that the descriptions of rivers in the 'Letter' are closely connected, in the details of their wording, to accounts of those same rivers in the *Remarks*. A similar linkage obtains at the level of theme, in the form of a recurrent concern with poetry's potential to mislead. Repeatedly in the

Remarks, the rivers of Italy feature as sites of conflict between ancient poetry and modern reality. Sometimes, the divide is registered more or less neutrally, as in the case of the "River *Adige*" which "runs thro" *Verona*; so much is the Situation of the Town chang'd from what it was in *Silius Italicus* his Time" (Addison cites Silius's reference in Book VIII of the *Punica* to "*Verona Athesi circumflua*"—"*Verona* by the circling *Adage* bound") (Addison 1705, 55). Elsewhere, Addison notes the disparity in slightly more fraught terms, as with the "Ticinus" which he describes as "excessively rapid", adding "I don't know therefore why *Silius Italicus* has represented it as so very gentle and still a River" (Addison 1705, 24–25), or the "River *Velino*" whose "astonishing ... *Cascade*", he reported, "looks at a distance like Clouds of smoak ascending from some vast furnace", so that:

> I could not but wonder when I first saw it that I had never met with it in any of the Old Poets, especially in *Claudian* who makes his Emperor *Honorarius* go out of his way to see the River *Nar* that runs just below it, and yet does not mention what would have been so great an Embellishment to his Poem. (Addison 1705, 157)
> (In most of those examples, *pace* D.R. Johnson, modern "historical reality" is more, not less, impressive than the ancient "literary accounts").

But in two cases—those of the Clitumnus and the Po—Addison addresses the failings of the Roman poets in describing them at greater length, and in a more explicitly critical tone. The Clitumnus is "celebrated by so many of the Poets for a particular Quality in its Waters of making the Cattle white that drink of it", a poetical belief shared by the modern inhabitants of the region because most of their cows are "of a whitish Colour", but which Addison curtly debunks: "they may as well fancy their Hogs turn black for some Reason of the same Nature because there are none in *Italy* of another Breed" (Addison 1705, 150–151).[3] And the Po is claimed by Lucan to be greater than the Nile or the Danube, on the basis of excluding the delta of the former and the tributaries of the latter from the calculation, a poetical sleight of hand Addison firmly exposes:

> That is, says *Scaliger*, the *Eridanis* [i.e. the Po] would be bigger than the *Nile* and *Danube*, if the *Nile* and *Danube* were not bigger than the *Eridanus*. What makes the Poet's Remark the more improper, the very Reason why the *Danube* is greater than the *Po*, as he designs it, is that which really makes the *Po* as great as it is; for before its fall into the Gulf it

3 Addison's scepticism is the more remarkable because (although he draws a veil over the fact) the source of this poetical belief was his beloved Virgil, at *Georgics* II. 146–148: 'hinc albi, Clitumne, greges et maxima taurus/victima, saepe tuo perfusi flumine sacro,/Romanos ad templa deum duxere triumphos' ('Hence your snowy flocks, Clitumnus, and the bull, that noblest victim, which, after been bathed repeatedly in your sacred stream, has been led to the shrines of the gods and the triumphs of Rome').

> receives into its channel the most considerable Rivers or *Piemont*, *Milan*, and the rest of *Lombardy*. (Addison 1705, 113)

The Clitumnus and the Po also feature in the 'Letter', and when describing them Addison reverses those poetical deceptions. The Clitumnus he calls "smooth" rather than white (Addison 1704, 2), thereby breaking any link with the area's famous cows; and he makes it clear that the Po's size is substantially due to its many tributaries: "The King of Floods! that rolling o're the Plains/The Towering Alps of half their moisture drains" (Addison 1704, 3).

The fifth paragraph of the poem, where Addison goes looking for "Streams immortaliz'd in Song/That lost in Silence and Oblivion lye", immediately follows the passage on the Po, and brings to a head the concerns about the relationship between poetry and reality which inform that passage and, to varying degrees, most of Addison's other descriptions of Italian rivers, both in the *Remarks* and the 'Letter'. The anxiety latent throughout those descriptions now emerges more fully into the open, as Addison complains of having been "misguided by the tuneful Throng". That's a sudden stab of satire, a spasm of resentment. And while it dissipates almost instantly (as if Addison needed to retreat from his own candour) into the familiar melancholy of the following lines, with their "Ruins of Rome" clichés about "Silence and Oblivion", "Dumb ... Fountains", and dried-up "Channels", there should be no mistaking the force of the phrase. Consider, for instance, the reference to the Roman poets as a "Throng". This noun is usually pejorative in Addison's poems, two of his other four uses of it coming in his translation of the Pentheus episode from Book III of the *Metamorphoses*, both applied to the Bacchic rout of Theban women ("the frantick Throng" [l. 683], "the distracted Throng" [l. 834]; Addison 1704, 551, 581), which tears Pentheus limb from limb, mistaking him in their frenzy for a savage boar. That translation, like the 'Letter from Italy', was first published in Tonson's *Poetical Miscellanies: the Fifth Part* (1704), so Addison may well have given both texts a final once-over towards the end of his European travels, in the autumn or winter of 1703. Without pushing the analogy too far, there is a Bacchic element to the scene in the 'Letter': Addison too is caught up in a collective delusion, induced by the Roman poets to expect to see rivers where there are none (the poets particularly merge into a "Throng" when writing about rivers because, as Addison points out in the *Remarks*, "when Virgil has mark'd any particular Quality in a River, the other Poets seldom fail of Copying after him"). (Addison 1705, 161–162)

"Misguided" too is a potent term. Here, the operative parallel comes not in Addison's verse (where he never used the verb) but in a letter he wrote to Bishop John Hough, President of his *Alma Mater* Magdalen, on 29 November 1700, shortly before crossing from France into Italy. Addison told Hough about his recent meeting with the great poet and critic Boileau, detailing their exchanges about the latest literary hit in Paris, Fénélon's *Télémaque* (1699):

> I askd him whether Telemach was not a good Modern piece; he spoke of it with a great deal of Esteem ... He said he thought the punishments inflicted on the Bad Kings in Hell might compare with anything in the Sixth Eneid, and that the deceit which is put upon Telemachs Pilot to make him misguide his Master is more Artfull and poetical than the Death of Palinurus. (Graham 1941, 26)

Fénélon's prose epic about Telemachus's travels under the guidance of the "knowledgeable and virtuous" Mentor (Riley 1994, xviii) was a work Addison had obvious reason to identify with as he journeyed around Europe, mentoring a series of young noblemen on the Grand Tour (Smithers 1968, 52–53). In Book VIII, Venus attempts to "misguide" Telemachus by getting Neptune to trick his steersman Athamas with "a deceitful Representation" (Fénélon 1699, 154), so that when the pilot believes he has brought them safely back to Ithaca, they are in fact landing on Crete. Boileau admired that "deceit" as highly "poetical"—that is, romantic or fanciful—but for Addison in the 'Letter from Italy' the prospect of being seduced off-course by poetic illusion could not be taken so lightly.

Like *Télémaque*, the 'Letter' is premised on the link between travel and education. Partly, Addison wrote the poem to guide the responses of well-to-do English tourists (like his pupils) to Italian history and culture; but more broadly, it also served to advertise his credentials as an adviser to the Whig ministry, which was sponsoring him on his travels, by means of a grant arranged through the poem's addressee, Halifax. In this process of self-advertisement, Addison's poetic formation played a double and contradictory role. In one sense, his deep familiarity with ancient Roman verse, as we've seen, spurred the patriotic narrative he offered in the 'Letter' about British modernity. At the same time, though, for Addison to conduct himself in front of his Whig pay-masters as an exemplary modern entailed distancing himself somewhat from his Oxonian past as an amateur of classical poetry. In *Télémaque*, Venus's enmity for Telemachus stems from the enlightened young hero's immunity to "Love and all its Charms" (Fénélon 1699, 146); likewise, in the fifth paragraph of the 'Letter', Addison shows that his experiences in Italy have taught him to resist the allure of the great Roman poets. "Sometimes misguided by the tuneful Throng,/I look for Streams immortaliz'd in Song,/That lost in Silence and Oblivion lye": a thread of assonance connects "misguided" through "immortaliz'd" to "lye", revealing the last of those three verbs as an instance of what Christopher Ricks in a famous essay collected in *The Force of Poetry* termed "the lie/lie pun", combining "rest" with "tell a falsehood"

(Ricks 1995, 369). Laid low by "Silence and Oblivion", the dried-up rivers give the "lie" to the ancient Roman poets who "immortaliz'd" them in "Song". In reality, nothing lasts forever. Poets, who can make it seem otherwise, are liars.

I need to add a coda to this section of my argument, about the concluding lines of the fifth paragraph. The once-great rivers have dried up; "Yet", Addison observes, "they run for ever by the Muses skill,/And in the smooth Description murmur still". That looks like a conventional compliment to the eternizing power of verse, which is to say an outright reversal of the criticism in the preceding lines.[4] However, "still", so near "run", comes to mean "unmoving" as well as "always", prompting us to ask what kind of defensive "skill" it is which serves to "still" a river, that archetype of vital energy and change. Sharper questions about poetry as a refuge from discomfiting realities arise out of the apparently unremarkable phrase "run for ever". It recalls one of the longest of the notes Addison appended to his translations from the *Metamorphoses*, and one of the richest, bearing out Samuel Johnson's view of the notes as containing "specimens of criticism sufficiently subtle and refined" (Lonsdale 2006, iii. 37). Considering poetic "descriptions of Pictures, Images, Dreams, Apparitions, Metamorphoses, and the like"—cases of what we would now call "ekphrasis"—Addison noted the tendency of "Latin Poets" at such moments to "bring together" what he memorably termed "two ... thwarting Ideas, by making one part of their descriptions relate to the representation, and the other to the thing that is represented" (Guthkelch 1914, i. 141). He gave three examples. The first is from Book VIII of the *Aeneid*, the moment where Aeneas shoulders the shield forged for him by Vulcan and inscribed with the glorious future of the Roman race ("Attolens humeris Famamque et Fata Nepotum"), which "though very odd and surprising", Addison remarked, "is plainly made out when we consider how these disagreeing Ideas are reconciled, and [Aeneas's] Posterity's fame and fate made portable by being engraven on the shield" (Guthkelch 1914, i. 141–142). Addison's second example comes

4 Indeed, these lines are quoted as an instance of the 'beautiful manner of speaking, usual with the Poets in praise of Poetry' (Rumbold 2007, 184) in the mock-commentary to *The Dunciad Variorum* (1729), in a note to a couplet in Book I (ll. 86–87) which parodies the convention: 'Now Night descending' (after the day of celebrations for the investitute of the new Lord Mayor of London) 'the proud scene was o'er,/But liv'd, in Settle's numbers, one day more.' It is an interesting question whether Pope's citation of Addison's lines, in the persona of the idiotic scholiast of *The Dunciad*, as 'praise of Poetry' for its eternizing power suggests he himself recognised that the tone of those lines, in their original context in the 'Letter', was not simply laudatory but edged with irony.

from the Arachne episode in Book VI of the *Metamorphoses*: "when *Ovid* tells us that *Pallas* tore in pieces *Arachne*'s work, where she had embroidered all the rapes that the Gods had committed, he says—*Rupit cœlestia Crimina* ["She rips up the celestial crimes"]" (Guthkelch 1914, i. 142). In this case, Addison doesn't say whether the "thwarting Ideas"—regarding the actual rapes committed by the Olympian gods on the one hand, and their depiction in Arachne's tapestry on the other—are ultimately "reconciled" or left jarringly at odds.

But in Addison's third example, artistic representation and reality are set irreconcilably athwart one another, with openly satiric intent. And this example, which comes from a poem by Charles Montagu (the addressee, of course, of the 'Letter'), hinges on the phrase "run for ever".

I shall conclude this tedious reflection with an excellent stroke of this nature, out of Mr. *Montagu*'s Poem to the King where he tells us how the King of France would have been celebrated by his subjects if he had ever gained such an honourable wound as King *William*'s at the fight of the *Boin*:

> His bleeding arm had furnish'd all their rooms,
> And *run* for ever *purple* in the Looms. (Guthkelch 1914, i. 142)

There can be little doubt that this note was somewhere in Addison's mind when he composed the fifth paragraph of the 'Letter'.[5] The two passages share their essential subject matter, both addressing art's pretention to immortalize, and its exposure by "reality". Furthermore, Addison must have been remembering the note rather than alluding directly to Montagu's lines, because the version of those lines given in the note is actually a misquotation. The lines are from Montagu's most famous poem, the *Epistle to Dorset* (1690), and what he wrote was not "run for ever" but "bleed for ever". Had Louis ever sustained a wound like that William III suffered at the Battle of the Boyne, it would have become a perennial theme for French poets and the weavers in the Gobelins tapestry factory in Paris:

> Their Plays, their Songs, wou'd dwell upon his Wound,
> And Opera's repeat no other Sound;
> *Boyne* wou'd, for Ages, be the Painter's Theme,

5 It's likely that the Ovid note preceded the 'Letter' rather than vice versa, the probability being that the notes were composed at the same time as the translations themselves (i.e., in 1694/5), at a time when the model of Dryden's Juvenal (1692) had made the provision of notes in translations of classical verse fashionable (and Addison himself was helping with the apparatus for the Virgil), rather than in 1703, ahead of their publication in Tonson's *Poetical Miscellanies: The Fifth Part*.

> The Goblin's Labour, and the Poet's Dream;
> The wounded Arm wou'd furnish all their Rooms,
> And bleed for ever Scarlet in their Looms. (Montagu 1690, 9)

Addison's "run" is a definite improvement on Montagu's "bleed", a verb more at home in the language of weaving (as in the "running" of thread, or the shuttle itself across the loom; OED 69a), and thereby achieving a subtler entangling of representation and reality.[6] In this context, the effect conveys a simple polemical message: the enlightened English reader can see through the deceitful illusions of absolutist French art, the "Poet's Dream". But the trace memory of the effect in the fifth paragraph of the 'Letter' suggests a more radical aesthetic recognition on Addison's part. At some level, apparently, he equated his own deference to the poets of ancient Rome with the sclerotic flattery paid to Louis XIV. As if classical poetry were a "Dream" he needed to awake from and find untruth.

The various threads of association and connotation I've been unravelling in the rivers section of the 'Letter from Italy', I believe, lead towards a view of this part of the poem as testifying to a phase of crisis in Addison's life and career. Not literally—I don't mean that he went to the site of a river he'd read about in Virgil or whoever, and upon finding it wasn't there any more had a breakdown on the spot. Rather, that scenario of disorientation and disillusionment can be seen as giving symbolic expression to the fundamental life changes that Addison underwent during the period of his travels in Italy, which prepared the ground for his eventual transformation from Oxonian scholar-poet to Whig politician. Prior to his departure for Europe in the late summer of 1699, he had lived virtually all his adult life within the purlieu of Magdalen College. Given that insular background, foreign travel must in itself have come as a shock to him, exacerbated by his monolingualism and intermittent money troubles (Smithers 1968, 48–49, 89). But most of all, the Europe he was travelling through was a war-zone

6 Testimony to Addison's achievement in re-writing Halifax's lines is supplied (perhaps unwittingly) by Pope, again in *The Dunciad*; during the mock-heroic games in Book II, Edmund Curll wins a carpet inscribed with the fates of hack booksellers, including the notorious episode in which Pope tricked him into drinking an emetic as punishment for his unauthorized publication of verse by Pope and Lady Mary Wortley Montagu in *Court Poems* (1716). Seeing his misery depicted in the carpet, Curll cries out: 'In ev'ry loom our labours shall be seen,/And the fresh vomit run for ever green!'; and a note in the mock-commentary identifies that couplet as 'A parody on these of a late noble author: 'His bleeding arm had furnish'd all their rooms,/And run for ever purple in the looms.' (Rumbold 2007, 231)—but in fact that's Addison's re-written version not Halifax's original text. My thanks to Henry Power for reminding me of this moment.

(for all these reasons, it is misleading to apply the genteel rubric of 'the Grand Tour' to Addison's European travels). The 'Letter from Italy' is where we would expect Addison to have registered these shocks to his system—a poem set in the fabled land of ancient poetry but written as that "classic ground" was being overrun by the modern military might of the French army, with the 'campaign in northern Italy ... beginning in earnest', as Addison "passed hastily through Bologna, Modena, Parma, and Savoy to gain the neutral shelter of Switzerland" (Smithers 1968, 70).

But, of course, Addison was a writer notoriously averse to autobiographical disclosure, his chronic 'avoidance of self-revelation' often cited as the main reason for his enduring unpopularity with present-day readers raised on Romantic or confessional literature (McCrea 1990, 152–153). In a well-known letter to his pupil Edward Wortley describing the genesis of the 'Letter', Addison elided the politically and personally unsettling circumstances of its composition into a witticism, noting suavely that in having produced a poem while crossing the Alps, 'I believe I am the first that ever thought of Parnassus on Mount Sennis' (Graham 1914, 30). He is no more likely to have addressed openly in the poem itself whatever "malaise" or "wounded spirits" (Smithers 1968, 48) he was experiencing when he wrote it. But if we were looking for an indirect expression of such feelings in the poem, the rivers section would be a natural place to try. When I referred to Addison's European travels a moment ago as a "phase of crisis" in his life and career, it was hard to avoid calling it a "watershed". And in fact the fluvial metaphor would be no idle play on words. Rivers have an age-old association with crises of life-choice, "rites of passage" or "new beginnings" (Herendeen 1986, 33), the prime example in the classical world being that of Caesar at the Rubicon—and sure enough, the Rubicon is another of those rivers which, in the *Remarks*, forces Addison to choose between poetry and reality, since it "is not so very contemptible as it is generally represented" (Addison 1705, 215). From Roman poetry, Addison would have absorbed a view of rivers as particularly emblematizing poetic choice, or "self-discovery" (Middleton 2012, 78–79), a link he activated with regard to the 'Letter' by choosing as its epigraph the passage from Book II of the *Georgics* where Virgil undertakes to "dare to unseal the sacred fountains of art" ("artem/... sanctos ausus recludere fontes"). The opening lines of the rivers section apparently announce Addison's own commitment to that Virgilian project:

How am I pleas'd to search the Hills and Woods
For rising Springs and celebrated Floods!
To view the *Nar*, tumultuous in his Course,
And trace the smooth *Clitumnus* to his Source. (Addison 1704, 2)

But to "search" the "springs" of Addison's poetry about the rivers of Italy, "trace" its "sources", is to arrive at the opposite conclusion. The conventional understanding of Addison's career has it that though he continued to write verse in later years, he to all intents and purposes turned his back on poetry in 1705, after the publication of *The Campaign* won him political preferment. But the riverrine journey of subtextual exploration we've been on in this chapter suggests that Addison already stood at the crossing-point between the domain of poetry and the world of affairs at the turn of 1701–1702.

References

ADDISON, Joseph: "A Letter from Italy". In: *Poetical Miscellanies: the Fifth Part.* London: Jacob Johnson 1704, 1–12.

ADDISON, Joseph: *Remarks on Several Parts of Italy*. London: Jacob Johnson 1705.

COURTHOPE, William J.: *Addison*. London: Macmillan 1884.

FÉNELON, François de Salignac de Lamothe: *The Adventures of Telemachus, the Son of Ulysses Translated from the French.* London: A. and J. Churchil 1700.

GRAHAM, Walter (ed.): *The Letters of Joseph Addison*. Oxford: Oxford University Press 1941.

GUTHKELCH, Adolph C. (ed.): *The Miscellaneous Works of Joseph Addison*. 2 vols. London: Bell and Sons Ltd 1914.

HERENDEEN, Wyman H.: *From Landscape to Literature: The River and the Myth of Geography*. Pittsburgh: Duquesne University Press 1986.

JOHNSON, Donald. R.: "Addison in Italy". *Modern Language Studies* 6, 1 (1976), 32–36.

LEWIS, Wilmarth Sheldon et al. (eds.): *Horace Walpole's Correspondence*. 48 vols. New Haven: Yale University Press 1937–1783.

LONSDALE, Roger (ed.): *Samuel Johnson: The Lives of the Poets*. 3 vols. Oxford: Oxford University Press 2006.

MCCREA, Brian: *Addison and Steele Are Dead: The English Department, Its Canon, and the Professionalization of Literary Criticism*. Newark: University of Delaware Press 1990.

MIDDLETON, Nick: *Rivers: A Very Short Introduction*. Oxford: Oxford University Press 2012.

MONTAGU, Charles: *An Epistle to the Right Honourable Charles Earl of Dorset and Middlesex, Lord Chamberlain of His Majesties Houshold.* London: Francis Saunders 1690.

REDFORD, Bruce: *Venice and the Grand Tour*. New Haven: Yale University Press 1996.

RICKS, Christopher: "Lies". In: Christopher Ricks: *The Force of Poetry*. Oxford: Oxford University Press 1995, 369–391.

RILEY, Patrick (trans. and ed.): *Telemachus, Son of Ulysses*. Cambridge: Cambridge University Press 1994.

RUMBOLD, Valerie (ed.): "The Dunciad (1728)" & "The Dunciad Variorum (1729)". *The Poems of Alexander Pope*. Vol. III. Harlow: Pearson Education 2007.

SMITHERS, Peter: *The Life of Joseph Addison*. Oxford: Oxford University Press 1968.

Klaus-Dieter Ertler

(University of Graz)

Addison, lecteur de Bayle

Il est généralement connu que Joseph Addison, un des représentants emblématiques du *Spectator*, avait trouvé une source féconde de son écriture dans les œuvres critiques de Pierre Bayle, professeur de philosophie calviniste d'origine occitane, qui avait émigré en 1681 à Rotterdam pour éviter les poursuites dans le contexte culturel de la Révocation de l'Édit de Nantes. Bayle avait cherché à réactiver le *Grand Dictionnaire historique* du jésuite Louis Moréri, publié en 1674, afin d'y introduire des voix et perspectives nouvelles, multiples, voire contradictoires, avec le but de créer une nouvelle écriture encyclopédique, qui devait aboutir au projet du *Dictionnaire historique et critique* de 1697. Nombreuses en étaient les éditions augmentées dans les années suivantes.

Il faut rappeler que la traduction du *Dictionnaire* en langue anglaise a été publiée à Londres en 1710 en quatre volumes, par un groupe d'éditeurs dont faisait partie un ami d'Addison, Jacob Tonson.[1] Celui-ci avait eu un rapport étroit avec Pierre Bayle pour préparer cette traduction, et il se peut que Joseph Addison, au cours de son Grand Tour en 1703, ait pu rencontrer le « the famous Monsieur Bayle »[2] dans le cadre de l'établissement de cette édition en Hollande. Pendant la rédaction des feuilles morales, Addison devait posséder une version en trois volumes de 1702, publiée à Amsterdam, et la version anglaise de 1710 mentionnée plus haut.[3]

Il existe une remarque connue dans les *Addisoniana* éditées par Richard Phillips (1803, 207), selon laquelle « old Jacob Tonson used to tell, that he seldom called upon Addison when he did not see Bayle's Dictionary lying open upon his table », ce qui confirme le lien étroit entre les deux formes d'écriture ainsi qu'une certaine disposition pour la migration des microrécits. Voilà le point de départ de notre étude, confirmée par Bond: « Many of the historical anecdotes in the *Spectator* can in fact be traced to the Dictionary ».[4]

1 Voir aussi l'introduction de Bond dans *The Spectator*, 1965, I/CXI.

2 *The Freeholder* 35, cit. d'après Smithers 1968, 84.

3 Peter Smithers: *The Life of Joseph Addison*. Oxford: Clarendon Press 1968, 84.

4 Note 4 de Bond dans *The Spectator*, 1965, I, 360.

Dans la présente analyse, nous nous concentrerons sur la presse spectatoriale de Joseph Addison et sur la forme narrative qui lui est propre, afin d'observer ses sources et les migrations intertextuelles de ses textes à travers les cultures et afin de décrire sa fonction à partir des écritures proto-encyclopédiques au début du siècle. Il s'agit de repérer les échanges culturels entre la France et l'Angleterre en ce qui concerne ces formes d'écriture, échanges qui ont lieu par l'intermédiaire des plateformes intellectuelles et matérielles des Pays-Bas. Nous nous pencherons aussi brièvement sur le réseau européen des feuilles volantes périodiques anglophones et francophones du XVIIIe siècle.

Dans la mesure où le modèle spectatorial anglais puise à son tour dans le corpus proto-encyclopédique de Pierre Bayle, il faudra s'interroger sur la question de l'écriture intertextuelle de cette presse et de ses traductions et adaptations à travers l'Europe : De quelle manière les textes spectatoriaux en anglais et en français contribuent-ils donc à la construction d'une nouvelle pratique d'écriture ? Comment intègrent-ils les microrécits du *Dictionnaire historique et critique* de Bayle afin de les utiliser à des fins morales ? Et comment préparent-ils le chemin conduisant vers les réseaux spectatoriaux européens[5] ?

Le corpus analysé ici concerne trois titres : les deux tomes du *Dictionnaire historique et critique* de Pierre Bayle de 1697, les 635 numéros du *Spectator* de Richard Steele et Joseph Addison (1711–1712 ; 1714), réunis en cinq tomes, et la traduction partielle en français des feuilles spectatoriales anglaises, sous le titre *Le Spectateur, ou le Socrate moderne* (1714–1726) réunies en six tomes, dont le traducteur est resté anonyme. Le recours au *Spectateur français* est important dans la mesure où celui-ci a fonctionné également comme une source non négligeable pour les entreprises de la République des Lettres en exportant le modèle spectatorial et ses pratiques d'écriture vers d'autres cultures européennes.

Avec leur réseau narratif dense et hautement complexe, les trois titres précoces de l'écriture proto-encyclopédique ou spectatoriale entretiennent donc des liens étroits qui rayonnent non seulement en aval de la chaîne communicationnelle, mais qui se nourrissent également en amont des sources européennes. N'oublions pas que Bayle, qui puise dans les ressources de la culture classique, se définit comme un compilateur, et qu'Addison et Steele se voient de leur côté comme les continuateurs des cultures antiques, grecque et latine, avec le recours à Socrate,

5 Pendant la seconde phase du *Spectator* en 1714, Addison pensait même à préparer un dictionnaire littéraire : « His experience in the writing of current English prose, added to his study of the literature of the past, of the critics and of Bayle, led him to contemplate the idea of compiling an English dictionary based upon extracts from the standard works of literature […] » (Smithers 1968, 292).

Caton, Juvénal ou Thucydide en tête, ou se considèrent comme inspirés par la culture classique dans le sillon de La Bruyère et La Rochefoucauld comme de Nicolas Boileau. Dans les trois titres, les microrécits circulent abondamment d'amont en aval, puisés dans toutes sortes de sources et transmis aux lecteurs des périodiques dans de nombreuses aires culturelles du continent. Ces récits courts ont souvent la fonction d'exemple pour appuyer une idée ou une argumentation avancée et s'inscrivent dans un contexte de modernisation discursive.

Les plus petits dénominateurs communs relevés dans l'architecture des deux genres bien distincts du corpus – c'est-à-dire le *Dictionnaire* et les « spectateurs » en général – se trouvent

1. dans leur intention de construire un espace public en intégrant une pluralité de voix pour démontrer une vérité ou une vertu. Cet intérêt pour une publicité participative crée un ensemble narratif dans lequel les récits courts ou les microrécits occupent une place centrale. Le Spectateur anglais invite ses amis et ses lecteurs à participer activement à l'entreprise journalistique pour enrichir le discours : « [...] as my Friends [du Club] have engaged me to stand in the Front, those who have a mind to correspond with me, may direct their Letters *To the Spectator*, at *Mr. Buckley's* in *Little Britain* » (*The Spectator* 1965, I, 6/Addison). Bayle réserve également un espace aux critiques de ses lecteurs : « *Si quelques-uns croyent qu'ils ont été critiquez mal-à-propos dans ce Dictionaire, & s'ils publient pour leur justification quelque petit imprimé [...], je m'assûre [...] je prenne la resolution de renvoyer tout cela à la suite de cet Ouvrage* » (Bayle 1697, Préface, 12). – « [...] *j'avois laissé au Libraire une pleine autorité d'inserer, même sans me consulter, les memoires que ses correspondans & ses amis lui enverroient* » (Bayle 1697, Préface, 7). On peut en déduire que la critique n'est plus réservée à une infime minorité de lecteurs, mais à un public instruit, à condition qu'elle porte sur une œuvre – en particulier dans le cas des satires – et non pas sur un auteur.
2. Bien que la tâche principale du travail incombe aux auteurs, ils s'attribuent un rôle modeste – ou même invisible – dans l'entreprise pour démontrer que les éditeurs et les lecteurs participent activement. Cela explique le jeu de l'anonymat chez les spectateurs ou la modestie de Bayle qui tient à ce que son nom ne figure pas sur la couverture du *Dictionnaire*. Le Spectateur invente une sorte de récit biofictionnel ou fiction d'éditeur pour satisfaire la curiosité de ses lecteurs : « As the chief Trouble of Compiling, Digesting and Correcting will fall to my Share, I must do Myself the Justice to open the Work with my own History. I was born to a small Hereditary Estate [...] » (*The Spectator* 1965, I, 1/Addison). – Bayle cherche à construire une œuvre sur la

couverture de laquelle son nom n'est pas mentionné et qui intègre les voix du public : « *Ceux qui verront mon nom à la tête de ce livre, & qui sauront que pendant le cours de l'impression j'ai dit en toutes rencontres, que je ne l'y mettrois pas, meritent un petit coin dans cette Preface* » (Bayle 1697, Préface, 10).

3. Les textes sont considérés avant tout en fonction de leur utilité pour un public plus large sans que les aspects esthétiques ou philosophiques aient à en souffrir. Cette fonction didactique relève du fond comme de la forme, en particulier dans les « spectateurs » où c'est le public en général – et avant tout les femmes – à qui on s'adresse et qu'on souhaite instruire. Le Spectateur anglais se réfère à Socrate comme modèle : "It was said of *Socrates*, that he brought Philosophy down from Heaven, to inhabit among Men; and I shall be ambitious to have it said of me, that I have brought Philosophy out of Closets and Libraries, Schools and Colleges, to dwell in Clubs and Assemblies, at Tea-Tables, and in Coffee-Houses" (*The Spectator* 1965, I/10, 44/Addison). – "But there are none to whom this Paper will be more useful, than to the female World" (*Ibid.*, 46). Bayle considère « [...] *qu'un Ouvrage comme celui-ci doit tenir lieu de Bibliothèque à un grand nombre de gens [...]* ». – « *[...] un Ouvrage de compilation tel que celui-ci où l'on se propose de narrer des faits, & puis de les illustrer par des commentaires* » (Bayle 1697, Préface, 6).
4. Les textes s'inscrivent dans un ensemble complexe abordant des domaines très variés en offrant des unités narratives, des exemples, qui fonctionnent comme des parties d'illustration dans un système de savoir ou d'éthique, souvent d'inspiration protestante.
5. Les considérations d'ordre économique ne sont pas absentes dans la mesure où les auteurs voient leurs lecteurs potentiels comme des clients qui assurent le succès de l'entreprise commerciale et sans lesquels l'écriture serait un échec.
6. Les textes sont présentés comme inachevés, sous une forme d'autogenèse soulignant leur caractère flexible, modulable, défendant leur statut d'improvisation afin de rester proche du lecteur.

Les nombreux dénominateurs communs relevés dans les œuvres considérées ici témoignent d'une perméabilité discursive entre les genres, qui se distinguent évidemment par leurs orientations particulières. N'oublions pas que la presse spectatoriale cherche à toucher le lectorat par des feuilles volantes avec des articles éphémères et divertissants, tel que le dictionnaire avec l'organisation de ses entrées indépendantes, bien que les deux genres opèrent également avec le format de recueil ou de volume. Les Spectateurs se présentent sous l'identité d'un auteur ou éditeur fictif tandis que Bayle opte de prime abord pour l'anonymat.

Les textes spectatoriaux sont étroitement liés à la vie publique, notamment aux milieux liés à la mode et au monde des cafés. Les « spectateurs » se présentent en observateurs discrètement participants, afin de fournir des orientations pour guider le comportement moral de la nouvelle société, tandis que le *Dictionnaire* de Bayle naît loin des « *divertissements, parties des loisirs, jeux, collations, voyages à la campagne, visites, & telles recréations* » (Bayle 1697, Préface, 5). Malgré ces distinctions – parmi d'autres –, on note un système discursif qui réunit les deux genres, non seulement par la construction complexe des récits, mais aussi par leur impact communicationnel. Il faut pourtant rappeler que, d'un côté, les journaux d'Addison et Steele seront publiés plus tard sous forme de volumes dont les nombreuses traductions marqueront la République des Lettres ; Bayle, quant à lui, opte pour l'ouverture de ses entrées à la discussion publique dont l'impact sera considérable dans les cultures européennes du XVIIIe siècle. Rappelons, enfin, la collaboration discrète d'Eustace Budgell, dont les contributions sont en étroite relation avec celles de Joseph Addison et qui a maintes fois recours aux textes de Bayle.[6]

La migration des récits

Dans la chaîne communicationnelle observée ici, nous pourrons constater que les auteurs et éditeurs du *Spectator* – notamment Joseph Addison – ont lu et recyclé les articles du *Dictionnaire historique et critique*, ce qui apparaît dans la traduction sélective du *Spectateur français* et la mode spectatoriale en Europe au cours du siècle.[7] Dans les trois titres en question, les récits courts et les microrécits ont un statut d'autant plus important que les auteurs se sont définis eux-mêmes comme des compilateurs afin de faire office d'instructeurs auprès de leur public. Ils puisent donc largement dans les sources du savoir européen pour le transmettre sous forme condensée à leurs lecteurs. Leur éthique de travail est très proche, car on lit dans la Préface du *Dictionnaire* que l'auteur modèle

6 Dans sa préface érudite dédiée au *Spectator*, Donald F. Bond rappelle ces liens entre Budgell, Addison et Bayle : « Four of these [papers] (Nos. 307, 313, 337 and 353) form a connected series on the subject of education. Others deal with such varied topics as beards, the Mohocks, women's vanity, Will Honeycomb's amours, friendship, dangers in the month of May, and the belief of God among the heathens. His essays are characterized by rather short paragraphs and a liberal sprinkling of out-of-the-way learning, much of it derived from Bayle's *Dictionary* » (Bond, in *The Spectator* 1965, LI–LII).

7 Addison avait la possibilité de voyager sur le continent européen et de rencontrer Boileau, Malebranche et Bayle. (Cf. Holzhey/Mudroch 2004, vol. 1., 287).

de Bayle se voyait « toujours en peine comment il pratiqueroit la vertu » (Bayle 1697, Préface, 11). Et il continue à défendre son statut de compilateur qui a été fortement attaqué par ses contemporains : « Mais les metiers les plus vils ne sont-ils pas necessaires ? [...] Il y a donc plus de vanité que de modestie, à ne vouloir pas passer pour un Auteur portefaix » (*Ibid.*). Ainsi le *Dictionnaire* représente-t-il déjà en soi une compilation très riche dans laquelle les auteurs ultérieurs iront puiser le savoir sous forme de récits. Bayle cherche à ne pas imiter ses précurseurs – tout en les citant fréquemment comme Louis Moréri et son *Grand Dictionnaire* (1674), Barthélemy d'Herbelot et sa *Bibliothèque orientale ou Dictionnaire universel* (1697) ou de Louis Ellies du Pin[8] avec la *Bibliothèque des auteurs ecclésiastiques* (1686–1691), mais à explorer d'autres sources de savoir. Pourtant il fait de la citation une stratégie centrale de son écriture : « Je cite souvent de très-longs passages : quelquefois j'en donne le sens en nôtre langue, & puis je le raporte & en Grec, & en Latin » (Bayle 1697, Préface, 5–6). Les entrées de Bayle suivent le principe socratique du dialogue, avec nombre d'opinions et de remarques illustrées par des exemples narratifs. On pourrait constater par conséquent que le *Dictionnaire* en soi représente l'aboutissement d'une forte influence de récits empruntés non seulement à l'Antiquité, mais aussi à des contemporains.

Dans l'appareil critique très fourni du *Spectator* de 1965, Donald F. Bond confirme ce constat par le grand nombre de références aux entrées du *Dictionnaire*, car on y compte une quarantaine de renvois à des articles de Bayle. Il faut relever que les textes d'Addison contiennent la plupart de ses références – comparés à ceux de Steele –, prouvant le recours le plus actif aux microrécits de Bayle. Pourtant les références explicites à l'auteur du *Dictionnaire* sont plutôt rares: « Mr. *Jacob Tonson, Jun*^{r}. is of Opinion, that *Bayle's Dictionary* might be of very great Use to the Ladies, in order to make them general Scholars » (*The Spectator* 1965, I/92, 390/Addison).[9] – « I will conclude my paper with the Words of Monsieur Bayle, who was a Man of great Freedom of Thought, as well as of exquisite Learnery and Judgement » (*The Spectator* 1965, IV/451, 89/Addison).[10] – « There is a noble

---

8 Dans ses éditions ultérieures, le *Dictionnaire* de Moréri s'enrichira de textes du *Dictionnaire historique et critique* de Bayle, de la *Bibliothèque orientale ou Dictionnaire universel* de Barthélemy d'Herbelot de Molainville et de la *Bibliothèque des auteurs ecclésiastique* de Louis Ellies du Pin.

9 « Mr. Jacob Tonson, le jeune, croit que le Dictionnaire de Mr. Bayle seroit fort utile aux Dames, pour leur donner une connoissance universelle » (*Spectateur* 1716, II/3, 16).

10 « D'ailleurs, afin qu'on ne me croie pas d'une opinion singuliere là-dessus, je vais citer un long passage de Mr. BAYLE, Homme d'esprit & d'érudition, qui n'avoit pas moins de bon goût, qu'il étoit libre de préjugez » (*Spectateur* 1716, IV, 75, 456).

Hymn in French, which Monsieur Bayle has celebrated for a very fine one … » (*The Spectator* 1965, V/513, 323–324/Addison).[11] En ce qui concerne le *Spectator*, la réception de Bayle passe donc essentiellement à travers les feuilles d'Addison, dont les textes se distinguent largement des autres contributions du point de vue du genre et de son intention, de sa qualité d'écriture et de son développement théorique.

Le passage de la version anglaise à la version française offre également des particularités, car chez *Le Spectateur* il s'agit d'une traduction sélectionnée selon les intérêts du traducteur ou de l'éditeur francophones. Nombreux sont les passages de textes et des numéros entiers qui ont été supprimés afin de répondre aux goûts du lectorat français. Ainsi beaucoup de récits du *Spectator* se voient exclus d'une transmission ultérieure par la voie francophone, tandis que d'autres parviennent à s'intégrer dans les cultures européennes et à se développer dans de nouvelles langues et couleurs locales. Dans la version française, il manque souvent les références à la politique anglaise contemporaine ainsi que des textes dont la disparition reste à élucider. En ce qui concerne la réception du *Dictionnaire* de Bayle et du recyclage de ses microrécits dans la version française du *Spectator*, on peut constater – entre autres – l'absence des articles concernant Sappho, Leucas, Alcaeus (Charaxos), Francis, Accursius, Périandre et Bossu. Ce sont surtout les histoires de Sappho et de Leucas qui ont été systématiquement supprimées.

Il est évident que ces microrécits manquent également – à titre d'exemple – dans les traductions ou les adaptations en Italie ou en Espagne, où les volumes portent le titre *Il Filosofo alla moda* (1727/28) de Cesare Frasponi, un pseudonyme, ou bien *El Filósofo a la Moda* (1788) établi par un traducteur anonyme. Il faut rappeler le caractère encyclopédique de ces deux adaptations, du moins en ce qui concerne le sous-titre italien : *ovvero il Maestro universale di quanto e oggidi proprio ad istruire, e divertire* (*ou le Maître universel de tout ce qu'il faut instruire et divertir aujourd'hui*). Finalement on peut relever que de nombreuses adaptations ainsi que traductions du *Spectateur* portent souvent des titres d'introduction explicites et offrent à leur public une version française des épigraphes – généralement en latin ou en grec – de chaque numéro.

11 « D'ailleurs Mr. BAYLE nous dit que c'est une Pièce *d'une grande beauté*, & le célébre Auteur de *la Rhétorique*, ou *l'Art de parler* la cite comme un Sonnet *admirable*. La voici » (*Spectateur* V/40, 245).

Les récits recyclés – quelques exemples

Les références au texte de Bayle avec les sujets recyclés par le *Spectator* et leur transmission à la version française et à d'autres versions révèlent quelques détails concernant l'écriture proto-encyclopédique du *Dictionnaire* et de sa réception dans la presse. Nous avons vu que la préoccupation pour la façon de raconter caractérise également la source de cette chaîne communicationnelle. Le choix des récits et leur emploi comme illustration exemplaire mettant en valeur des faits historiques ou sociaux y jouent un rôle important. La question essentielle portera sur le degré de traduction ou d'adaptation des unités narratives de texte. Sont-elles traduites plus ou moins fidèlement, ou subissent-elles des adaptations quelconques ; servent-elles à d'autres contextes culturels, ou bien disparaissent-elles entièrement ? Nous trouverons donc à la source un processus de recyclage initial qui sera relevé par le *Spectator*, en particulier par Addison qui, par sa qualité d'adaptation, valorise considérablement ce nouveau genre périodique. Les traductions françaises ou autres, par contre, restent dans le domaine de la copie sélective sans ajouter d'éléments notables.[12]

Mahomet et les Devins

Un des récits courts les plus diffusés dans les « spectateurs » porte sur différents aspects de l'histoire de Mahomet et de son interprétation dans les cultures européennes. L'intérêt porté à ce personnage s'appuie partiellement sur les lectures du jeune Addison qui s'intéressait à la bibliothèque de son père, Lancelot Addison, dont la fonction militaire britannique à Tanger avait laissé des traces notables dans son écriture, en particulier dans son livre « costumbriste » de *West Barbary, or a Short Narrative of the Revolutions of the Kingdoms of Fez and Morocco* (1671). Le texte contient le cadre topique qui sera cher à Joseph Addison et à la tradition spectatoriale ultérieure, par exemple le lien entre le nom de Mahomet et la fonction d'imposteur dans l'incipit ou bien la lettre du Roi de Maroc au Roi d'Angleterre (1671, 9).

Dans notre premier exemple illustrant les liens entre les œuvres d'Addison et de Bayle, le sujet se réfère au cœur et aux intestins de Mahomet, qui ont été nettoyés par les Anges et restent purs et propres comparés à ceux de l'homme ordinaire, dont le corps reste généralement souillé par des substances nocives, ce qui le condamne à une existence peu vertueuse. Ce microrécit a été largement

12 « [...] one should mention Bayle's Dictionnaire, which Addison frequently consulted, and which is itself another teeming, generative work » (Junqua 2012, 36).

repris dans les Spectateurs du XVIIIe siècle, en particulier en Espagne, où les vices sont étudiés dans le cerveau des hommes mondains, les petits-maîtres en tant que représentants de la mode.

Si nous consultons une des sources possibles d'Addison, le *Dictionnaire* de Bayle, nous constatons que l'article sur « Mahomet » y développe l'histoire du cœur et des intestins de Mahomet d'une façon critique, même ironique. Dans la première remarque, ce microrécit constitue une base pour le développement ultérieur dans les réseaux spectatoriaux.

> Mahomet (Remarque I)
> Il n'y a rien de plus risible que ce qu'on veut qu'ayent fait les Anges gardiens de Mahomet. Ils (b) le transporterent sur une montagne, & ils lui fendirent le ventre, il lui laverent si bien les boyaux qu'ils les rendirent plus blancs que la neige, ils lui ouvrirent la poitrine, & lui ôterent du cœur le grain noir, ou la goutte noire qui est une semence diabolique, qui tourmente tous les autres hommes ; ils lui firent tout cela sans qu'il sentît aucune douleur, & ayant été ainsi lavé & nettoyé au dedans du corps, il s'en retourna de lui-même au logis. Notez qu'il n'avoit alors que quatre ans. (Bayle 1697, II, 428/429)
> SIR, I was the other Day reading the Life of *Mahomet*. Among many other Extravagancies, I find it recorded of that Impostor, that in the fourth Year of his Age the Angel *Gabriel* caught him up, while he was among his Play-fellows, and carrying him aside, cut open his Breast, plucked out his Heart, and wrung out of it that black Drop of Blood in which, say the *Turkish* Divines, is contained the *Fomes Peccati*, so that he was free from Sin ever after. I immediately said to my self, tho' this Story be a Fiction, a very good Moral may be drawn from it, would every Man but apply it to himself, and endeavor to squeeze out of his Heart whatever Sins or ill Qualities he finds in it. (*The Spectator* 1965, V/587, 7/ Addison)[13]

MONSIEUR,

> Occupé l'autre jour à lire la Vie de Mahomet, j'y trouvai, entre plusieurs autres extravagances, qu'à l'âge de quatre ans, cet Imposteur fut enlevé, pendant qu'il badinoit avec ses Camarades, par l'Ange Gabriel, qui le transporta dans quelque endroit à l'écart, lui ouvrit la poitrine, en tira son Cœur, qu'il tordit pour en exprimer cette goûte de sang noir, où reside, suivant les Théologiens *Turcs*, ce qu'on appelle *fomes peccati*, ou *le germe du Péché* ; en sorte que Mahomet en fut delivré le reste de ses jours. Je me dis aussitôt à moi-même, Quoi que ce ne soit qu'un Conte, on pourroit en tirer une fort bonne

13 *Cf. ibid.* Remarque dans l'édition critique, n° 2 : « The anecdote is told in the *Turkish Spy*, book iii, letter xx, ed. 1702, v. 200, and Bayle art. *Mahomet*, Remark I. In neither of these accounts, however, is *Fomes peccati* used. The phrase occurs in Prudentius, *Apophthegmata*, 942, and elsewhere ».

> Morale, si chacun vouloit s'en faire l'aplication, & tâcher d'exprimer hors de son Cœur tous les Vices & les Défauts qu'il y trouve (*Le Spectateur* 1724, VI, 133).[14]

Comme nous avons pu le constater, le ton de la première remarque de Pierre Bayle contient une forte critique culturelle de la construction du mythe de Mahomet. L'évaluation initiatrice sur le caractère risible de ce récit entraîne le lecteur vers une position axiologique préétablie. La remarque finale de ce microrécit fait écho au scepticisme exprimé au début. Il faut rappeler que, dans le *Spectator*, Mahomet passe systématiquement pour un imposteur. Comme ce texte de Bayle peut être attribué à une plume étrangère, stratégie largement pratiquée par l'auteur et éditeur du *Dictionnaire*, Mr. Spectator opère également une extrapolation dans la mesure où le récit présenté ici se voit placé au début de la lettre d'un correspondant. Les événements sont présentés avec plus de détail, le style est plus enjoué et enrichi de noms qui ne figurent pas dans le *Dictionnaire*. D'autre part, le texte fait abstraction du lavage des intestins de Mahomet tout en se concentrant sur l'organe emblématique de la chrétienté, le cœur. On y trouve également une référence à d'autres sources de la narration comme à des devins turcs, dont l'auteur de la lettre tire ses informations sur les *Fomes Peccati,* expression accompagnée d'un commentaire libre « free of Sin » dans le *Spectator*, et traduite dans la version française par « germes du péché ». Ce qui est « semence diabolique » devient dans un contexte protestant en quelque sorte le péché originel. À la fin du microrécit, le Spectator – ou bien son correspondant – profite de l'exemple avancé sur Mahomet pour le recycler dans le sens moral de la feuille : à partir de cette narration peut se construire une leçon utile pour tout lecteur, qui devrait faire son introspection et chercher à débarrasser son cœur de ses impuretés.

Quant à la version française, elle suit dans l'ensemble son modèle anglais. Il faut relever pourtant que les « devins turcs » deviennent des « Théologiens Turcs », que la « fiction » est remplacée par le terme de « conte » et que le concept « Sin » se transforme en « vices ». Il s'agit donc d'un récit court fortement enraciné en amont et en aval de la réception de ces trois textes et mis par les « spectateurs » au service du concept d'une vie vertueuse. Le cas de Mahomet cherche une fois de plus à illustrer cette idée omniprésente dans l'univers spectatorial selon laquelle les préceptes horaciens du « prodesse et delectare » ainsi que la méthode socratique du dialogue représentent les voies royales de l'enseignement de la vertu.

14 Titre ajouté de la feuille : « Vision allégorique sur le Germe du Péché, qui se trouve plus ou moins dans tous les Cœurs ».

Les rêves et leur fonction

Le sujet qui a le plus marqué l'écriture spectatoriale, à savoir la narration du rêve, constitue un aspect essentiel à relever dans le travail de réécriture des récits courts et des microrécits du *Dictionnaire*. Les exemples sont nombreux où les rêves se voient employés comme allégories ou comme élément fondamental et nécessaire au développement de l'imagination, un concept systématiquement défendu par Addison. L'article de Bayle sur Junianus Majus décrit le savant italien comme un éminent « onirocritique » (ou mieux interprète des rêves en son temps). Dans la remarque A, le lecteur trouve une critique acerbe de cette interprétation des songes, vu que ceux-ci servent généralement de présages pour l'avenir, nourrissant ainsi la superstition chez les contemporains. Addison reprend cette idée pour la réfuter en développant sa propre théorie de l'interprétation des rêves qui contribueraient, selon lui, à enrichir l'imaginaire.

> Majus (Junianus), gentilhomme napolitain, enseigna les belles lettres dans Naples vers la fin du XV. siecle *. Il eût entre autres disciples le celebre (A) Sannazar. Il contribua beaucoup par ses leçons & par ses livres à retablir le bel (B) usage de la langue Latine, mais il se distingua encore plus par l'explication (C) des songes. Ce fut le plus grand Onirocritique de son siecle, & l'on recouroit à lui de toutes parts, pour savoir ce que présageoient tels et tels songes. Plusieurs prétendaient que ses réponses leur avoient été fort utiles. Ce n'est pas indigne d'une (D) réflexion. Reflexion A : [...] [Note à part : Reflexion sur les songes] Il seroit à souhaiter pour le bien & pour le repos d'esprit d'une infinité de gens, que l'on n'eût jamais parlé des songes comme une chose qui presage l'avenir ; car les personnes qui sont une fois imbuës de cette pensée, s'imaginent que la plûpart des images qui leur passent par l'esprit pendant leur sommeil, sont autant de predictions le plus souvent menaçantes : de là naissent mille inquietudes, & pour un homme qui n'est point sujet à ses foiblesses, il y en a mille qui ne sauroient s'en defendre. (Bayle 1697, II, 509–510)
>
> Tho' there are many Authors, who have written in Dreams, they have generally considered them only as Revelations of what has already happened in distant Parts in the World, or as Presages of what is to happen in future Periods of Time. I shall consider this subject in another Light, as Dreams may give us some Idea of the great Excellency of an Human Soul, and some Intimations of its Independency on Matter. In the first Place, our Dreams are great Instances of that Activity which is Natural to the Human Soul, and which is not in the Power of sleep to deaden or abate (*The Spectator* 1965, IV/487, 226/Addison).[15]

15 L'épigraphe de ce chapitre se marie bien avec le discours sur les rêves : « ... cùm prostrata sopore/Urget membra quies, & mens sine pondere ludit. Petronius, *Satyricon*. » (*Ibid.*)

> [Réflexion sur la nature de l'Ame à l'occasion des Rêves.] Quoi qu'il y ait divers Auteurs, qui ont écrit sur les Songes, ils les ont presque tous regardez comme des Révélations de ce qui est arrivé en certains Païs fort éloignez du nôtre, ou comme des Présages de ce qui doit arriver dans la suite. Je les vai considérer ici sous une tout autre vûe, en ce qu'ils peuvent nous donner quelque idée de l'excellence de nos Ames, & nous insinuer qu'elles sont indépendantes de la matiere. En premier lieu, nos Rêves nous fournissent de bonnes preuves de l'Activité qui est naturelle à l'Ame, & qu'il n'est pas au pouvoir du Sommeil d'éteindre ou de ralentir (*Le Spectateur* 1724, V/26, 158–159).[16]

Si on considère que l'utilisation des rêves dans l'écriture des « spectateurs » occupe une place importante, cette interprétation des thèses de Justinianus Major est d'autant plus révélatrice. Pourtant, cette fois, le recyclage se fait plus discrètement dans la mesure où le lecteur n'apprend pas le nom de la source. Addison se tient plutôt à une riche tradition d'écrits sur les rêves, tout en prenant une position claire dans cet essai pour comprendre le phénomène onirique. Cette attitude ne manque pas de constituer un certain paradoxe dans la mesure où les feuilles volantes témoignent d'une grande aversion contre le genre des almanachs, qui suivent généralement la ligne de l'onirocritique telle qu'elle a été présentée dans l'article sur Justinianus Major. Mais, en même temps, elles reconnaissent à l'activité onirique une faculté d'enrichissement de l'imaginaire, le cheval de bataille par excellence de Joseph Addison. L'épigraphe tirée d'une œuvre antique, le *Satyricon* de Pétrone, et choisie pour introduire ce numéro 487, renforce la thèse de l'auteur des « Pleasures of Imagination », publiés dans les numéros 410–420, du « mens sine pondere ludit ». Au métatexte initial, la version française ajoute une traduction de la citation et un titre introducteur : « Réflexion sur la nature de l'Ame à l'occasion des Rêves ».

Conclusion

La migration des récits courts du *Dictionnaire* de Bayle, exemple d'une écriture proto-encyclopédique, a trouvé un terrain fertile dans les feuilles volantes spectatoriales en Angleterre et plus tard de nouveau sur le continent européen. Il s'agit là d'une réception très performante dans la mesure où la presse d'Addison et Steele a contribué à une diffusion très large, non seulement par des traductions,

16 « Lors qu'un profond sommeil nous ferme la paupiere,/L'Esprit, se trouvant libre, agit sans la matiere,/Il retrace dans l'ombre à notre Entendement,/Les objets qu'à nos Sens presente la lumiere » (*Ibid.*).

mais par un grand nombre d'adaptations dans les feuilles autonomes en Europe, allant des Provinces Unies jusqu'en Russie, du Portugal jusqu'à l'Empire des Habsbourg et la Scandinavie. Ainsi la traduction française a largement contribué à leur excellente distribution. La raison essentielle de leur succès réside dans le récit court ou dans le microrécit ainsi que dans la fictionnalisation de l'auteur et de l'éditeur.

Dans notre analyse, nous avons pu constater l'existence de liens très étroits entre les deux genres, une nouvelle version de l'écriture proto-encyclopédique fonctionnant sous une forme à la fois éphémère et durable. Les récits passent par un processus de recyclage discursif en servant généralement d'exemple ou de modèle pour développer un cas de figure en faveur de la vertu proposée. Soulignons néanmoins que Joseph Addison, par son éducation protestante et ses intérêts littéraires, occupa une place essentielle dans cette transformation de l'écriture intergénérique. Il trouva dans le *Dictionnaire* de Pierre Bayle non seulement une source féconde d'unités narratives qu'il pouvait facilement retravailler, mais aussi un esprit génétique, ouvert au dialogue et avec un intérêt didactique de formation de son lectorat, autrement dit soucieux de lui transmettre les éléments du savoir moderne sous forme proto-encyclopédique. Là où Bayle utilise les exemples narratifs pour bien représenter des personnages notables de l'histoire humaine afin de les intégrer dans le vaste champ d'une vérité, les feuilles volantes addisoniennes les reprennent pour créer un univers moral et pédagogique qui préparera ses lecteurs, et notamment ses lectrices, à un comportement adapté à la vie publique du monde moderne.[17]

Références bibliographiques

ADDISON, Lancelot : *West Barbary, or a Short Narrative of the Revolutions of the Kingdoms of Fez and Morocco. With an Account of the Present Customs, Sacred, Civil and Domestick*. Oxford: John Wilmot 1671.

An Historical and Critical Dictionary. By Monsieur [Pierre] Bayle. Translated into English [by Pierre de Maizeaux], with many Additions and Corrections,

17 Une version de cette étude se trouve aussi dans Klaus-Dieter Ertler : « Les aspects encyclopédiques dans l'écriture des feuilles périodiques morales du XVIIIe siècle : le traitement et la migration des micro-récits ». In : Hans-Jürgen Lüsebrink/Susanne Greilich. *Écrire l'encyclopédisme, des Lumières à nos jours*. Paris : Classiques Garnier 2020, sous presse.

made by the Author himself, that are not in the French Edition. London: C. Harper, D. Brown, J. Tonson, A. and J. Churchill, T. Horne [and 8 others in London] 1710, 4 vol.

Bibliothèque des auteurs ecclésiastique, par Louis Ellies du Pin. Paris: A. Pralart 1686–1691.

Bibliothèque orientale ou Dictionnaire universel, contenant tout ce qui regarde la connoissance des peuples de l'Orient, par Barthélemy d'Herbelot de Molainville [complétée par Antoine Galland]. Paris: Compagnie des Libraires 1697.

Diction[n]aire historique et critique, par Monsieur Bayle. Seconde édition revuë, corrigée & augmentée par l'auteur. Rotterdam: Reinier Leers 1702, 3 vol. (avec 2 livres par vol. : A–B, C–G ; H–O, P–Z).

Dictionnaire historique et critique, par Monsieur Bayle. Rotterdam: Reinier Leers 1697, 2 vol. (avec 2 livres par vol. : A–B, C–G ; H–O, P–Z).

El Filósofo a la Moda o el Maestro universal: Obra periódica que se distribuye al público los lunes y los jueves de cada semana: Sacada de la obra francesa intitulada Le Spectateur ou le Socrate moderne. Madrid: Benito Cano 1788.

ERTLER, Klaus-Dieter : « Les aspects encyclopédiques dans l'écriture des feuilles périodiques morales du XVIIIe siècle : le traitement et la migration des micro-récits ». In: *Écrire l'encyclopédisme, des Lumières à nos jours.* Paris: Classiques Garnier 2020, sous presse.

HOLZHEY, Helmut/Vilem Mudroch: *Die Philosophie des 18. Jahrhunderts.* Vol. 1. Bâle : Schwabe Verlag 2004.

Il Filosofo alla Moda, ovvero il Maestro universale di quanto e oggidi proprio ad istruire, e divertire: ricavato all'opera di varij scrittori anonimi, intitulato Le Spectateur, ou Le Socrate moderne, par Cesare Frasponi. Venice: Giovanni Malachineo 1727/28.

JUNQUA, Amélie: « A Stranger's Strength – The Spectator in the crowd ». In: *Regards sur les 'spectateurs'. Periodical Essay – Feuilles volantes – Moralische Wochenschriften – Foglie moralistici – Prensa moral.* Eds. Klaus-Dieter Ertler/Alexis Lévrier/Michaela Fischer. Frankfurt/Main: Petr Lang 2012, 25–40.

Le Grand dictionnaire historique ou mélange curieux de l'histoire sacrée et profane, qui contient en abregé, les vies et les actions remarquables des Patriarches, des Juges, des Rois des Juifs…, par Louis Moréri. Lyon: J. Girin et B. Rivière 1674.

Le Spectateur, ou le Socrate moderne. Où l'on voit un Portrait naïf des Mœurs de ce Siècle, traduit de l'anglois. Amsterdam, vols. 1–3, David Mortier, vols. 4–6, Frères Wetstein, 1714–1726 [Paris 1716–1726].

PHILLIPS, Richard (ed.): *Addisoniana*. London: T. Davison 1803.

The Spectator. Donald F. Bond (ed.). Oxford: Clarendon Press 1965, 5 vol.

The Spectator: To be continued every Day [1ère série] [Richard Steele/Joseph Addison] : London, Samuel Buckley/Jacob Tonson [1er mars] 1711-[6 décembre] 1712, n° 1–555, <http://www.gutenberg.org/ebooks/12030> [05.01.2012].

The Spectator [2e série] [Joseph Addison/Eustache Budgell/Thomas Tickell]: London, Samuel Buckley, Jacob Tonson [18 juin] 1714-[20 décembre] 1714, n 556–635, <http://www.gutenberg.org/ebooks/12030> [01.11.2018].

Addison's legacy to Europe/L'héritage addisonien en Europe

María José Rodríguez Sánchez de León

(University of Salamanca)

"Varying life": The idea of fiction in the Spanish version of Joseph Addison's *The Pleasures of the Imagination*[1]

1. Introduction

One of the most frequently cited texts in the fields of history of art, literature, aesthetics and journalism at the end of the 18th century and the beginning of the 19th century is the essay called *The Pleasures of the Imagination*, by the British intellectual and politician Joseph Addison (1672–1719). The text was first published in the British poetical essay *The Spectator* in consecutive issues from Saturday, June 21 to Tuesday, July 3, 1712. The text came to Spain relatively early through its translation into French, which made it possible for different authors to get to know it, including Luzán (Sebold 1989, 128), Jovellanos (Aguilar Piñal 1984, 132) and, thanks to the latter, Meléndez Valdés (Lorenzo Álvarez 2017, 103–119). However, his aesthetic proposal became more widely known when Hugh Blair's famous *Lectures on Rhetoric and Belles Lettres* were published in Spanish. The translation of this treatise was carried out by José Luis Munárriz from 1798 to 1801 and, as in the original, the Spanish version contained the key ideas of Addison's text (Blair 1804, 55–72).[2] Nevertheless, the *Essay* itself would not be published in full until 1804. The Madrid-based journal *Variedades de ciencias, literatura y artes*, founded in 1803, published every two weeks and edited by Manuel José Quintana (Gil Novales 1959), included it in its third volume, corresponding to 1804, in the issues XIII, XIV and XV (27–46; 82–99; 159–176).

---

1 This work has been executed within the framework of the Research Project *Teoría de la lectura y hermenéutica literaria en la Ilustración: edición de fuentes documentales y literarias (1750–1808)* [Theory of literary reading and hermeneutics in the Enlightenment: edition of documentary and literary sources (1750–1808) (FFI2016-80168-P)] of the Spanish Ministry of Economy and Competitiveness.

2 José Luis Munárriz took an interest in Addison because he was one of the sources used by Hugh Blair in his *Lectures on Rhetoric and Belles Lettres*, which he started to publish in 1783. In Spain, the first translation appeared in the years 1798 and 1799. I will quote here the second Spanish edition, whose first volume was published in 1804.

Munárriz, who had also translated this text, offered it to the public because he believed that it represented "a worthy theory, in all senses" and because, according to him, the aim of the *Variedades* was to feature in its pages articles and debates "on the most useful and enjoyable parts of the areas included under the generic term of *literature*" (1804, III, 28).[3]

In the pages of this publication, José Luis Munárriz declares that he is aware of the value of Addison's small work, which he framed within Lecture III of the first volume of the Spanish translation of Blair's *Lectures*. It is not by chance that he explains there different notions of "Criticism, genius, pleasures of taste and sublimity in objects" (Blair 1804, 46–72). When discussing the pleasures of taste, he finds that Addison provides a simple and yet valid answer with which he can enlighten his readers, and he says:

> We are far from having yet attained to any system concerning this subject [the pleasures of taste]. Mr. Addison was the first who attempted a *methodical enquiry*, in his *Essay on the Pleasures of the Imagination*. [...]. He has reduced these Pleasures under three heads; Beauty, Grandeur, and Novelty. His speculations on this subject, if not exceedingly profound, are, however, very beautiful and entertaining; and he has the merit of having opened a tract, which was before unbeaten (Blair 1804, 55).[4]

However, a reading of the text in its entirety explains the justification provided by Munárriz to the translation. The *Pleasures* are a short treatise of aesthetics,

---

3 A Spanish translation of the English text was created by Tonia Raquejo in the book *Los placeres de la imaginación y otros ensayos de The Spectator* [*The pleasures of the imagination and other essays from The Spectator*] (Madrid: Visor 1991), where she also analyses the differences between the original version and the Spanish translation from 1803. The English version of *The Pleasures of the Imagination* published in *The Spectator* (*Tastes and the Pleasures of the Imagination*, London, 1834) can be read online in google books.

4 We need to highlight the ideas of "system" and "method" contained in the Spanish quote. Blair, Addison and other critics of the Scottish Enlightenment were concerned with finding a "logic of imagination" that could organize and explain the participation of imagination, taste and other faculties as a solution to the existing reluctance regarding their participation in literature and arts. The exact word in the English version is: "regular enquiry" but the general meaning is what we note. The Spanish version states: "Estamos aún muy distantes de tener un sistema relativo a este asunto [los placeres del gusto]. Addison fue el primero que emprendió acerca de él una indagación metódica en su *Ensayo sobre los placeres de la imaginación*. Él redujo estos placeres a tres clases: belleza, grandeza y novedad. Sus especulaciones en esta parte, si no son profundas, son como quiera muy bellas y entretenidas y tienen el mérito de haber abierto un camino aún no hollado".

and, therefore, it does not limit its comments to the field of literature. On the contrary, it can be classified in a general context in which the ideas it contains acquire an artistic-literary sense. That is precisely what caught Munárriz's attention (Youngren 1982, 267–283).

A close friend of Goya's, who painted his portrait in 1815, Munárriz was a member of the San Fernando Royal Academy of Fine Arts, and he also worked as the secretary and then director of the Royal Company of the Philippines.[5] As a regular collaborator with Quintana's journal, Munárriz was the figure who introduced the British aesthetic and literary line of thought in Spain at the turn of the century, and he granted it a position of superiority with regard to the classicist ideas rooted in Aristotelian doctrine that came from France and whose most orthodox version was championed by Abbé Charles Batteux (Blair 1804, xv; Rodríguez Sánchez de León 1993, 227–235 and 2011, 449–464). For Munárriz, who had read Batteux's work and who also valued it, the traditional rationalism on which the theory of arts and letters had been erected had to be completed with the ideas proposed by British authors, who were less known in Spain, partly as a consequence of the Seven Year's War (1761–1763) and later, from 1779 to 1783, because of the Great Siege of Gibraltar (Blair 1804, xii). The historical alliance between France and Spain had consequences beyond the military and political spheres. The presence of English ideas and authors was much less common than in the case of the French, regardless of language differences. The access to British sources was always more limited and it almost always came through French editions, translations and interpretations.[6]

2. On imagination as a concept and its problems

Poetic reason, that is, the foundation of all Western poetological thinking on the classical idea of imitation, did not represent the only interpretation, or even the most appropriate one, if we take into account the evolutionary stage of literary ideas in the 18th century. Together with it, there was also the belief that there was a creative reasoning rooted in Leibniz. As the philosophical thought moved on, the absolutizing belief in the existence of a single logical norm became increasingly problematic. The philosophical access to knowledge required the inclusion

5 His biography can be accessed online at the digital edition of the *Diccionario Biográfico Español* of the Spanish Royal Academy of History: <http://dbe.rah.es/biografias/19595/jose-luis-munarriz-iraizoz>.

6 Munárriz himself says so in the "[Dedication] to Doctor Hugo Blair from the translator of his lessons [...]" (1804, h.1r).

of the universe of sensibility and taste. This, in the field of aesthetics and literary studies, involved a will to solve or at least recognize the existing contradictions between logical and aesthetic knowledge (Hernández Marcos 2003, 81–121). The existence of antithetical dualities such as *norm* and *genius* or *reason* and *imagination* was reviewed in order to acknowledge the need for logic and aesthetics to stop sharing the same intellectual origin and, therefore, to acknowledge the fact that they had to find their own identity within themselves, beyond that unitary origin of knowledge that was inherited from Descartes (Cassirer 2000, 112–128).

In this context, we may point out that the British thinking, as well as part of the French thinking (Rousseau, Diderot, Voltaire…), grants a certain degree of autonomy to beauty and, through it, it introduces a review of different concepts in the aesthetic-literary debate, such as *genius*, *taste* or *imagination*, which are related to the creative subjectivity. Munárriz admires the fact that Blair, and the sources that his treatise is based on—Addison included—go beyond the study of arts and letters founded on a purely intellectualist perception of reason (1804, I, xlv–xlvi). Creation and art are constructed on an irrational or psychological feeling in which imagination plays an important role which was properly acknowledged by the English philosophy of the 18th century, from Hume to Locke, Hutcheson, Adam Smith, Gerard and Addison (a list in which we may add in France the figure of Voltaire and in Germany the philosophers Leibniz, Wolf and, of course, Kant), and about which the Spanish readers had to be informed.[7]

Indeed, when works of art are considered the result of the creator's capacity to showcase both his relationship with nature and with beauty, then literature and arts stop being understood as the result of the poetic intelligence of the author. On the contrary, their interpretation is based on the intervention of imagination and feeling into that cognitive and representative process; and they are also a reflection of the particular *genius* of the artist. Consequently, the faculty to imagine is presented as a higher order skill, because it allows not only an analogic and/or abstract recreation of human actions, emotions or the passions contained within the limits of nature, but also a widening of the world, either through its longing or idealization, or through the invention of other worlds that are as sensitive as possible (Bowra 1972, 13–36; Lapoujade 1988, 21).

The proclamation of the power to imagine as the origin of poetic creation underlines the existence of an anthropological foundation in fiction from which literary creation and communication emerge. After taking every possible

7 For authors like Addison, Locke became a philosophical reference for their postulates, based on which they could formulate a new epistemology (Tueson 1960, 5–26).

precaution, this suggests the idea of fictionalization as a formal representation of human creativity (Iser 1997, 43–65). This means that creative activity is considered the art of imitation that leads to beauty. In this regard, both the research in aesthetics and in poetics adopts a genetic approach to this question.[8] The main concern of aesthetes and theorists is to explain the mechanism that leads human beings to the feeling of beauty. For this reason, they try to systematize or, at least, analyse the sources that cause it, because the creation and reception of works of art will depend on them. Beauty is, therefore, interpreted as an inherent quality of the object.[9] This will be the moment in which preceptists find themselves again faced with the need to impose different rules that generate artistic pleasure on literary discourse. Consequently, this will be the point in which they return over and over again towards the idea of the "logic of imitation". Batteux's dogmatic version states that everything that represents beauty must be an imitation. The more ductile view, suggested by Addison, contends that artistic imitation is, in itself, one of the sources of the pleasures of taste and imagination.

3. The Addisonian theory of the pleasures: Principles and configuration

Addison's *Essay* can be interpreted, among other possibilities, as an elementary theory of fiction that considers imagination as an essential element in it. His approach presents in simple terms a general theory on the perception of arts that explains the process that leads human beings to feel pleasure when they are faced with them. The purpose of his discourse is to find out what the sources of that pleasure are and how that pleasurable feeling that causes delight takes shape in the human mind. For Addison, who is after all an empiricist, the relevant factor is not the knowledge of the works of art in itself, but the state in which the subjects find themselves when they create and receive them. His interest does not only focus on the pieces of art and their shape (on whether they represent nature or not and remain faithful to the Aristotelian principle, that is, on their academicism), but rather on the psychical process that leads to the experience of the artist and the pleasurable feelings they evoke on the observers. What concerns

---

8 This idea comes from Francis Hutcheson, *An Inquiry into the Original of Our Ideas of Beauty and Virtue*, as Arregui explains in his edition (Madrid: Tecnos 1992).

9 The concept of the sublime had a major theoretical significance in the United Kingdom thanks to the works of authors such as Holmes, Burke, Kames or Blair himself. See Monk 1960 and, for the French scenario, Litman 1971. On the presence of this concept in the theory and its formulation in Kant, see Guerlac 1991.

him, therefore, is the analysis of the effect on the subject of the contemplation or the experience not only of nature (that which exists), but also of the artistic work (that which has been artificially created). From this perspective, art is conceived as an expression of beauty, and this cannot be mistaken for the description of the materiality of objects.[10] On the contrary, understanding beauty means studying how the feeling of pleasure comes true in the subject, and how grasping it is not the result of a merely logic comprehension, but of an anthropological capture in which other faculties and senses take part.[11] The beauty that arts bring is clearly a source of pleasure, but it is necessary to investigate the nature of such pleasure.

Addison places the starting point of any kind of pleasure on sight, which is the most perfect of senses, and the one that provides imagination with ideas.[12] He thinks that the origin of any image, be it real or created by an individual, comes from it: "We cannot, indeed, have a single image in the fancy that did not make its first entrance through the sight" (1803, 30). The creation of images through *fancy/imagination* is only possible because visible objects generate images for

10 This idea of what is beautiful contradicts what is defended by authors such as Yves-Marie André, who defines it as follows: "I call *beauty*, in a work of the mind, not what pleases the first glance of the imagination in certain particular dispositions of the faculties of the soul or the organs of the body, but what is entitled to appeal to reason and reflection by its own excellence, by its light or by its exactness, and, if I am allowed this term, by its intrinsic pleasantness" (2010, 31).

11 We may mention here the hermeneutics of the affections formulated by Johann Jakob Rambach (1693–1735) which anticipates the process of psychologization of interpretation that evolved during the Enlightenment and Romanticism (Ferraris 2000, 58–61). See also the proposal of a *sympathetic imagination* in Jackson Bate 1945, 144–164.

12 This idea can be found in Avicenna, who provides that same description for the activity of sight in its relationship with the brain. Also Feijoo, in his *Cartas eruditas*, when discussing whether air is visible, points out that its perception depends on sight, and he adds: "Seeing an object is not the same as perceiving that it may be seen. Generally, whenever an object causes the slightest impression in the external senses, the perception of said impression does not leave a mark in the understanding, the imagination or the common sense" ("Carta primera", 1765, I, 12). For his part, Jovellanos, in his *Curso de humanidades castellanas*, when referring to pastoral poetry, points out that the poet must present nature with an aura of beauty, but he must never disfigure it, because those are objects that "sometimes entrance our sight and our imagination". He claims that poetic description cannot distort the image that the reader may have of prairies, forests, streams and other bucolic elements (1858, I, 141). That same relationship between sight and imagination can be found in several 19th-century treatises on legislation or medicine (1834, I, 31) or in Alibert (1826, 19). In fact, imagination was associated with some diseases of sight (Hurtado de Mendoza, 1821, II, 455).

us, real or not, with their presence or their absence.[13] This is due to the fact that they are able, without any effort, to evoke feelings that allow us in turn to recognize the beauty of objects: "We are struck, we know not how, with the symmetry of anything *we see, and immediately assent* to the beauty of an object, without inquiring into the particular causes and occasions of it" (1804, III, 31). Perception in this first stage is instinctive, or even inherent in the act of recognition. This last process involves bringing to mind a previous image or the idea of an entity.[14] Imagination activates the brain and it has, as Feijoo explained—albeit in the opposite sense—a powerful and admirable impact on the perception of the world.[15] That is what happens when we contemplate an impressive landscape. Its magnificence causes awe:

---

13 Both qualities, *fancy* and *imagination*, are interpreted in the context of poetics as faculties that are opposed to the concepts of *reason*, *judgement* and even *memory*. Both are often used as synonyms and refer to what is perceived by the senses and can be subject to new combinatorial possibilities. The difference between both concepts, fancy and imagination, lies in the fact that *fancy* represents a memory that is free from time and space. According to Ferraris' *L'immaginazione*, in Neo-Latin languages there is an idea of imagination as the retention of what is absent, and of fancy as its recreation (Spanish version 1999, 11). However, he admits that the translation of both terms is troublesome, and that their meanings are often confused (12–19). When he explains this concept in Hobbes, Pascal and Spinoza, he claims that imagination plays a role in which it revives what is absent, and it can become a source of illusion (90–92).

14 This image represents the re-establishment of an image within the mind which is recovered by it through memory or through an analogical relationship, thus associating what is presented before it with what it knows or with that of which it has an experience or a memory. It involves identifying an entity through memory without having judgement take part in the process, or at least not consciously. That is precisely the reason why Feijoo complained about the effects of imagination, which he associated with an overflowing of passions. In his "Carta VIII" of the *Cartas eruditas y curiosas*, he tries to put an end to the power attributed to imagination to explain unknown or supernatural events (IV, 85). In addition, he denies the force of imagination over passions. He explains that "Despotism of imagination" by saying: "It [imagination] moves them [passions: love, hate, anger, concupiscence] or calms them, lights them up or puts them out. It causes the violence of passions" (1770, IV, 83).

15 When discussing the "Remedies of love" in his *Theatro crítico universal*, Feijoo says: "I think that with some passions, even when the object is present, imagination is the element that grants the fibres of the brain all their impulse, or else the object moves the fibres of the brain only through imagination alone. [...] This influence of imagination on the brain is the source of most of the evil consequences brought by our passions". The reason why this happens is that images or feelings remain in memory, and imagination allows them to be relived (1778 [1736], VII, 410; <http://www.filosofia.org/bjf/

> We are flung into a pleasing astonishment at such unbounded views, and feel a delightful stillness and amazement in the soul at the apprehension of them. [...] Everything that is new or uncommon raises a pleasure in the imagination, because it fills the soul with an agreeable surprise, gratifies its curiosity, and gives it an idea of which it was not before possessed (1804, III, 34–35).[16]

The pleasure provided by these views of nature (huge mountains, precipices, deserts, seas) derives from their exceptionality, which leads them to cause surprise and admiration. Therefore, this first perception gives birth to the feeling of beauty, which occupies a second stage, because it involves imagination in order to capture it. It is a unique and spontaneous discovery. When referring to beauty, Addison says: "The very first discovery of it strikes the mind with an inward joy, and spreads a cheerfulness and delight through all its faculties" (1804, III, 36). Nevertheless, Addison wonders about the reason behind such pleasure. His religious fervour moves him to declare that the admiration and delight that he describes are surprising because they are interpreted as the sublime work of the Supreme Being:

> Our admiration, which is a very pleasing motion of the mind, immediately rises at the consideration of any object that takes up a great deal of room in the fancy, and by consequence will improve into the highest pitch of astonishment and devotion [...The Supreme Being] has given almost everything about us the power of raising an agreeable idea in the imagination: so that is impossible for us to behold his works with coldness or indifference, and to survey so many beauties without secret satisfaction and complacency. (1804, III, 40; Tuveson 1960, 5–16; Zeitz 1992, 493–502)

As a first consequence, Addison establishes that the works of nature and art have the power to entertain the imagination, although the former, which are extraordinary creations due to their divine origin, are much superior to the latter.[17] The grandiosity and immensity of nature can be copied by art, but art can only come close to it, never matching it (1804, III, 42). However, when both elements

---

bjft716.htm>). This explains why Alibert, in his *Fisiología de las pasiones* [*Physiologie des passions*] claims that "imagination is memory, excited and made beautiful by feeling" (1826, 19).

16 The relationship between the view of nature and the creation of an aesthetic effect can be found in Kant's *Critique of Judgment*, which is also associated with imagination. It includes the idea of complacence, but this could assume the existence of an ignorant admiration, that is, one that is simple and trivial.

17 This approach, which is originally Platonic, can also be found in the Neoplatonism of Plotinus, who reserves some space for imagination, because, in a sense, this faculty connects humans to the rest of creation.

converge, for example, when poets imitate nature, then the works of nature are more enjoyable the more they resemble the works of art. The reason is that the comparison provides a unique type of delight that comes from recognizing the perfect similitude between the natural beauty and the artistic beauty (1804, III, 44).[18] The prodigies of nature reveal its perfection, and it is so admirable that it seems to have been produced by art, that is, it looks artificial. This is also the origin of the desire to imitate nature, and it explains the fact that he considers architecture its closest form of art and, consequently, the human production that can more easily evoke the primary pleasures of the imagination, that is, admiration and surprise before the extraordinary. He describes primary pleasures as those that "entirely proceed from such objects as are before our eyes", whereas secondary pleasures flow "from the ideas of visible objects, when the objects are not actually before the eye, but are called up into our memories, or formed into agreeable visions of things that are either absent or fictitious" (1804, III, 30). The pyramids of Egypt, the Great Wall of China or a Gothic church evoke great thoughts and belong to the first category. On the other hand, sculptures and descriptions cause the second category of pleasures:

> When I say the ideas we receive from statues, descriptions, or such like occasions, are the same that were once actually in our view, it must not be understood that we had once seen the very place, action, or person which are carved or described. It is sufficient that we have seen places, persons, or actions, in general, which bear a resemblance, or at least some remote analogy with what we find represented. Since it is in the power of the imagination, when it is once stocked with particular ideas, to enlarge, compound, and vary them at her own pleasure. (1804, III, 89)

What all these arts have in common is the fact that they are forms of representation that range from sculpture, which would be the closest one to nature, given its similitude with the object that is portrayed, to painting, description and sounds (1804, III, 89). Pleasure emerges when these creations allow the imagination to remember the exceptional properties of the originals. Therefore, what we admire is the talent of those who best manage to come close to the ideas that the originals have erected in our minds and which are stored there after we had direct natural contact with them. The pleasure of the imagination comes then

18 This reasoning states that nature can surprise men so much that it makes them think that this natural perfection, with a divine origin, is so unfathomable that it seems to be the result of an artistic production that is staged, false or imagined (1804, III, 43–44). As a result, the admiration for the consciousness that men have of the dimension of the divine work is endless.

from the awareness of the memory and its power to reshape or to create, and it in turns reflects an intellectual knowledge (1804, IV, 91).[19]

In this context, language acquires enormous value. Addison almost contradicts what he claimed before when he says that:

> Words, when well chosen, have so great a force in them, that a description often gives us more lively ideas than the sight of things themselves. [...] As we look on any object our idea of it is, perhaps, made up of two or three simple ideas; but when the poet represents it, he may either give us a more complex idea of it, or only raise in us such ideas as are most apt to affect the imagination. (1804, III, 92–93)

This role as a mediator between nature and new ideas implies that, while creating an artificial representation, poets can provide a more complex and elaborate representation than what is caused by the direct impression of objects themselves. This means that they possess an immense imagination, while at the same time they must have a good mastery of the language. Artificially, they must be able to create images that enter the reality of objects and go beyond what a common individual is able to perceive. They appeal to imagination alone by building images that readers will relive, regardless of whether they had previously received them or not. However, poets are not only gifted with privileged imagination, which is used to retain the images they receive and to recreate them or pretend that they do with the power of words. They also have to master the language and, by extension, the artistic technique:

> [...] For to have a true relish and form a right judgment of a description, a man should be born with a good imagination, and must have well weighed the force and energy that lie in the several words of a language, so as to be able to distinguish which are most significant and expressive of their proper ideas, and what additional strength and beauty they are capable of receiving from conjunction with others. (1804, III, 93)

Every author worth his salt must possess an excellent imagination—a productive imagination—because that is the basis of his ability to remember the impressions he received, to translate them in language and to propose different words that are not related to that experience, but that are created by him:

---

19 Addison-Munárriz explains it by saying: "The final cause, probably, of annexing pleasure to this operation of the mind was to quicken and encourage us in our searches after truth, since the distinguishing one thing from another, and the right discerning betwixt our ideas, depends wholly upon our comparing them together, and observing the congruity or disagreement that appears among the several works of Nature" (1804, III, 92).

> […] A noble writer should be born with this faculty in its full strength and vigour, so as to be able to receive lively ideas from outward objects, to retain them long, and to range them together, upon occasion, in such figures and representations as are most likely to hit the fancy of the reader. (1804, III, 95)

The author he believes is sublime is Milton with his poem *Paradise Lost*.[20] In that text, according to Addison, Milton masterfully portrays the creation of the world and the hardships of fallen angels, and specifically Lucifer. "No other subject could have furnished a poet with scenes so proper to strike the imagination, as no other poet could have painted those scenes in more strong and lively colours" (1804, III, 99). The goal of literature—he concludes—is to create a strong impact on the spirit, to evoke unforgettable images from which the human soul can feed. However, the means to achieve this in the poet and in the reader can also be found in the talent and the skills of the former.[21] It is, in sum, the result of an equal combination of fantasy and judgement:

> The fancy must be warm to retain the print of those images it hath received from outward objects; and the judgment discerning, to know what expressions are most proper to clothe and adorn them to the best advantage (1804, III, 93).[22]

4. The secondary pleasures: Towards an idea of fiction

With this approach, in the final part of his *Essay*, Addison focuses on studying what secondary pleasures are and how they originate. In fact, one of the topics that concern him is finding out the reason why things that are disagreeable, unpleasant or grotesque may also provide pleasure. The first explanation he offers states that secondary pleasures are "wider", and the second explanation establishes that those things are used for comparisons. This principle makes them seem pleasing to the imagination if the image is represented by means

20 On the images of this poem, see Dobranski (2015).

21 When referring to the different allusions [similitudes, metaphors and allegories] he says: "The great art of a writer shows itself in the choice of pleasing allusions, which are generally to be taken from the great or beautiful works of art or Nature" (1804, III, 173).

22 Addison wonders whether the power of imagination is due to the way in which images take shape in the brain—that is, whether it is a physical question—or, on the contrary, whether it belongs to the realm of the soul (1804, III, 95). In any case, he concludes by saying that the poet must create his own imagination (by contemplating nature), but at the same time he must know how to choose the most appropriate form for his discourse (1804, III, 95). He also points out that an injury in the brain can hurt the fancy and generate negative and confusing ideas (1804, III, 175).

of expression. In fact, what Addison claims is that the pleasing element is what makes it aesthetic, because the image of a dungeon[23] or of hell are not perceived as they are, but through the way in which the poet can evoke an object through the power of words. For this reason, he even says that it may be more properly called the pleasure of understanding than of imagination:

> Perhaps, this may be more properly called the pleasure of the understanding than of the fancy, because we are not so much delighted with the image that is contained in the description, as with the aptness of the description to excite the image. (1804, III, 159)

However, he qualifies this statement and adds that what is great, new or beautiful is more delightful. Addison is presenting a problem that is far from trivial: that of literary referentiality. In his case, he refers to truth and to associative memory as the ultimate reference to which he believes that the human mind turns when it tries to understand fiction. However, his words seem to say that the aesthetic experience has—apart from an admiring dimension which is clearly material or that can become material since it can remind us of what we have lived and what we have seen—an imaginable dimension as well. According to this last approach, fiction becomes alive in the mind of the readers when the poetic images are credible or beautiful, regardless of whether they have a correlate in real life or, more specifically, in their own life experience. Its value derives from the fact that the way in which the objects are portrayed is able to move the spirit. Regardless of classical references, the matter is that fiction attempts "to raise a secret ferment in the mind of the reader, and to work with violence upon his passions" (1803, III, 160). In this case, the admiration lies in the fact that fiction reaches an element that is uniquely human; it touches its sensitivity and its passions, rather than an imitating similitude with nature:

> It is not strange that we should take delight in such passages as are apt to produce hope, joy, admiration, love, or the like emotions in us, because they never rise in the mind without an inward pleasure which attends them. (1804, III, 160)

In this context, and although his Christian view of existence emerges again, he believes that in the case of feelings such as terror, pleasure appears when we realize that they are not real, and to this we must add the inner gratitude that we feel when we know we are safe. In fact, fiction must not be so real as to cause a commotion:

---

23 It's a mistake. In the English version, Addison uses the instance of a "dunghill", not of a dungeon. <http://web.mnstate.edu/gracyk/courses/web%20publishing/addison418.htm)>.

> [...] We consider the misfortunes we read in history or poetry, either as past, or as fictitious, so that the reflection upon ourselves rises in us insensibly, and overbears the sorrow we conceive for the sufferings of the afflicted. (1804, III, 162)

This accounts for the fact that we can also feel pleasure when the poet "entertains his reader's imagination with the characters and actions of such persons as have many of them no existence but what he bestows on them" (1804, 164). The poet also creates creatures and scenarios that do not refer to the real world, such as fairies. It depends on the poet's fancy, "because he has no pattern to follow in it, and they must work altogether out of his own invention" (1804, 164). He is the creator of a possible world which, in this specific case, has no other reference than popular imagery. Since it is impossible to imitate nature, what literature makes up is a universe of beliefs, which are popular in many cases, with an inexistent relationship of proximity to the real world. His reasoning could not be more enlightening:

> We are pleased with surveying the different habits and behaviours of foreign countries, how much more must we be delighted and surprised when we are led, as it were, into a new creation, and see the persons and manners of another species? Men of cold fancies, and philosophical dispositions, object to this kind of poetry, that it has not probability enough to affect the imagination. But to this it may be answered, that we are sure, in general, there are many intellectual beings in the world besides ourselves, and several species of spirits, who are subject to different laws and economies from those of mankind; when we see, therefore, any of these represented naturally, we cannot look upon the representation as altogether impossible; nay, many are prepossessed with such false opinions, as dispose them to believe these particular delusions; at least, we have all heard so many pleasing relations in favour of them, that we do not care for seeing through the falsehood and willingly give ourselves up to so agreeable an imposture. (1804, III, 165)

Actually, Addison accepts that the process of reading or reception may involve a suspension of belief. The reader does not question whether the characters or the events are real, but instead he considers them fictionally possible and, for that reason, his interpretation of them is not based on logic or natural laws (Rodríguez Sánchez de León 2014). It is enough that they seem internally coherent (Garrido Domínguez 1997, 20). In order to participate in the game of fiction, it is necessary to assume the world of the imaginary as it is presented. The only difference is that the fictional experience, as explained by Martínez Bonati, becomes a lived experience and, in this kind of works, that is achieved through the memory of the stories that are part of the popular heritage that have been transmitted generation after generation (Martínez Bonati 1997, 159–170).[24] In this regard, it is

24 In the words of Addison: "They bring up into our memory the stories we have heard in

clear that Addison does not formulate a fictional theory in its strict sense. He always looks for a justification with the existence of mental parameters which, in one way or another, involve the activation of a memory to which fiction can refer. Fiction only manages to create the reference of a psychical experience, although he suggests that the veracity or falsehood of what is told is not brought into question. Moreover, Addison admits that fictional falsehood does not prevent artistic interpretation or, consequently, the achievement of aesthetic pleasure (Ferraris 1999, 112–114).

It is also true that when he provides an example he is not able to explain it very accurately. The poets more likely to create this sort of fiction are English and, more specifically, Shakespeare:

> That noble extravagance of fancy, which he had in so great perfection, thoroughly qualified him to touch this weak superstitious part of his reader's imagination, and made him capable of succeeding, where he had nothing to support him besides the strength of his own genius. There is something so wild and yet so solemn in the speeches of his ghosts, fairies, witches, and the like imaginary persons, that we cannot forbear thinking them natural, though we have no rule by which to judge of them, and must confess, if there are such beings in the world, it looks highly probable they should talk and act as he has represented them. (1804, III, 166–167)

As we can see from this quote, a poet gifted with inventiveness can raise above nature and, when creating, can make the readers not question the veracity of what is being told or, according to his words, can make them accept them as natural because of their coherence. As Jovellanos explains when he refers to Velázquez's *Las Meninas*, the artist stands out because of his excellence. This is what happens when genius overcomes nature and reveals what can be seen with the spirit rather than with the eyes (Jovellanos 1976, 198).

Conclusions

The Addisonian theory leads us to a conclusion that was formulated by Addison himself, and then shared by Munárriz: "A man of polite imagination is let into a great many pleasures, that the vulgar are not capable of receiving" (1804, III, 31). Although the presence of imagination arrived late at the Spanish aesthetic-literary debate, the most important thing is that, at the beginning of the 21st century it was perfectly integrated into the literary debate around the traditional logical-classicist parameters to which Spaniards were so reluctant, since they

---

our childhood, and favour those secret terrors and apprehensions to which the mind of man is naturally subject" (1804, III, 165).

championed the poetic norm and discursive rationality alike. In 1806, volume VIII of the *Correo literario y económico de Sevilla* included different articles that explained human imagination. Those texts analyse the advantages of imagination as well as the pleasures it provides. The text closely follows Addison's ideas, and it summarizes and adopts them.[25] Imagination is valued as a prerogative with which nature—and divinity through it—has gifted humans. Thanks to it, "everything is enlarged, enlivened and multiplied. Everything becomes beautiful, appealing and interesting" (1806, VIII, n° 245, 5). In fact, the text accepts the idea that convincing our reason and creating noble feelings are tasks that can only be achieved by using imagination as an intermediary. In addition, it states that without imagination, men would be unhappy (1806, VIII, n° 247, 20). In any case, in the words of Addison, imagination is essential to "vary human life". Humans no longer look at nature to reproduce it, but rather rise above it to match its creator by creating new worlds that emerge from art, imagination and technique.

References

ADDISON, Joseph: *Los placeres de la imaginación y otros ensayos de* The Spectator. Ed Tonia Requejo Madrid: 1991.

ADDISON, Joseph: *Tastes and the Pleasures of the Imagination*. London, 1834.

ALIBERT, J. L.: *Fisiología de las pasiones, o Teoría de los sentimientos morales*. t. I. Trad. C. A. Bordeaux: Carlos Lawalle Sobrino 1826.

ANDRÉ, Yves-Marie: *Ensayo sobre lo bello*. València: Universitat de València 2003.

ANDRÉ, Yves-Marie: *Essay on Beauty*. Alan J. Cain (trans.). Porto: 2018 [2010] (The most recent versión: <www-groups.mcs.st-and.ac.uk/~alanc/pub/c_andreessai>).

AGUILAR PIÑAL, Francisco: *La biblioteca de Jovellanos* (1778). Madrid: CSIC 1984.

BLAIR, Hugh: *Lecciones sobre la Retórica y las Bellas Letras [...]. Las tradujo del inglés Don Joséf Luis Munárriz*. Madrid: Imprenta Real 1804, 4 tomos.

BOWRA, C. M.: *La imaginación romántica*. Madrid: Taurus 1972 [1969].

CASSIRER, Ernst: *La filosofía de la Ilustración*. México: FCE 2000.

25 That same journal featured translations of texts by Adam Smith on dance as the art of imitation (1806, VII, n° 240, 244–246).

Correo literario y económico de Sevilla. t. VII-VIII. Sevilla: Viuda de Hidalgo y Sobrino 1806.

DOBRANSKI, Stephen B.: *Milton's Visual Imagination. Imagery in* Paradise Lost. Cambridge: Cambridge University Press 2015.

FEIJOO, Benito Jerónimo: *Cartas eruditas, y curiosas.* Madrid: Imprenta Real de la Gaceta 1777 [1742], t. I, and Madrid: Ibarra, 1770 [1753], t. IV. <http://www.filosofia.org/bjf/bjfc101. htm>.

FEIJOO, Benito Jerónimo: *Theatro crítico universal,* t. VII. Madrid: Andrés Ortega 1778 [1736]. <http://www. filosofia.org/bjf/bjft700.htm>.

FERRARIS, Maurizio: *Historia de la Hermenéutica.* Madrid: Akal 2000.

FERRARIS, Maurizio: *La imaginación.* Madrid: Visor 1999.

GARRIDO DOMÍNGUEZ, Antonio (comp.): *Teorías de la ficción literaria.* Madrid: Arco Libros 1997.

GIL NOVALES, Alberto: "Un periódico de 1803". *Las pequeñas Atlántidas.* Barcelona: Seix-Barral 1959, 113–124.

GUERLAC, Suzanne: "The Sublime in Theory". *MLN* 106, 5 (1991), 895–909.

HERNÁNDEZ MARCOS, Maximiliano: "Teoría de la sensibilidad, Teoría de las humanidades. El proyecto filosófico de la Estética en A. G. Baumgartem". *Cuadernos dieciochistas* 4 (2003), 81–121.

HURTADO DE MENDOZA, Manuel y Celedonio Martínez Caballero: *Suplemento al Diccionario de Medicina y Cirugía del profesor D. Antonio Ballano,* t. II. Madrid: Viuda de Barco López 1821.

HUTCHESON, Francis. *Una investigación sobre el origen de nuestra idea de belleza.* Madrid: Tecnos 1992.

ISER, Wolfgang: "La ficcionalización: dimensión antropológica de las ficciones literarias". In: Antonio Garrido Domínguez (comp.): *Teorías de la ficción literaria.* Madrid: Arco Libros 1997, 43–65.

JACKSON BATE, Walter: "The Sympathetic Imagination in Eighteenth-Century Cristicism". *ELE* 12, 2 (1945), 144–164.

JOVELLANOS, Melchor Gaspar de: *Obras en prosa.* José Caso González (ed.). Madrid: Castalia 1976.

JOVELLANOS, Melchor Gaspar de: *Obras publicadas e inéditas*, t. I. Cándido Nocedal (ed.). Madrid: Rivadeneyra 1858.

LAPOUJADE, María Noel: *Filosofía de la imaginación.* México: Siglo XXI 1988.

LITMAN, Théodore A.: *Le Sublime en France: 1660–1714.* Paris: A. G. Nizet 1971.

LORENZO ÁLVAREZ, Elena de: "Lo sublime cómico en la poesía de Juan Meléndez Valdés". *Cuadernos dieciochistas* 18 (2017), 101–156.

MARTÍNEZ BONATI, Félix: "El acto de escribir ficciones". In: Antonio Garrido Domínguez (ed.): *Teorías de la ficción literaria*. Madrid: Arco Libros 1997, 159–170.

MONK, Samuel: *The Sublime: A Study of Critical Theories in XVIII-Century England*. Ann Arbor: University of Michigan Press 1960.

MUNÁRRIZ, José Luis: "Ensayo sobre los placeres de la imaginación escrito por Addison". *Variedades de Ciencias, Literatura y Artes*, t. III, 1804, núms. xiii, xiv y xv, 27–46; 82–99; 159–176.

RODRÍGUEZ SÁNCHEZ DE LEÓN, María José: "Batteux y Blair en la vida literaria española a comienzos del siglo xix". *EntreSiglos* 2 (1993), 227–235.

RODRÍGUEZ SÁNCHEZ DE LEÓN, María José: "Hugh Blair y la introducción en España de la poética creacionista". In: Álvarez Barrientos, J. y J. Herrera (eds.): *Para Emilio Palacios Fernández: 25 estudios sobre el siglo XVIII español*. Madrid: FUE 2011, 449–464.

RODRÍGUEZ SÁNCHEZ DE LEÓN, María José: "Teoría de los mundos posibles y modernidad litearia: la creación de un nuevo paradigma". In: Domingo Sánchez Mesa et alii. (eds.): *Teoría y comparatismo: Tradición y nuevos espacios*. Granada/Salamanca/Cáceres: Universidad de Granada/Universidad de Salamanca/Universidad de Extremadura 2014, 55–70.

SEBOLD, Russell P.: "Análisis estadístico de las ideas poéticas de Luzán: sus orígenes y su naturaleza". *El rapto de la mente*. Barcelona: Anthropos 1989, 98–128.

TUVESON, Ernst Lee: *The Imagination as a Means of Grace. Locke and the Aesthetics of Romanticism*. Berkeley/Los Angeles: University of California Press 1960.

YOUNGREN, William H.: "Addison and the Birth of Eighteenthe-Century Aesthetics". *MP* 79 (1982), 26–283.

ZEITZ, Lisa M. "Addison's 'imagination' papers and the design argument". *English Studies* 73, 6 (1992), 493–502.

Klara Leszczynska

(University of Warsaw)

How Mr. Spectator became the father of the Polish essay

In December 1803, an announcement was published in *Nowy Pamiętnik Warszawski* containing the information that the sixth volume of Ignacy Krasicki's "Dzieła" was available for purchase and that, for the first time, it included "dissertations on various philosophical, moral and academic issues" (Goliński 2011, 1085). It was titled "Uwagi" (Comments). It was the first Polish collection of essays, and—what is even more interesting—it was based not so much on Montaigne's personal model of the essay, as on the periodical observational essay genre created by Addison and Steele, and made famous by *The Spectator*. This collection of 304 pages was published for the first time two years after Krasicki's death, and contains 48 texts, most of which were "regular" essays and 6 were a small collection of aphorisms.[1] Contrary to their model, these Polish essays were not headed by a motto, but by one word describing the main topic such as: "Letters", "Amour-propre", or "Piety". Eleven such essays written by Krasicki had previously been published in the periodical *Co Tydzień* (*Every week*) written by Krasicki along with short texts about the most famous poets,[2] fables, short oriental novels and dialogues of the dead inspired by Lucian. Krasicki's "Uwagi" focused on three fields: morality ("Virtue", "Patience"), literature ("Criticism") and everyday life ("Gardens").[3] The research to-date on the impact of the English

1 Which can also be regarded as some kind of essay, as Scott Black has written: "*Such work is dense with quotations, using others, self-consciously, to say what one means*". And sums up his thoughts: "Essays do not discover new things but compound old stuff". See Black 2006, 27 and 29. Furthermore, Theodore P. Fraser (1986, 46–49) gives La Rochefoucauld's *Maximes* as an example of seventeenth-century essay.

2 Some of them become parts of such encyclopedia-like volumes of literature and writers as *O rymotworstwie i rymotworcach*.

3 *Uwagi* is not very popular among the scholars in Poland. Besides short mentions in biographies of Krasicki by Cazin 1940; 1986, 273–280, Pokrzywniak 1992, Goliński 1979, 356–357, 403, there are some articles such as: Gajzler 2009, 37–42; Pusz 2002, 133–147; Górska 2014, 513–534, 485–503; Kalinowski 2002, 27–40; Libera 1997, 5–17.

periodical on Polish writing has dealt mainly with *Monitor*,[4] the first journal in Poland that focused on morality. The aim of this article is to trace the impact of *The Spectator* on the essay genre which was being conceived in Poland.

The author of "Uwagi", who, having died in March 1801, did not live to see his work in print, was one of the most eminent figures of the Polish Enlightenment—a dignitary of the Catholic Church, Bishop of Warmia, later Archbishop of Gniezno, and a friend of the last king of Poland—Stanisław August Poniatowski. Krasicki was also the author of the first Polish novel, an excellent poet and co-editor of *Monitor*. It was at that time—at the beginning of his illustrious career—that he became acquainted with Addison's and Steele's work—*Le Spectateur ou le Socrate Moderne*,[5] (Sinko 1956, 34–38) which was popular throughout the whole of Europe. Despite the fact that he only read it in its French translation as published in the first annals of *Monitor*—to which he cooperated—he was the author of the largest number of adaptations and translations derived from it (Sinko 1956, 71).[6] Although the *Spectator* was both a model and inspiration, neither the young author nor the readers were prepared for the transfer to Poland of one of the most successful achievements of the English publishers, namely the genre known as the *periodical essay*.[7] The articles which were translated and adapted took on a form which was more or less akin to the only known method of communicating in the Polish public sphere—a rhetorical discourse based on principles of speech dating back to classical antiquity.[8] However, in Poland, the experience Krasicki gained from reading *Le Spectateur Moderne* did not come to naught. It remained

4 Sinko 1956; Aleksandrowska 1976, V–CXL.

5 In Krasicki's library remains one copy of this translation: *Le Spectateur ou le Socrate moderne trad. de l'anglais*. Paris: Merigot 1754, vol. 9, 8vo, in calf. We can assume that this was the edition he used in his youth.

6 In Ignacy Krasicki's library catalogue there is no sign of other works by Joseph Addison although Krasicki could have been familiar with them thanks to Adam Kazimierz Czartoryski, coeditor of the "Monitor" papers.

7 Brian Cowan wrote: "By the age of the American Revolution, the Whig political purpose behind the Spectator project had become opaque and it was legacy of the polite periodical prose essay which remained first and foremost in the minds of Addison's and Steele's readers" (Cowan 2004, 360). See also Black 1999, 21–42.

8 When Krasicki translated articles from *The Spectator*, he usually cut off all digressions. Whenever an essay started *in medias res*, he would add some kind of introduction to put stress on the main topic. He would find and collect arguments concerning possible loss or gain – which is typical of deliberative rhetoric – from Addison's essays and he would order them. About the role of ancient rhetoric in the Polish society in the eighteenth century, read Axer 1996, 134–143.

in the author's memory for many years, and had a decisive impact on his "Uwagi". Why was it that Mr. Spectator, and not Montaigne—the creator of the essay as a literary genre—played such a significant role in the nascence of the first Polish essay? The reasons can be sought in two sources—the similarity of the creative methods of the eccentric Englishman and of the Prince-Bishop of Warmia, and the latter aiming at the same goal—influencing the readers, improving the world and shaping reality.

Mr. Spectator and Mr. Krasicki

Scholars have often emphasized that one of the characteristics of the *Spectator* was the special atmosphere the authors were able to evoke in the relationship between the narrator and the reader:

> The *Spectator*'s relationship with its readers suggest the same intimacy that we see in the club. The *Spectator* papers are distributed to a large, public audience, yet they also sustain the illusion of an intimate circle of readers [...]. (Ketcham 1985, 17)

Michael G. Ketcham wrote, while Scott Black emphasized that the essay form used by the eccentric Englishman was based on the principles of friendship, even if there was no friendship between the parties (Black 1999, 30). Iona Italia noticed that, apart from the fictitious club created in the pages of the *Spectator*—the periodical itself established a specific type of club within its readership:

> It is a club that is, of course, both exclusive - composed of people of particular discernment - and open - to feel part of this club you only need to regard yourself as a regular *Spectator* reader. (Italia 2005, 91)

Therefore—to sum up the aforementioned observations—relationships between Mr. Spectator and his readers are based on common beliefs and mutual kindness. There is no place in the relationship for authoritarianism, for creating a distance between the author—who is perfect and authorized to instruct—and the morally weaker reader who is dependent on him. In the works of Krasicki, not only in "Uwagi", there is a similar manner of creating relationships between the narrator and the reader: they are not detached, but full of mutual understanding; it is more a partnership than a master and student dependency: "The status of a writer, which is magnificent by its proper essence of a master and a teacher, gives him a certain authority over a reader [...] it is a charming thing to be a master, yet a difficult one to perform. Authority and superiority humiliate, thus they, by their essence, are not pleasant for those who are subordinated" (Krasicki 1997, 54). Krasicki's conviction that persuasion is more effective when it does not offend the recipient's *amour propre* undoubtedly had an impact on building such contact with the reader. This was why he so valued the fable as a genre, because it made it possible to point out the flaws that needed improving in such a way that the reader was unable 'to see the hand that supported him' (*Monitor*, 1766, no. 104).

The community spirit among readers of the *Spectator* was achieved through the fact they felt like they were members of a club. Addison wrote about these associations which were characteristic of eighteenth-century England:

> When Men are thus knit together, by a Love of Society, not a Spirit of Faction, and do not meet to censure or annoy those that are absent, but to enjoy one another: When they are thus combined for their own Improvement, or for the Good of others, or at least to relax themselves from the Business of the Day, by an innocent and chearful Conversation, there may be something very useful in these little Institutions and Establishments. (Addison 1891, no. 9)

Krasicki was unable to enter into this type of relationship with the readers in his *Uwagi* because, unlike *The Spectator*, *Uwagi* was a hermetic publication[9]; it was not possible to exchange views with correspondents who would become co-authors. He had to use other means to instil a spirit of amity; above all he had to refer to what was common to both him and his readers—the fact of belonging to one nation, culture, language, and living in the era in which the text was written. These factors were all the more unifying in that they enabled a community of people who had just been deprived of their political existence[10] to identify with something concrete. As a result, Krasicki's essays contain many references to colloquial language, which reflects the mentality of the readers. Along with references to common phenomena, native literature and customs, there were references to Polish and classical history which the representatives of the *szlachta*[11] mastered well and considered to be part of their heritage (Grześkowiak-Krwawicz 2006,

9 Although Krasicki knew *The Spectator* thanks to the French translations as the editor of *Monitor* he was aware that its original periodical form was written by Addison and Steele in "cooperation" with their correspondents. It is possible that the idea of editing the *Monitor* in its best-known shape came from Adam Kazimierz Czartoryski who edited several numbers of *Monitor* "father", a paper modelled on English papers too. Kaleta 1953, 7–160; Rudnicka 1955, 211–221.

10 This was after the third partition of Poland which was literally erased from the European map since its territory was taken by its neighbours: Russia, Habsburg's Austria and Prussia.

11 'Szlachta' was the name given to the nobility in the Polish-Lithuanian Commonwealth. As they had privileges they had real power over the country: they created laws, elected kings and held offices.

18–47 passim). Another method of gaining trust and building close relationships was the concept of openness adopted by the writer; Krasicki not only appeared as the author of the texts but also tried to give the impression of creating them, so to speak, in the presence of the reader, as a result of mutual reflections. He constantly agreed with his readers about the code implicit in the text by emphasizing and explaining the metaphors used, providing definitions and revealing his intentions.

> Another trick used to create this particular atmosphere of intimacy was to make the printed text sound like conversation. This may be why Krasicki used the periodical essay developed by the editors of *The Spectator* as a model for his work. Scholars (Italia 2005, 85) of *The Spectator* emphasize the similarity between an essay and a conversation:
> A friend allows one to measure oneself through one's relation to another human being [...] and essays are organised by this kind of relationship, offering a mode of literary reflection organized by the mutuality and interactivity of such 'conversation' and – its exact cognate in the eighteenth century – 'commerce'. (Black 1999, 27)

Reciprocity and interaction are the key words for the goals set by Krasicki and, consequently, he emphasized the conversational nature of his statements by constantly stressing the presence of a co-participant in the act of communication. Even if the co-participant could not really converse, the author tried to anticipate his doubts, allay his reservations and coax him into participating in his musings, also by asking questions which required the co-participant to have an independent stance on the topic. Additionally, he would sometimes ask him to speak on his behalf:

> A will to be good and happy is our first thought, since we can think about ourselves. If I asked everyone who reads me about this truth, everyone would agree that he thought that about himself, and everyone who knows less about himself would say that he did it, and everyone who knows himself would say that eventually it happened differently than he promised himself. (Krasicki 1997, 417)

Another tool to create the illusion of a conversation was the impression of a free flow of thoughts inscribed into the poetics of an essay from the very nascence of the genre. This manner of writing could help build a relationship which would facilitate accepting the moral pressure which the author so cared about. All the more so since, like the English authors of *The Spectator*, he valued the wisdom of Socrates (Ketcham 1985, 33–35) and with the help of conversation the latter refreshed the memory of his contemporaries and improved them.

Another feature common to Mr. Spectator and Krasicki is the tendency to choose subjects for their works drawing on observations of reality. The writings of the eccentric Englishman were written in London, inspired by the life of its citizens and wholly dedicated to forming and influencing them (Cowan 2004, 345–366). His name—one of the characteristic names of a magazine or newspaper with didactic assumptions—indicated that observation was the dominant trait of his personality. And indeed, when presenting himself to his readers, he wrote:

> Thus I live in the World, rather as a Spectator of Mankind, than as one of the Species; [...] In short, I have acted in all the parts of my Life as a Looker-on, which is the Character I intend to preserve in this Paper. (Addison 1891, no.1)

Of course, Krasicki was not as uninvolved in life as the eccentric English gentleman, but he also had a keen sense of observation which was reflected in his entire oeuvre. The sharp eye of the Polish writer was able to capture and transfer to the pages of his novel "Mikołaja Doświadczyńskiego przypadki" (Adventures of Nicolas Doświadczyński) (1776) the atmosphere and customs of Polish tribunals with its abundance of personalities, languages and behaviours. He was able to discern common features shared by particular individuals to create unique portraits in his satires of a drunkard or a fashionable wife, and to discern the general principles governing the human world hidden in repetitive situations and events which were later shown using animal allegories in his famous "Bajki i przypowieści" (Fables and Parables) (1779). The world of people, their behaviour, customs and day-to-day life provided a source of ceaseless inspiration for Krasicki; trivial and serious flaws were a compelling reason—as they were for Mr. Spectator—to appeal, ridicule, point out, and persuade. Perhaps the most important difference between the observations transferred to paper in the letters of Mr. Spectator and in *Uwagi* lies in their presentation. When analysing the *short fiction* in the consecutive numbers of *The Spectator*, Hiroyuki Ito noticed in them the same simplicity and dignity of language, as well as the authenticity, and congruence with reality, which characterizes the language of the English novel. Yet, he emphasized their discursive nature and lack of concreteness:

> [...] the authors appear to delineate a character or an event as factual and stative rather than as direct and tangible, or as a result accompanying an event than the event itself. (Ito 1986, 87)

Although the language of Polish prose in novels was only just beginning to be developed and be distinguishable, Krasicki's descriptions are striking and dynamic. They convey visual and auditory impressions, they focus on events rather than on states, and show attention to detail. For Mr. Spectator, a lover of the theatre, people were characterized by their dress and gestures, while for

Krasicki, by their actions and speech. However, apart from the manner of their presentation, the principle was the same since both Krasicki and Mr. Spectator departed from observation of the real world: the latter broached topics and was a source of inspiration for reflection.

The last feature shared by the character of Mr. Spectator and Krasicki is their propensity for satire and irony. Ketcham associates them with Socrates' raillery, which enables a comparison between the loftiest of things and the everyday, one being explained by the other (Ketcham 1985, 21). Italia emphasized their usefulness as a means of influencing readers, mentioning that, according to Steele, for readers of moral journals the fear of satire was greater than the fear of hell because it was not a question of the future, but rather of the present (Italia 2005, 145–146). For Krasicki that was the very purpose of irony, satire and mockery—ridiculing faults to encourage the practice of virtue. Irony is, first and foremost, one of the ways in which the narrator negatively assesses the phenomenon he is describing: "[…] unrighteous Vandals sometimes demolish the tombstones of their own ancestors, and to show respect to its fragments, they turn them into stairs or doorsteps of their houses" (Krasicki 1997, 341). In other cases, it is used to adopt the perspective of the person who is being improved, and to present their arguments 'in good faith' in a manner which clearly emphasizes their inconsistency with reality or common sense. He sometimes also used hyperboles which grotesquely featured the reality that was described. However, in *Uwagi* the narrator had fewer possibilities than the editors of the *Spectator* to threaten the shortcomings and degenerateness he was portraying with general ridicule because the latter had the advantage of its established popularity (Sinko 1957, XLII); it was, in a sense, a local paper addressed primarily to the milieu which frequented the cafés and it was closely connected with London (Italia, 2005, 76–79). Therefore, as well as exposing the ludicrousness in his essays, Krasicki warned against the condemnation of other people's private life. It was the opinion of others, the role of a person in society, and their own feeling of well-being resulting from compliance, or non-compliance, with social idea of propriety that was supposed to convince people:

> The second type of wicked and offensive behaviour is when things that are inappropriate for this company, are expressed. This habit seems to be the most common for educated people […] They over-ornament colloquial conversations with mathematical expressions and, as if it would be the kindest gift for the female sex, they quote Latin and Greek authors there, where thing needs only be charming […]. Such a manner of speaking causes two things: boredom and anger. (Krasicki 1997, 192–193)

And this was yet another—although it was implemented somewhat differently[12]—common stratagem used by Krasicki in his *Uwagi* and Addison and Steele in *The Spectator*.

These features connecting the character created by the editors of *The Spectator* and the Polish writer—the propensity to shorten the distance and create intimate relationships between the narrator and the reader, a conversational tone based on the involvement of the reader, drawing inspiration from observations of the world and of people, and mockery and humour as didactic means—are related primarily to certain internal predispositions, and a writing technique which reflects the author's beliefs and temperament. However, there was another reason for Krasicki to select the *periodical essay* form and that was the desire to achieve the goal which Mr. Spectator managed to accomplish—influencing non-textual reality with written discourse.

On ways to improve the world

Ignacy Krasicki was deeply convinced that it was possible to influence reality using words, especially through written texts (printed, and therefore widely distributable) (Kostkiewiczowa 1997). He expressed this conviction in almost all of his works, from *Monitor* to "Uwagi". As such, he constantly returned to the problem of the responsibility of authors and readers, the proper way of writing and reading, literary criticism, imitation and translation, even setting up libraries so they could be used for self-improvement, rather than holding a merely representative function. Although the latter purpose was also important especially for aristocrats (Górska 2014), it was not of prime importance in comparison with knowledge and morality which one could acquire from books. Krasicki's awareness of the significance of literature and its influence on life, as well as his talent for clear and accurate expression, constituted a point of admiration for his contemporaries appreciated by posterity. In the eyes of many scholars, it made him a moralist (Cazin 1986, 264–265). "Uwagi" is one of his last works and, in fact, one might be tempted to perceive it as a kind of

12 Readers of *The Spectator* were able to find in their neighbourhood or in the in coffeehouses they would go to a person who matched the characters described in the paper. It was Mr. Spectator who opened their eyes to the ridiculousness of some behaviours, ways of thinking day after day. In the case of Krasicki's "Uwagi", it was common sense, customs, politeness and so on, which exposed the ridiculousness of some kind of behaviour. It was not fear of being exposed in the paper but of being perceived by others in wrong or ridiculous ways which reformed readers.

testament since it contains nothing new with regard to the issues raised and the opinions expressed. However, what distinguishes it from other works is its form. It is not surprising that Krasicki used a model which was successful—the tricks and techniques developed by Addison and Steele, the founders of a paper which was so admired and avidly read in England, and translated, imitated and praised throughout Europe.

When analysing Mr Spectator's strategy, Ketcham drew attention to one of its founders' most important tasks: developing a new language which its readers could use to describe the world and which would help them to understand it. This language sought to restore the proper meaning to words and their 'moral weight', and would influence readers' behaviour, because words, like gestures, are like an act played out in public, and thus have an impact on the behaviour of individuals (Ketcham 1985, 124 passim). To create this new language, they used parallel meanings and antithesis, synonyms and multiple subordinate clauses. As a result, the meanings of particular words were established in terms of the meaning of other words, creating a coherent network of connections.[13] In order to make it easier for readers to adapt this language for their own use, they repeated each of its parts over and over—both the particular elements of the system as well as ways of connecting entire sentence structures and expressions (Ketcham 1985, 144–155). Krasicki adopted a similar strategy. The dispersed and inconsistent terms he uses at the beginning of his literary work become clearer in "Uwagi" and form a single system based on the interdependencies between its individual elements.

Two concepts lie at the centre of this system: virtue and excess. The first is the main goal of man because it leads to happiness while the second—excess—is the main obstacle to achieving it. Virtue is defined as doing what must be done and is related to constancy, patience, kind-heartedness, piety, which is kind-heartedness on a 'higher level'. The latter is actually a synonym of virtue. Other concepts are equally important in Krasicki's system: Duty – as one has to be dutiful to be virtuous; Bravery—the main 'component' of which is constancy. And perhaps the most important—moderation. Intellect, prudence and reason are also important lexemes; their task is to tame passions and show what is good. The reward for pursuing a path of virtue is inner satisfaction, which is even more than peace of mind, a type of stoic inner independence. The group

13 "Each word has value within this verbal system, but none of them can be defined except in terms of others. If we look at any of these words, we find its definition spreading out to incorporate the other words in the field" (Ketcham 1985, 155).

of positive values revolves around those concepts. For example, patience and constancy protect one from despair, virtue and duty result in respect for parents and elders, piety helps to bear adversities, constancy is necessary to change one's life for better (also practical life, as among the *szlachta* one had to be courageous and constant to go against established customs and, for example, build houses equipped with chimneys for his peasants), reason and intellect make one and enable to gain self-knowledge; self-knowledge gives rise to politeness and humility and so on.

With regard to negative values, the key word is "excess". Of course, excessive *amour propre* is the most dangerous. In itself it is natural but if it crosses the boundaries determined by virtue and reason it leads to an excessive understanding of oneself. It lies at the root of all 'social' vices—loquaciousness, defamation, derision—and 'personal' ones—pride, jealousy, false modesty, and others. However, according to Aristotle's theory of the golden mean between the extremes of the "Nicomachean ethics" (Arystoteles 2000, 113)—virtue in excess is even more dangerous. Excess in the virtue of constancy leads to stubbornness, excess in the virtue of prudence leads to parsimoniousness, and so on. The difference between the strategy used by Mr. Spectator and that wielded by Krasicki—as Wiesław Pusz aptly remarked—lies in the latter's somewhat different technique of creating a network of terms. While Addison and Steele used synonyms, parallel meanings, analogies and repetition, Krasicki's domain was contradistinction and hierarchization.[14]

Another technique which Krasicki partially adapted in "Uwagi" is that of self-creation. Addison and Steele created the character of Mr. Spectator, mainly—as Iona Italia claimed—to be able to freely give advice and tips of a moral nature without being accused of hypocrisy (Italia 2005, 149). Apart from his impeccable moral integrity, they gave him yet another trait, more important for these deliberations—an eccentric nature. Richard Squibbs believes that this was an attempt to contend with standardization and people mindlessly following changes in fashion which resulted from the development of the luxury goods market, and to encourage people to opt for more constant values instead:

> Understood in these terms the reflexive personality modelled in periodicals aims to shake readers out of such a consumerist torpor, and to reorient them toward a civic

14 Here is an example of contradistinction: courage—a feature which people have in common with animals—versus valor—a noble kind of courage, which is specific to humankind. An example of hierarchization is, for example, given by kind-heartedness and piety – the latter being a higher form of kind-heartedness (Pusz 2002, 143–144).

> awareness that social life is not a mere dumb show of saleable goods guaranteed to make their owners stand out from the crowd by, paradoxically, 'follow[ing]the crowd' in pursuit of novelty. (Squibbs 2008, 403)

Common sense and truth were supposed to be a test of eccentricity—deciding whether or not it tended towards 'untamed' individualism—and the common measure of 'outlandishness' for all those who were eccentric and capricious (that is those who were not followers of fashion). In brief, Mr. Spectator's unusual behaviour and habits gave him the opportunity to look at the life which he was describing from a distance, and to divulge anything that did not agree with reason or morality. This attitude was close to Krasicki's heart. On many occasions when recommending various actions, he warned his readers that they would be considered peculiar, unfashionable, volatile, simply because they were trying to find new solutions, because they dared to show their attachment to old values or dared to change their behaviour for the better. In *Uwagi*, as befits the author of essays, he did not use a *persona*; he spoke openly, on his own behalf; however, he used a technique which made him, like Mr. Spectator, stand out from the crowd and look at things which were seemingly obvious from a distance thus bringing to the fore any falsehood and stupidity. This technique consisted in adopting the attitude of a simple man, which—as used by Krasicki—had the same function in *Uwagi* as foreigners who came from far away to visit Europe, and the same role as noble savages in Polish and foreign literature (Hazard 1972, 24–26). Similarly, to them, as a narrator, he used common sense and was full of good faith with which he unmasked all the absurdities and irregularities he encountered on his way. Astonishment at people's irrational deeds is not the only device the author uses. The common-sense views of a simple man allowed him to expose many problems to which people no longer paid attention, and to ask questions which many a refined man would probably not dare ask. There was one more reason why Krasicki 'wore a mask'—irony. His sentences which are expressed, allegedly in good faith, are suffused with irony due to the discrepancy between a willingness to serve or to respect the practices of the readers and the actual state of affairs: "Ladies should not be offended, when I explain to them, that it is rude to laugh [...] about an old style of dress that has gone out of fashion [...] there may be a time when, while in the countryside, they will miss information about a new trend and their neighbour who has just come from the spa will find her in a dress that had been out of fashion for three or six months. After one such situation, of her own fault, she would become an object of ridicule and have to bear a parish gawkiness, that is the last stage of humiliation" (Krasicki 1997, 272–273).

It is interesting to note that in using *The Spectator*'s techniques, Krasicki went so far as to use devices which seemed out of place in a collection of essays. Essays of a 'practical' nature, about the construction of houses, planting gardens or roadworks, show similarities to those written by the eccentric Englishman to his readers regarding the treatment of servants or caring for property (Addison, 1711, no.107). In this way, they can be seen as going beyond the subject matter characteristic of Montaigne's style of essay. Moreover, another ploy is worth mentioning, often used in the English periodical, which also appears in *Uwagi*, but which is not often used in essays: letters. There are three of them for 48 texts. The first one is a typical letter addressed to the editors, but it is a forgery. The sender presents the difficulty with which he is confronted and asks the addressee for advice. Meanwhile, the sender himself presents his knowledge about the topic and his standpoint which is the same as that of the author of the essay.[15] The second letter is also a fake and becomes the pretext for writing about a particular subject.[16] The last one uses a device that is common in the moral essay: it quotes a compassionate letter from Servius Supicius to Cicero to teach the reader how to comfort a friend in distress.[17] It is difficult to say why Krasicki actually used these two techniques which were inadequate for his oeuvre. Perhaps he wanted to convince his contemporaries that all the advice and thoughts contained in his collection of writings, also including those on ageless subjects, were addressed to them and written with them in mind. Or perhaps it was to be a factor which helped him to evoke an atmosphere of intimacy and trust, to sustain the reader's involvement and an illusion of conversation, which—as has been mentioned—characterized the paper of the eccentric Englishman.

---

15 This is one possible sort of letters sent to the paper. In *Monitor*, some correspondents presented standpoints which were opposite to the editors'. This occasionally gave them the occasion to expose the irrationality of their point of view.

16 In *Uwagi*, it is a letter from one cardsharper to another and the subject of essay is of course gambling.

17 Addison used ancient letter as a model too in *The Spectator*. See Addison, *Spectator* 1712, no. 292 [4 February]. That was one of Addison's essays which was adapted in Krasicki's *Monitor*. *Monitor* 1766, no. 98 [6 December]. Krasicki in *Monitor* also translated other letters from *Le Spectateur* (e.g., letters about education), a letter from a constantly ill reader (from *Spectator* 1711, no. 25), the letter "To Cloe" (from *Spectator* 1712, no. 301) and he adapted a letter about women's education (from *Spectator* 1712, no. 328b). In "Uwagi", he inserted just three letters and what's more one of these letters (a fake letter from a cardsharper) had been published earlier in his periodical *Co Tydzień*.

In summarizing the above deliberations, we cannot omit the characteristic features of *Uwagi*, which were related to the heritage of the Montaigne-style essay (Libera 1997, 6–10). One is the erudition of Krasicki's essays; in addition to Latin and Greek texts, *Uwagi* also contained references to the Bible and modern authors, including *Le Spectateur.* Because his works were addressed to readers who had a similar educational background (Grell 1995), he did not have to leave out references to literature and culture. Krasicki also 'inherited' an approach to the world which was characteristic of Montaigne's genre—one full of cautious reserve and shunning prejudice. It is also worth emphasizing the fact that he appears in his essays in person, as himself, without the need to create a *porte parole*. And although, in contrast to the First Essayist, he does not focus on getting to know himself, he sometimes reveals his most personal likes and dislikes in the pages of *Uwagi*.

In addition to these features, which attest to the connection between the first collection of Polish essays and the classic model of the genre, as a writer, Krasicki deliberately turned to the model of *The Spectator* not only because of a certain temperamental relationship which connected him with the character created by Addison and Steele, but also—above all—because of their similar goals, the desire to change the world around him, to convince his readers and shape their manner of thinking and behaviour. He was to be aided in this task by the atmosphere of intimacy characteristic of the English periodical, which was achieved, among other means, by the conversational tone of the essays, drawing on subjects and examples from extra-textual reality, using humour. Following the example of his English colleagues, he created a system of interdefinable terms for this purpose that restored the 'moral weight' of words. Like Mr. Spectator, he also presented himself as an eccentric, and even touched on practical issues or imitated the letters sent to the English periodical. He wanted his reflections to bring about a response from the readers in their day-to-day lives. Scott Black, writing about the essay as a genre, gave the most apt description of this desire: "It's not about acquiring knowledge but using it" (Black 2006, 25). In this way, Krasicki's essay became the precursor of all Polish essays striving to change the world.

References

ADDISON, Joseph/Richard Steele: *The Spectator. A New Edition. Reproducing the Original Text Both as First Issued and as Corrected by Its Authors with Introduction, Notes and Index*. Henry Morley (ed.) 1891, 3 vols. <https://www.gutenberg.org/files/9334/9334-h/9334-h.htm# toc>. [12.05.2018].

ALEKSANDROWSKA, Elżbieta: "Wstęp". In: Elżbieta Aleksandrowska (ed.): *Monitor 1765–1785. Wybór*. Wrocław: Zakład Narodowy im. Ossolińskich 1976, V–CXL.

ANON: *Le Spectateur ou le Socrate moderne trad. de l'anglais*. Vol. 9. Paris: Merigot 1754.

ARYSTOTELES: "*Etyka nikomachejska*". In: D. Gromska (trans.): Arystoteles: *Dzieła wszystkie*. Vol. 5. Warszawa: PWN 2000, 113.

AXER, Jerzy: "Latinitas jako składnik polskiej tożsamości kulturowej". In: *Tradycje antyczne w kulturze europejskiej – perspektywa polska*. Warszawa: OBTA 1995, 71–81.

AXER, Jerzy: "Trening oratorski jako składnik wychowania obywatelskiego w systemie republikańskim. Przypadek Polski". In: *Retoryka antyczna i jej dziedzictwo*. Warszawa: OBTA 1996, 39–51.

AXER, Jerzy: "Łacina jako drugi język narodu szlacheckiego Rzeczypospolitej". In: Jerzy Axer (ed.): *Łacina jako język elit*. Warszawa: Wydawnictwo DiG 2004, 151–156.

BLACK, Scott: "Social and Literary Form in the 'Spectator'". *Eighteenth-Century Studies* 33, 1 (1999), 21–42.

BLACK, Scott: *Of Essays and Reading in Early Modern Britain*. Basingstoke: Palgrave Macmillan 2006.

CAZIN, Paul: *Książę biskup warmiński Ignacy Krasicki (1735–1801)*. Michał Mroziński (trans.). Olsztyn: Wydawnictwo Pojezierze 1986.

COWAN, Brian: "Mr. Spectator and the Coffehouse Public Sphere". *Eighteenth-Century Studies* 37, 3 (2004), 345–366.

FRASER, Theodore P.: *The French Essay*. Boston: Twayne Publishers 1986.

GAJZLER, Eliza: "Ignacy Krasicki – pierwszy polski eseista". *Polonistyka* 6 (2009), 37–42.

GOLIŃSKI, Zbigniew: *Ignacy Krasicki*. Warszawa: PIW 1979.

GOLIŃSKI, Zbigniew: *Kalendarz życia i twórczości Ignacego Krasickiego*. Vol. 2. Magdalena Górska (ed.). Poznań: Poznańskie Towarzystwo Przyjaciół Nauk 2011.

GÓRSKA, Magdalena: "O wyborze ksiąg i bibliomanii: Biblioteki". In: Teresa Kostkiewiczowa/Bożena Mazurkowa/Roman Doktór (eds.): *Czytanie Krasickiego*. Warszawa: Wydawnictwo IBL PAN 2014, 513–534.

NORKOWSKA, Aleksandra: "Na straży kobiecego piękna? Damskie nauki". In: Teresa Kostkiewiczowa/Bożena Mazurkowa/Roman Doktór (eds.): *Czytanie Krasickiego*. Warszawa: Wydawnictwo IBL PAN 2014, 485–503.

GRELL, Chantal: *Le Dix-huitième siècle et l'antiquité en France 1680–1789*. Oxford: Voltaire Foundation 1995.

GRZEŚKOWIAK-KRWAWICZ, Anna: *Regina libertas. Wolność w polskiej myśli politycznej XVIII wieku*. Gdańsk: Wydawnictwo Słowo/Obraz Terytoria 2006.

HAZARD, Paul: *Myśl europejska w XVIII wieku. Od Monteskiusza do Lessinga*. Halina Suwała (trans.). Preface: Stanisław Pietraszko. Warszawa: PIW 1972.

ITALIA, Iona: *The Rise of Literary Journalism in the Eighteenth Century. Anxious Employment*. London: Routledge 2005.

ITO, Hiroyuki: "The Language of The Spectator; As Seen in the Movement of English Prose towards the Rise of the Novel". *Poetica: International Journal of Linguistic-literary Studies* 23 (1986), 81–97.

KALETA, Roman: "Monitor z roku 1763 na tle swoich czasów". In: Roman Kaleta/Mieczysław Klimowicz: *Prekursorzy Oświecenia. "Monitor" z roku 1763 na tle swoich czasów*. Mitzler de Kolof, redaktor i wydawca. Wrocław: Zakład Narodowy im. Ossolińskich 1953, 7–160.

KALINOWSKI, Daniel: "Uwagi Ignacego Krasickiego na tle europejskiej tradycji pism moralistycznych". *Słupskie Prace Filologiczne. Seria Filologia Polska* 1 (2002), 27–40.

KETCHAM, Michael G.: *Transparent Designs. Reading, Performance, and Form in the Spectator Papers*. Ateny: The University of Georgia Press 1985.

KOSTKIEWICZOWA, Teresa: " 'Księgi, wiersze, dzienniki…'. O poglądach na książki i czytanie w epoce oświecenia i pismach Ignacego Krasickiego". In: Teresa Kostkiewiczowa (ed.) *Studia o Krasickim*. Warszawa: Wydawnictwo IBL PAN 1997, 31–60.

KRASICKI, Ignacy: *Monitor*. Warszawa: s.e. 1766.

KRASICKI, Ignacy: *Uwagi*. Zbigniew Libera (ed.). Warszawa: Czytelnik 1997.

KURDYBACHA, Łukasz: *Staropolski ideał wychowawczy*. Lwów: Księgarnia A. Krawczyńskiego 1938.

LIBERA, Zbigniew: "Ignacy Krasicki – myśliciel". In: Z. Libera (ed.): Ignacy Krasicki: *Uwagi*. Warszawa: Czytelnik 1997, 5–17.

MOKRZECKI, Lech/Puchowski, Kazimierz: "Programy szkolnictwa staropolskiego w XVI i XVII wieku. Kierunki zmian". *Kwartalnik Pedagogiczny* 3 (1995), 89–110.

POKRZYWNIAK, Tomasz: *Ignacy Krasicki*. Warszawa: WSiP 1992.

PUCHOWSKI, Kazimierz: "Antyk w edukacji elit Rzeczypospolitej epoki oświecenia". In: Tomasz Chachulski (ed.): *Antyk oświeconych. Studia i rozprawy o miejscu starożytności w kulturze polskiej XVIII wieku*. Warszawa: Wydawnictwo IBL PAN 2012, 97–144.

PUSZ Wiesław: "Zastanowić się potrzeba… – czyli uwagi o Uwagach Ignacego Krasickiego". *Wiek Oświecenia* 18 (2002), 133–147.

RUDNICKA, Jadwiga: "Z genealogii 'Monitora' z roku 1763". *Pamiętnik Literacki* 1 (1955), 211–221.

SINKO, Zofia: "Wstęp". In: Zofia Sinko (ed.): *Spectator*. Wrocław: Zakład Narodowy im. Ossolińskich 1957, V–CXIV.

SINKO, Zofia: "*Monitor wobec angielskiego Spectatora*". Wrocław: Zakład Narodowy im. Ossolińskich 1956.

SQUIBBS, Richard: "Civic Humorism and the Eighteenth-Century Periodical Essay". *ELH* 75, 2 (2008), 389–413.

Carmen García Cela

(Université de Salamanque)

La Spectatrice (1728–1729): scènes de lecture ?

1. Plumes de femmes[1]

« Le culte voué au *Spectator* en Angleterre en faisait un modèle écrasant », affirme Alexis Lévrier : « tous les épigones ont souffert de la comparaison avec le périodique de Steele et Addison » car « les lecteurs n'ont d'ailleurs pas manqué de rappeler aux imitateurs la supériorité de leur prédécesseur » (Lévrier 2007, 38). Le *Spectator* de Joseph Addison et Richard Steele, paru en 1711, vint au monde sous le signe du succès. Le retentissement formidable du journal repose sans doute sur l'invention d'une forme d'écriture s'accordant aux demandes d'une société en mutation. Son essor est tel qu'il se propage rapidement à travers l'Europe voire jusque dans le continent américain, notamment grâce aux traductions en français réalisées en Hollande[2] qui en assurèrent la circulation tout en inspirant une pléiade de continuateurs. La puissance du prototype est telle que l'on peut même parler d'un phénomène spectatorial qui hante le XVIIIe siècle.

Au siècle des Lumières, l'activité journalistique n'exclut pas les femmes. *The Female Tatler* (1709–1710), est l'un des premiers journaux adressés à un public éminemment féminin en Angleterre. Pour ce qui est de la France, il faut, ainsi que l'affirme Marion Brétéché, remonter jusqu'en 1703[3] pour repérer le premier

---

1 Cet article s'inscrit dans le cadre du Groupe de recherche « Estudios de Literatura y Pensamiento » (IEMYRhd, Universidad de Salamanca) ainsi que du projet de recherche national MINCI « Teoría de la lectura y hermenéutica literaria en la Ilustración (1750–1808): edición y estudio de fuentes documentales y literarias » (FFI2016-80168-P), tous deux dirigés par María José Rodríguez Sánchez de León.

2 Tel que le précise Klaus-Dieter Ertler, l'entrée des 'spectateurs' « dans le continent européen s'est réalisée par la Hollande, où de nombreux émigrants français avaient trouvé refuge après la Révocation de l'Edit de Nantes en 1685. C'est donc à La Haye et à Amsterdam que sortirent les premiers spectateurs en langue française, avant même de passer par Paris » (Ertler 2014, 3).

3 En effet, le parcours de Marion Brétéché débute sur un « étonnement historiographique » dans la mesure où, de manière générale, on situe l'acte de naissance de la presse féminine française en 1759, date de la parution du premier numéro du *Journal des Dames*, La Haye [Paris], divers éd.,1759–1778, mensuel, 36 vol. in 8°. « Cette datation – selon Marion Brétéché – s'explique sans doute par le fait que ces auteurs n'envisagent que les

exemple d'une figure de femme-journaliste (2013, 247). C'est en effet en 1703 que la nièce de Charles Perrault, Marie-Jeanne L'Héritier de Villandon (1664–1734),[4] fait paraître les trois livraisons de *L'érudition enjouée.*[5] Suivra, en 1710, *Le Nouveau Mercure galant des cours de l'Europe* d'Anne-Marguerite Dunoyer (1663–1719). Né en novembre 1710 chez Étienne Foulque à la Haye, *Le Nouveau Mercure Galant* est présenté comme un périodique mensuel qui s'éteindra après la publication de la deuxième remise suite au décès de l'imprimeur (Brétéché 2013, 247).[6] À partir de 1711, Denoyer deviendra la rédactrice de la *Quintessence des Nouvelles*, un périodique bihebdomadaire édité chez Uytwerf à La Haye.[7]

C'est aussi dans le premier tiers du siècle, en 1728, que paraît la première feuille de *La Spectatrice* (1728–1729). Ce périodique anonyme trouva un écho modeste dans la presse littéraire de son temps. En juin 1728, lors du tirage de sa cinquième feuille, le *Mercure de France* lui consacre un article saluant un « petit ouvrage écrit légèrement mais avec soin » (*Mercure*, 1204) qui « saisit l'occasion pour faire l'apologie » du sexe féminin et « le défendre de l'injustice des hommes ». Deux ans plus tard, en 1730, les quinze feuilles de *La Spectatrice* sont rassemblées dans un volume intitulé *Recueil de toutes les feuilles de la Spectatrice qui ont paru et de celles qui n'ont point paru*. En 1733, l'abbé Desfontaines, dans *Le Pour et le contre*, fera le détail des périodiques moraux et littéraires français

---

périodiques destinés aux femmes, quand elles ne sont pas à la recherche d'ouvrages pouvant être considérés comme 'féministes' » (Brétéché 2013, 247).

4 Marie-Jeanne L'Héritier a adhéré au mouvement des Précieuses et, en 1711, elle hérite du salon de Melle de Scudéry. Son premier ouvrage, *Œuvres meslées : contenant L'innocente tromperie, L'avare puny, Les enchantemens de l'eloquence, Les avantures de Finette : nouvelles et autres ouvrages en vers et en prose*, est publié en 1695 chez Jean Guignard à Paris.

5 *Le périodique paraît à Paris chez Pierre Ribou entre juin et octobre 1703. Les numéros deux et trois ajoutent un sous-titre : ou Nouvelles sçavantes, satiriques et galantes, écrites à une Dame Françoise, qui est à Madrid. Voir Jean Sgard : Dictionnaire des journaux 1600–1789, en ligne.*

6 Anne-Marguerite du Noyer (1663–1719). Sa vie mouvementée est bien connue grâce à ses *Mémoires de Madame Du N*** écrits par elle-même, dont les 5 volumes furent publiés à* Cologne, chez Pierre Marteau, entre 1709 et 1710. Le personnage est intéressant en ce qu'il représente la professionnalisation du métier de journaliste (Voir à ce sujet Brétéché 2011).

7 Signalons au passage que l'apparition des « spectateurs » en Espagne est plus tardive. Elle n'aura lieu qu'à partir des années 60. Le premier, *El duende especulativo sobre la Vida Civil*, paraît en 1761. Le premier périodique féminin, *La Pensadora Gaditana*, sera publié entre 1763 et 1764, alors que *La pensatriz de Salamanca*, dont un seul numéro est conservé verra le jour en 1777.

« que tout le monde connaît », à savoir *Le Spectateur Français* (1721–1724) de Marivaux, *La Spectatrice* et *Le Nouvelliste du Parnasse* (1730–1732) (Desfontaines 1733, 339). Malgré le rang qu'accorde Desfontaines à l'ouvrage,[8] le silence finira par retomber sur lui. Presque trois siècles devront s'écouler avant de voir paraître l'édition critique qu'Alexis Lévrier et une équipe de chercheurs lui consacrent pour « mettre en évidence la place ambiguë, à la fois importante et marginale, que les feuilles de *La Spectatrice* occupent dans l'histoire de la presse littéraire du XVIIIe siècle » (Lévrier 2013, 225).

La Spectatrice comporte quinze feuilles organisées en autant de *Semaines*. Dans l'avertissement de la Première Semaine on apprend que les feuilles paraîtront les lundis, deux fois par mois (S. 1, 30).[9] La première feuille voit le jour le 29 mars 1728 et l'auteur s'en tient à la régularité annoncée jusqu'à la Neuvième Semaine datée du 24 juillet 1728. À partir de la Dixième Semaine, du 28 août 1728, les livraisons s'espacent et le périodique disparaît treize mois après sa naissance, en mars 1729.

2. *La Spectatrice* dans le champ spectatorial

Dans *La Plume et le Plomb. Espaces de l'imprimé et du manuscrit au siècle des Lumières* (2006), François Moureau affirmait, à propos des « spectateurs », que le mot « journal » n'est pas le plus juste pour désigner ces productions périodiques qui se distinguent de la presse d'information générale – gazettes et mercures – et des périodiques « savants » ou « techniques » dont le rôle était de diffuser les nouveautés scientifiques (2006, 385). Si journalisme il y a dans les périodiques du type « spectateur », c'est qu'il s'agit, comme le veut Moureau, de « véritable[s] journa[ux] au sens premier du terme » (2006, 388) puisqu'ils sont écrits à la première personne. D'autre part, la parution de ces journaux, dispersée dans le temps et dont le support physique est la feuille, est soumise à une régularité programmée par l'auteur. Ces conditions de publication matérielles déterminent à leur tour l'inachèvement, l'improvisation et le naturel qui caractérisent ce genre d'ouvrages.

Ce sont là des traits que *La Spectatrice* et *The Spectator* ont en partage. Dans le *Spectator*, le narrateur du périodique, Mr. Spectator, assure, de remise en remise, la continuité des feuilles qui se succèdent à un rythme trépidant. Mais, instance

---

8 Voir Alexis Lévrier (2013, 223–224) et Élise Revon-Rivière (2013) qui analyse le plagiat de *La Spectatrice* dans les *Chiffons de Javotte* de Mague de Saint Aubin.

9 Les références à *La Spectatrice* renvoient à l'édition de Lévrier et indiquent, entre parenthèses, le numéro de la Semaine (S. n°) suivi de la page.

fictive, il se distingue des auteurs réels. Ayant cependant observé combien les lecteurs sont curieux de connaître la vie de l'auteur pour pouvoir juger de son texte (Addison 1987, I, 1), il leur offre, dans le premier essai, une ébauche de son autobiographie tout en se gardant de dévoiler son nom, son âge et son adresse (Addison 1987, I, 5). La révélation d'anecdotes cocasses compense par l'humour l'éventuelle déception du lecteur.

En tête du discours et à la première personne, Mr Spectator se donne la mission d'observer la société dont il prétend réformer les mœurs. Or il ne le fait pas à la manière des moralistes qui imposent leurs règles. Au contraire, Mr Spectator séduit le lecteur, s'entretient avec lui en s'attirant sa sympathie et lui demande même expressément de lui envoyer des lettres qu'il devra adresser à son éditeur Mr Buckley (Addison 1987, I, 6). Ce narrateur qui encourage les échanges écrits s'avère être en manque de parole : plutôt qu'un membre du genre humain (Addison 1987, I, 4), il en est l'observateur ainsi qu'il l'annonce à la première ligne de l'ouvrage. Personnage qui ne supporte ni la parole des interlocuteurs ni le regard d'autrui posé sur lui, il ne participe à d'autres échanges verbaux que ceux qui se tiennent au sein d'un Club d'amis. Ne voulant pas se résigner à mourir sans avoir transmis les résultats de ses observations, il décide de le faire par écrit. Dès lors, il se faufile en témoin muet dans les espaces de sociabilité de son entourage, en silence et placé à une certaine distance, sans intervenir dans les conversations de ses concitoyens, sans participer aux événements qu'il transmet dans ses essais.

La première personne, commune aux « spectateurs », se donne un nouvel avatar avec *La Spectatrice*, dont l'auteur réel est à ce jour inconnu. Bien que le sexe de l'auteur réel demeure indécidable, le « je » de ses discours renvoie à une instance féminine qui revendique sa place parmi les auteurs masculins. Les démarches d'écriture du périodique ont beau jouxter celles de ses prédécesseurs, l'introduction d'une voix féminine est déjà un geste transgresseur. Cependant, existe-t-il vraiment une intention d'imiter ou de déranger le modèle ? Aucune référence dans le texte ne confirme que l'auteur réel de la *Spectatrice* ait lu le *Spectator* ni même sa première traduction en français, connue comme *Le Socrate moderne* (1714–1726). Toutefois, la forme du périodique prouve qu'il connaît bien le genre. Dès le début de la première feuille, la rédactrice montre sa volonté de s'intégrer à la liste des « spectateurs » par le choix d'un ton polémique puisqu'elle s'affronte d'emblée à la gente masculine en souhaitant l'emporter sur ces quelques auteurs français qui ont échoué là où elle espère l'emporter :

> Trois ou quatre Spectateurs qui ont paru en France nous ont donné quelques brochures, et en sont demeurés là – dit-elle –. N'auront-ils point de honte qu'une femme fournisse mieux cette carrière ? Car j'espère bien aller plus loin que ces Messieurs. (S. 1, 21)

Dans cette compétition pour apparaître dans le champ spectatorial, il n'est pas que des opposants à dépasser. La narratrice fait savoir qu'elle entretient un rapport avec un correspondant de Paris, « une espèce de Spectateur » (S. 5, 77), ayant apparemment la même occupation que celle qui veut devenir « Spectatrice et contrôleuse du genre humain » (S. 3, 41–42). Le texte n'offre aucune piste pour déterminer si ce correspondant est un personnage fictif ou réel. Le contexte réel émergera plus loin, lorsqu'elle se montrera élogieuse avec son « confrère » *Le Spectateur Français* – que Marivaux publia entre 1721 et 1724 (S. 7, 109) –. Le recueil ne fait allusion à nul autre « spectateur ». C'est donc probablement par le truchement d'imitateurs ou de continuateurs interposés que l'auteur de *La Spectatrice* conçoit une rédactrice déterminée à se hisser à la hauteur de ceux qu'elle aspire à égaler.

Comme Mr Spectator, elle se contente de se présenter en Spectatrice, voilant son nom ainsi que son adresse : on sait qu'elle passe la première partie de sa vie à la campagne et qu'elle déménage plus tard à Paris, mais les précisions géographiques font défaut. Quant à son âge, elle n'en dit mot dans sa présentation mais, peut-être par mégarde, elle laisse entendre qu'elle a trente ans à la Septième Semaine (S. 7, 110).

Toujours proche du modèle, elle s'attarde également à faire le détail de ses origines : elle ignore l'identité de son père mais se sait probablement la fille d'un baron qui « comptait sa noblesse depuis plusieurs siècles » (S. 1, 23) et n'avait jamais daigné épouser sa mère. Lorsqu'elle vint au monde, elle ressemblait « aussi peu [à sa mère] qu'au Baron et à un autre noble » que celle-ci avoue avoir aimé « un peu » (S. 1, 26). Aucun de ces deux pères présomptifs ne la reconnaît comme fille légitime, mais le Baron lui lègue de quoi vivre aisément : « Fille de deux personnes de qualité », elle se trouve être « méprisable par [s]a naissance » (S. 1, 26). Quant à son état civil, si elle échappe au joug du mariage – qu'elle considère incompatible avec la liberté indispensable à son désir de s'ériger en Auteur et philosophe –, les règles sociales, qui pèsent lourd sur les femmes, retombent sur elle car le célibat et la bâtardise la laissent deux fois dans les marges de la société.[10]

L'éducation qu'elle reçoit ne fera pas mieux. Malgré un intérêt précoce pour la réflexion, à la campagne, sa mère « ayant été élevée avec tous les animaux de

10 « Quand une fille qui aspire au joug du mariage, vient à passer pour philosophe, adieu les épouseurs, á moins qu'elle ne soit assez riche pour acheter la patience du futur. Si elle est auteur, c'est bien pis » (S. 2, 40), pose la Spectatrice. Plus loin, elle s'avise que ce trait la rapproche de la lignée des philosophes à qui « la nature n'a pas prodigué [...] le talent ni le goût de peupler le monde », leur mission étant plutôt celle de le « corriger » (S. 2, 41).

la basse-cour et de la société des Dames Dindonnières » (S. 1, 24), considérait l'éducation de sa fille « une affaire moins pressante que celle de ses poulets » (S. 1, 27). Le Baron, de son côté, lui fit apprendre à lire et à chasser (S. 1, 27). Avec lui, elle devint « chasseuse » et « quelque chose de mieux » grâce au Curé qui l'initia aux rudiments du latin et lui procura les livres des grands auteurs classiques. Elle devint donc « un peu latine, à force d'étude et de temps » (S.1, 28), tout comme Mr Spectateur, à cette différence près que celui-ci s'est formé à l'université (Addison 1987, I, 2). En effet, la narratrice ne possède pas le rang académique de Mr Spectateur mais elle est prête à tout faire pour être reconnue par ses pairs comme Auteur. En l'absence d'autres maîtres, elle se trouve préférer le « livre de la Nature […] rempli d'une infinité de sujets de réflexion » où elle lisait « avec plus de plaisir que dans les livres artificiels ». Livrée à elle-même, c'est tout compte fait la nature qui façonne la Spectatrice : « je sentis que la nature m'avait fait Spectatrice » (S. 1, 27), dit-elle lorsqu'elle découvre que l'observation fait naître en elle « une infinité de petits raisonnements (S. 1, 27).

Pour sa mise en scène, la Spectatrice tire avantage de son aspect androgyne : « je suis – dit-elle – une figure un peu équivoque, propre à paraître homme ou femme dans un extérieur postiche » (S. 1, 29). Elle se travestit donc en homme pour échapper à la « misère d'être attachée à un corps féminin » (S. 1, 29). Ce faisant elle transgresse l'ordre social, sans pour autant le mettre en cause, tout en poussant d'un degré la superposition des masques du narrateur spectatorial, par cohérence envers sa « vocation » (S. 10, 144) de Spectatrice qui voudrait qu'aucun endroit n'échappe à son observation, y compris ceux auxquels les femmes n'ont pas accès.

3. Avantages moraux des plaisirs de l'imagination

S'il est un aspect sur lequel s'accordent les « spectateurs » c'est l'espace privilégié qu'ils réservent à l'observation et au sens de la vue. Dans *Les plaisirs de l'imagination* – un ensemble d'essais marquants parus dans le *Spectator*[11] – Addison énonce les mécanismes d'un engrenage poétique et scientifique centré sur le sens de la vue :

> Our sight – dit-il – is the most perfect and the most delightful of all our senses. It fills the mind with the largest varieties of ideas, converses with its objects at the greatest distance, and continues the longest in action without being tired satiated with its proper enjoyments. (Addison 1987, III, 536)

11 *Les plaisirs de l'imagination* sont parus dans *The Spectator* en 1712 entre le 2 juin et le 3 juillet 1712 et s'étendent entre les essais n° 411 et n° 421 (1987, III).

Pour Addison, l'origine des idées ne réside pas dans l'entendement mais dans la perception visuelle qui emplit l'esprit d'idées en dialogue avec les objets du monde extérieur. Il revient aussi à ces idées appréhendées par la vue de meubler l'imagination ou la fantaisie, les deux termes étant synonymes chez Addison :

> It is this sense which furnishes the imagination with its ideas; so that by the pleasures of the imagination or fancy (which I shall use promiscuously) I here mean such as arise from visible objects, either when we have them actually in our view, or when we call up their ideas into our minds by paintings, statues, descriptions, or any the like occasion. We cannot, indeed, have a single image in the fancy that did not make its first entrance through the sight; but we have the power of retaining, altering and compounding those images, which we have once received, into all the varieties of picture and vision that are most agreeable to the imagination. (Addison 1987, III, 537)

Issues de la perception, ces idées sont le fondement des plaisirs de l'imagination. Ces plaisirs sont primaires lorsque l'objet perçu est actuellement présent ; secondaires (Addison 1987, III, 537) si l'objet est évoqué au moyen de représentations telles que les tableaux, les statues ou les descriptions. L'imagination opère ainsi une sorte d'appropriation de l'objet qu'elle transforme en image, en matériau qu'elle peut retenir grâce à la mémoire, modifier et combiner autrement dans d'autres œuvres d'art ou dans d'autres visions de choses absentes ou fictives (Addison 1987, III 537). Ces plaisirs que procure l'imagination sont donc moins « grossiers » que ceux que fournissent les sens mais moins « raffinés » que ceux de l'entendement (Addison 1987, III, 537), « indeed more preferable, because they are founded on some new knowledge or improvement in the mind of man » (Addison 1987, III, 537).

Addison décrit ainsi les trois sphères de l'esprit humain : à la base, la perception ; plus haut, l'imagination ; au sommet, l'entendement. Du bas vers le haut ou, si l'on veut, du concret vers l'abstrait, il reproduit le parcours de la logique inductive fondée sur l'observation, appelée à rendre désuète la logique déductive de la scholastique. C'est sur l'induction que reposent la nouvelle philosophie et la nouvelle science prônant l'empirisme qu'Addison tient, entre autres, de John Locke à qui il renvoie ses lecteurs pour continuer à approfondir certains aspects de la philosophie naturelle (Addison 1987, III, 547).

Cependant, bien que les plaisirs de l'entendement occupent le premier rang de la hiérarchie, Addison avoue que ceux de l'imagination peuvent égaler les premiers en ce qu'ils sont « as great and as transporting as the other » car « a beautiful prospect delights the soul, as much as a demonstration » (Addison 1987, III, 538). L'imagination a même cet avantage à l'égard de l'entendement que ses objets sont plus évidents et plus faciles à acquérir car il suffit d'ouvrir les yeux pour qu'ils entrent dans l'esprit (Addison 1987, III, 538).

C'est sur les prémices de la plus grande efficacité de l'imagination que le *Spectator* est bâti : Mr Spectator n'est pas enfermé dans son cabinet occupé à penser en systèmes abstraits la complexité du monde. Il pose, au contraire, son regard sur la société et aspire à la transformer au moyen d'essais qu'il envoie jour après jour à la société de son temps pour tenter de l'améliorer. En ce sens, Addison et Steele ont réussi à vulgariser la philosophie. Si Mr Spectator séduit une foule de lecteurs,[12] c'est qu'il n'est pas le philosophe imbu de théories inaccessibles aux non-initiés ; c'est qu'il est lui-même un personnage inventé ; c'est aussi que la pédagogie sociale du *Spectator* loge dans une large mesure dans les récits fictifs intercalés dans ses essais. Ces objets de l'imagination interpellent le lecteur dans une cordialité intelligente capable de produire les effets de ce que plus tard Diderot nommera la « morale en action », dans son *Éloge de Richardson* (Diderot 1959, 29). Richardson, autre passionné d'Addison ! Morale en action, autant dire une morale visant à transformer la conduite du lecteur en contournant l'imposition aprioristique de principes, une morale toute centrée en revanche sur la conviction que suscite chez le récepteur l'adhésion par sympathie. Les préceptes laissent ainsi leur place à une éducation des sens et des émotions édifiée à travers la fiction.

4. La mosaïque de micro-fictions

La *Spectatrice* n'est pas étrangère à cette éducation émotionnelle si tant est, comme le pose la narratrice, « qu'on est de meilleur commerce par le cœur que par l'esprit » (S. 3, 60) lorsqu'on se donne pour but d'« apprendre l'utile et l'agréable » (S. 1, 27). Mais c'est aussi dans un projet poétique que la rédactrice du périodique inscrit sa pédagogie morale tel qu'elle l'affirme dès la Première Semaine : « La suite de mes discours – dit-elle – formera un ouvrage mêlé, souvent sans ordre » (S. 1, 30).

Un retour sur les conditions de production et de réception matérielles du périodique peut aider à saisir la mise en œuvre de ces « pièces rapportées ». On y apprend que quinze jours séparent l'approbation – 14 mars 1728 – et la parution de la première feuille, le lundi 29 mars 1728 (S. 1, 30). Ainsi, les dates qui accompagnent chaque feuille – celles de l'approbation pour le reste des feuilles – indiquent l'ordre chronologique des livraisons tout comme l'intervalle temporel qui sépare leur publication. Il en découle que l'écriture des feuilles

12 Le *Spectator* était tiré à 4.000 exemplaires journaliers, mais on sait que le nombre des lecteurs s'élevait à 60.000.

et leur réception sont pratiquement contemporaines.[13] Ce sont donc ces dates qui affichent, pour le lecteur actuel, qu'il se trouve bien devant un périodique. Cependant, cette signalisation temporelle ne fournit aucun renseignement révélant un éventuel fil narratif reliant les feuilles entre elles.

Ce fil narratif est également introuvable dans le contenu des feuilles. En effet, le recueil n'est pas structuré autour d'un vecteur temporel sur lequel reposerait une systématisation sémiotique d'appels et de rappels. D'un côté, les mécanismes mnémotechniques sont faibles puisque les rares cas d'évocation d'événements ou de personnages ne suffisent pas à l'établissement de rapports anaphoriques cadencés,[14] alors que, d'autre part, les quelques renvois anticipant le contenu de feuilles ultérieures demeurent parfois sans écho.[15] Reste que, du point de vue structurel, l'addition de Semaines forme une série inachevée – puisque la narratrice ne dit jamais qu'elle va interrompre la publication des feuilles – obéissant à une juxtaposition cumulative où la cohérence anaphorique-cataphorique (Hamon 1983, 108) reposant sur des marques stables de temporalisation est pratiquement neutralisée, où aucun signe n'indique, par conséquent, que les quinze Semaines de *La Spectatrice* puissent constituer les quinze chapitres dans lesquels s'organiserait un récit.

En effet, considérée de manière individuelle, chaque feuille s'avère être un segment indépendant. Or ce n'est pas une logique narrative reposant sur l'enchaînement d'événements que révèle la lecture de chacune des Semaines mais un aménagement spatial où déferlent toute sorte d'anecdotes voire même de récits enchâssés, de nature et de longueur variables. Certes, les micro-fictions intercalées ouvrent à l'intérieur du texte un intervalle où l'écoulement temps ne dépasse guère la durée de l'histoire rapportée. Mais, en-deçà et au-delà de ces micro-fictions, le texte se plie à l'espace car ces greffes textuelles s'insèrent dans un discours voué à la démonstration. Ainsi, leur fonction sera celle de creuser le hiatus temporel afin de mieux servir au déroulement du raisonnement qui, avant de devenir une spéculation abstraite, cherche plus bas, plus près des objets

---

13 En l'occurrence, l'approbation de la Quatorzième Semaine porte la date du 5 janvier 1729 (S. 14, 195) et la rédactrice affirme l'avoir écrite le lendemain du premier jour de l'année où a eu lieu l'événement rapporté.

14 Dans la Quatorzième Semaine, la Spectatrice rencontre un parent de son père présomptif qui s'intéresse à sa fortune. Il s'agit de l'un des rares cas où le feedback établit un lien de continuité entre les feuilles (S. 14, 198).

15 En l'occurrence, la Spectatrice ne tient pas sa parole lorsqu'elle annonce, à la Quatorzième Semaine, qu'un « plaidoyer » à propos des « friandises de l'esprit » et du « bonheur idéal » (S. 14, 202) paraîtra dans une autre feuille.

observables, ses preuves à conviction : « Voilà ma manière de philosopher – annonce la Spectatrice –. Je ne touche point à ces quelques questions subtiles ou relevées des philosophes au grand air. Je raisonne par des sujets simples, et si simples qu'ils pourront bien paraître bas à quelques lecteurs » (S. 3, 56). Les idées dont se nourrit l'entendement n'existent donc pas de manière indépendante mais sont nécessairement capturées au moyen de l'observation, ce que confirme la Spectatrice : « les Spectateurs observent les caractères même les plus communs. C'est leur vocation : et là-dessus, ils se font des idées dont ils se repaissent » (S. 10, 144).

L'on sait, après Addison, que ces idées émanant de la perception peuvent également être saisies à travers les plaisirs de l'imagination qui représentent au second degré les objets perçus. Les micro-fictions qui jonchent *La Spectatrice* appartiennent à cette seconde catégorie d'objets que le texte s'offre en multipliant les mécanismes d'insertion. Car ici, ce qui intrigue le regard du lecteur ne réside pas seulement dans l'argument des histoires racontées, mais bien dans la manière dont l'imagination trace des lieux de passage entre le visible et le lisible à travers lesquels transite incessamment l'observation.

Parfois, les récits enchâssés s'enclenchent sur des événements réels comme celui du concert des Tuileries où le spectacle est interrompu par la pluie. Ainsi que le montre A. Lévrier, la feuille qui accueille le récit est approuvée le 28 août, soit trois jours après que le concert réel ait eu lieu (S. 10, 143, note 2). Mais le contexte est souvent évoqué au moyen de l'observation des mœurs. Ainsi lorsque le lecteur découvre la Spectatrice habillée en homme dans une boutique de perruques où une vendeuse lui apprend, à son grand étonnement, que la tête, le siège de la raison, n'est pas de même facture chez les hommes et chez les femmes (S. 12, 169). Quelques particularités culinaires sont également étalées chez un aubergiste, homme franc et loyal, chez qui la narratrice se procure de la nourriture. Et pour faire preuve que « les philosophes ne méprisent point la nature, pas même dans les plus petites choses » (S. 15, 207), la quinzième feuille donne à voir une scène où une femme, qui alimente l'un de ses enfants à la bouillie pendant qu'un deuxième est accroché au sein d'une nourrice, se méfiant des philosophes qui croient mieux savoir que les femmes comment il faut élever les enfants, demande à la Spectatrice de se mêler de ses livres (S. 15, 207–208). Dans tous les cas, la Spectatrice se regarde elle-même agir à l'intérieur de l'histoire rapportée, en s'éloignant par là du rôle assumé par Mr Spectator.

La vue n'est pas le seul sens convoqué par la perception qui circule parfois à travers la seule écoute. C'est le cas de l'épisode où la Spectatrice entend « le bruit d'une voisine qui se fait battre régulièrement tous les jours par son mari, mais dont les invectives ne cessent point pendant que les coups se donnent » (S. 12,

170). La scène, rapportée comme allant de soi, dénonce la fureur de certaines femmes « à qui les hommes sont obligés de céder, parce qu'ils ne veulent pas les tuer, et qu'il faudrait, pour les obliger à céder d'elles-mêmes » (S. 12, 170). Et la Spectatrice d'approuver sans broncher une méthode qui blesse le féminisme actuel.

Or la perception peut tout aussi bien solliciter les sens de la vue et de l'ouïe, en particulier dans certains épisodes où les échanges de paroles entre les personnages sont perçus par le lecteur comme des mico-scènes de théâtre. Ainsi, la Sixième Semaine découvre la Spectatrice dans un café en discussion avec un Mahométan et trois jeunes Français à propos des mœurs en matière d'amour : la narratrice a beau maudire « le sérail où les femmes sont enfermées au service d'un seul homme (S. 6, 94), c'est le sérail que préfèrent tous ses interlocuteurs, sans égard à leur origine. Plus loin, dans la Quatorzième Semaine, la narratrice, attablée avec un cousin normand, engage une conversation, bien arrosée et devant des plats bien garnis, où le convive, philosophe épicurien et « matériel » (S. 14, 201), fait prévaloir ses vues sur la philosophie spirituelle que pratique son interlocutrice. La conversation peut même devenir une sorte de laboratoire où la narratrice met en place une expérience empirique « qui régale sa philosophie » : en promenade avec deux hommes, elle provoque une « *bataille d'esprits* » entre l'un, qui « avait du vin dans la tête », et l'autre dont l'esprit est de ceux qui pensent « singulièrement et souvent faux » (S. 13, 181). À travers ces conversations, le lecteur voit la scène qui livre les denrées philosophiques tout en jouant le jeu synesthésique qui le met à l'écoute des paroles prononcées par les personnages. L'opération synesthésique peut se complexifier davantage, notamment dans certains récits insérés décelant, en profondeur, différents niveaux de prise de parole comme l'histoire de Léonor – une jeune fille impulsive qui tua « un de ses frères pour l'avoir outragée » et dut, pour se cacher, s'enrôler dans l'armée déguisée en homme (S. 4, 68) –, que la rédactrice a entendue et qu'elle rapporte ensuite au lecteur : le lisible y voit en abyme l'écoute du visible.

Visible et lisible s'imbriquent à nouveau dès que le texte fait comparaître d'autres ouvrages. La Troisième Semaine, en l'occurrence, porte le lecteur à croire que le visible à lui seul est sollicité dans l'observation de la basse-cour prouvant des avantages moraux de la conduite des animaux, alors que, en trompe-l'œil, sont lisibles les moralistes que sont Pascal (S. 3, 53) ou La Bruyère (S. 3, 57). L'intertexte peut être autrement productif. Annoncée par une instance extérieure au texte – le correspondant de la Spectatrice à Paris – fait son entrée sur scène, à la Cinquième Semaine, *La méchante femme*, une brochure de Louis de Loquet parue en 1728 chez Jacques Longlois. L'auteur y « blâme vigoureusement les préjugés de l'homme contre les méchantes femmes [...] causés [...] par la lecture d'un tas d'auteurs qui ont écrit en prose et en vers contre ce sexe charmant » (S. 5, 77). Au moyen de la citation, le texte capture dans le volume de Loquet la cohorte de moralisateurs misogynes que forment La Bruyère, Despréaux – autre nom de Boileau – Molière, Sarrazin, entre autres (S. 5, 78) ; et l'intertexte d'étaler devant les yeux du lecteur une écriture lisant le texte de Loquet et finissant par se l'approprier en s'adonnant au plagiat.[16] Ainsi incorporée au régime du texte, *La méchante femme* sera évoquée une deuxième fois dans une boutique où deux femmes se querellent après avoir répondu à la question posée par un bourgeois qui leur demanda « laquelle des deux pourrait aspirer à l'honneur d'être l'héroïne de cet ouvrage » (S. 5, 80).

La Spectatrice n'hésitera pas non plus à transporter son lecteur dans les coulisses de l'imagination : c'est la genèse d'un songe qui transparaît lorsqu'elle confie à son lecteur le secret d'un « commerce de vision » (S. 8, 117) où la lecture devient fournisseuse de l'imagination. Le métadiscours révèle le procédé exigeant une disposition du corps – elle se « couche sans souper afin de rêver beaucoup » (S. 8, 118) – puis de l'esprit – « afin de rêver à certains morts pour qui j'ai de la prédilection, je lis un morceau de leur histoire, ou je médite sur leur sujet » (S. 8, 118). Ainsi imprégnée de ces idées, l'imagination les augmente, les combine et les transforme dans le songe qui transporte la narratrice sur les Champs Élysées, où elle voit des ombres et des choses, de quoi « repaître » et « régaler » (S. 8, 119) son esprit. Se conduisant en Spectatrice silencieuse, elle se laisse guider par une ombre « malicieuse » (S. 8, 122) et « babillarde » (S. 8, 125) dans un parcours où elle croise les ombres de Caron, Sénèque et Montaigne en conversation avec Saint-Évremont sous un arbre. Pénétrée d'une forte émotion, elle demeure interdite devant Montaigne mais aura moins d'égards pour sa « fille d'alliance », Marie de Gournay, dont une digression rappelle que tout en ayant « quelque mérite » elle était « un peu folle » (S. 8, 124). La Spectatrice s'incline devant Montaigne tandis qu'elle refuse sa connivence à la seule femme auteur citée dans le recueil – celle qui conçut avant elle l'*Égalité des hommes et des femmes* (1622).

Un dernier exemple montre le cheminement de la perception vers l'entendement en passant par l'imagination. À la Neuvième Semaine, la Spectatrice perçoit dans la rue un « pauvre diable [...] mené en prison suivi de son créancier ainsi qu'un arracheur de dents. Deux fois elle détourne son regard pour ne pas à avoir à contempler la douleur des deux personnages et

16 Voir les notes de la Cinquième Semaine où Alexis Lévrier décortique les reprises de la brochure de Loquet.

s'enfuit ne comprenant pas « cette maligne curiosité de voir jusqu'au bout la peine d'un homme qui ne vous a jamais fait de mal » (S. 9, 132). Les idées qui découlent de la perception sont nuancées dans une histoire qu'elle rapporte elle-même où il est question d'un jeune homme se refusant à hériter de la charge de magistrat occupée par son père. S'avisant que son fils se laissait aller à la compassion devant les condamnés, le père le soumet à une éducation des sens pour l'aider à « surmonter sa répugnance » (S. 9, 133). « Il faut commencer par vous essayer » (S. 9, 133), lui dit-il en laissant à découvert la dimension empirique son expérience. Par induction, le fils découvrira que deux sortes de « voir » entrent en collision devant les condamnés : le premier cède à la pitié ; le second exige une véritable analyse des signes révélant les émotions obscures des malfaiteurs. La fiction dévoile de la sorte une herméneutique des émotions à fondement sémiotique modifiant la conduite du fils qui finit par « [s'] accoutume[r] à faire du mal à ceux qui font le mal, et pour en empêcher un plus grand » (S. 9, 136). Au sortir de la narration, c'est aussi le raisonnement de la narratrice qui s'est transformé : « L'habitude contractée par raison, ou par éducation, disculpe, et le juge et celui qui par ses ordres fait un mal nécessaire. Rien ne disculpe celui qui voit faire ce mal, sans autre raison que sa curiosité » (S. 9, 136), en conclut-elle. Le jugement moral de la narratrice boucle un parcours où l'empirisme a donné ses fruits.

L'ensemble des micro-récits enchâssés forment un socle sur lequel devra s'ancrer la pédagogie moralisante de *La Spectatrice*. La mosaïque de couches textuelles enchevêtrées nourrit l'entendement par le biais de l'imagination afin que le récepteur morde à l'appât et n'abandonne pas la lecture à la suivante remise du périodique.

5. La quête du lecteur

Aujourd'hui, les lecteurs de *La Spectatrice* ont sous les yeux un objet clos ayant perdu en chemin la matérialité des feuilles volantes : le recueil forme bien un livre pouvant être parcouru d'un trait au fil de ses quinze Semaines. En absence de logique narrative, une seconde dimension du projet poétique esquissé dans la Première Semaine pourrait donner à voir une autre sorte de fil conducteur reliant les feuilles entre elles : « La suite de mes discours formera [...] – affirme la Spectatrice – un ouvrage de pièces rapportées, qui [...] ne manqueront point à exciter tour à tour l'approbation et la critique des lecteurs » (S. 1, 30). En effet, si concaténation il y a entre les quinze Semaines, celle-ci ne résidera pas dans le déroulement d'une histoire, mais dans l'interpellation qu'incessamment la Spectatrice adresse à son lecteur.

De manière récurrente l'énonciation du texte est en proie au lecteur, instance servant à la fois à dépasser la contingence de la rédactrice ainsi qu'à produire le métadiscours qui juge et le texte et les manières de son auteur. Il arrive ainsi à la Spectatrice d'accepter que le lecteur guide ses pas pour remédier à certains défauts dans l'organisation de sa pensée (S. 1, 23) ou bien pour redresser sa prose si d'aventure il se moque d'elle (S. 1, 23).[17] Mais c'est le lecteur réel qui est visé au premier chef, plus précisément un public masculin à qui elle « ne fera pas sa cour pour obtenir des suffrages » (S. 1, 22). Et, forte d'un désir d'impartialité, elle annonce qu'elle n'aura point d'indulgence ni pour son sexe ni pour elle-même (S. 1, 22). Cependant, l'incertitude quant à la réception plane sur le recueil. En désespoir de cause, si son ouvrage ne plaît pas aux hommes, elle pourrait se contenter de la lecture des femmes voire même se passer de tout lecteur (S. 2, 42).

Malgré l'impérieux besoin d'attirer son destinataire sur la scène de l'écriture, la narratrice se risque sans cesse à briser les seuils d'entente avec lui et si, à l'instar de Mr. Spectator, elle le vise émotionnellement, elle ne cherchera pas pour autant à le séduire. Son ton véhément semble plutôt vouloir le secouer afin de le faire réagir à son texte :

> [...] pour me faire dire mes vérités – insiste la Spectatrice –, j'agacerai mes lecteurs : je les humilierai par la vue de certaines infirmités assez générales [...]. Je leur ferai voir leur moi, qu'ils ne regardent que du beau côté, si faux, si pauvre, si sot, si misérable, qu'ils m'en voudront assurément du mal, qu'ils chercheront à démêler mon caractère dans mon babil, et qu'ils relèveront mes sottises à leur tour. (S. 2, 42)

L'énonciation pragmatise la réception, or le lecteur, attendu à tous les niveaux du texte, demeure hypothétique. Il s'inscrit souvent en interlocuteur fictif dont les répliques sont imaginées par la rédactrice : « Courage, madame la Spectatrice – lui lance-t-il –, vous faites bien la cour à vos lecteurs, [...] vous trouverez le secret de réduire les centaines en centième » (S. 2, 42). Même procédure dans la scène où, déguisée en homme, elle est seule à condamner le sérail et conçoit un « lecteur chicaneur » lui rappelant que son déguisement ne suffit pas à savoir ce qu'elle penserait si elle était vraiment un homme (S. 6, 95). Pour renforcer son argument, elle évoquera l'existence d'un Sénat de femmes à l'époque de Néron dans une réflexion censurée par un sénateur imaginaire qui « se moquer[ait] de sa spéculation » (S. 6, 98).

17 « Si quelqu'un se moque de moi à bonnes enseignes – ajoute dans la Deuxième Semaine la Spectatrice –, il m'instruira ; j'en profiterai et peut-être contre mon intention » (S. 2, 42).

Le lecteur apparaît également comme personnage des récits enchâssés. La rédactrice l'aperçoit, par exemple, dans une séance de lecture à haute voix de l'une ses feuilles.[18] Elle y entend les contestations des auditeurs : « cette feuille est pleine de sophismes », dit l'un ; « les raisonnements étaient purement sceptiques », affirme l'autre (S. 15, 210). Mais c'est dans une conversation de café à propos de *La Spectatrice* que les égarements de sa conduite de Spectatrice sont mis en évidence : « Je m'attendais – dit le lecteur – à trouver dans ce petit ouvrage des aventures réjouissantes et je n'y vois que des réflexions : cette femme n'est que philosophe, un peu égayée à la vérité ; mais cela n'est pas assez divertissant » (S. 4, 65). Sensibles aux conventions du genre spectatorial, les lecteurs se plaignent des écarts et réclament leur dû. La Spectatrice, de son côté, décidée à se corriger, promet « quelques aventures quand il s'en présentera », (S. 4, 65), tout en se montrant prête à renoncer à son public.

Le lecteur rouspète ; la Spectatrice provoque. Les ripostes se donnant le relais d'une Semaine à l'autre créent une tension croissante qui agence une fictionnalisation de la lecture.

Car la Spectatrice aspire à une autre sorte de lecteur dont le profil est esquissé à la Onzième Semaine. Pendant une nuit d'insomnie, elle entame l'observation de son esprit, littéralement détaché de son corps, où elle voit agir les facultés de son âme (S. 11, 157). Le lecteur idéal dont elle rêve serait sensible à ce genre de spéculations auxquelles s'adonnerait également son esprit. D'une part, Montaigne s'esquisse comme cet alter ego de la Spectatrice, en ce sens où l'objet de celui qui « étudiait l'homme en s'étudiant lui-même » (S. 2, 39) est aussi le sien. Or, ainsi que le précise Amélie Junqua, Montaigne est un « auteur solitaire presque enfermé dans son propre discours » dont Mr Spectator rejetait le « monologue erratique » (Junqua 2013, 272). Réglé sur la tradition philosophique française et à distance d'Addison, le solipsisme spéculatif dans lequel s'engage parfois la Spectatrice s'appuie, d'autre part, sur la méthode cartésienne. Certes, la Spectatrice encourage son lecteur à se fier à sa vision (S. 4, 65), mais elle ne fait pas de même en ce qui concerne son jugement : « ne jugez point par votre seul jugement – dit-elle –. Doutez » (S. 4, 65), dit-elle. Ainsi que l'a vu Claire Boulard-Jouslin, la supériorité de la Spectatrice réside précisément dans sa « capacité à douter » en ce sens où « pour parvenir à l'autorité il lui faut douter de sa propre autorité, c'est-à-dire douter de sa capacité à raisonner correctement » (Boulard-Jouslin 2013, 288). Ce faisant, elle s'oppose, poursuit Boulard-Jouslin, au *Spectator* en ce que « l'assurance masculine d'une vision parfaite que le *Spectator*

18 Il s'agirait, d'après Alexis Lévrier, de la septième feuille (2013, 210, note 7).

revendiquait comme facteur d'autorité devient ainsi un préjugé qui fait obstacle à la bonne connaissance du monde » (2013, 289).

Dans *La Spectatrice*, la mise en cause de la figure auctoriale féminine est autrement préjugée par un modèle social hiérarchique et étanche où priment les privilèges : ceux des aristocrates qui regardent le bourgeois comme « une espèce de subalterne » (S. 6, 97) ; ceux des savants, « autre espèce de Grands » (S. 2, 46), se comportant en « monarque[s] de la République des Lettres » (S. 2, 47) à l'égard des ignorants ; ceux, enfin, de certains esprits qui considèrent les femmes « des êtres moins pensants, moins parfaits que les hommes » (S. 6, 97). C'est au prix du renversement de l'ordre établi qu'un paysan pourrait devenir gouverneur de la Insula Barataria, comme Sancho Panza dans le *Quixotte* (S. 6, 99) ; qu'une femme se verrait gouverner un État (S. 6, 97) ; qu'une Spectatrice, déshonorée par son origine et par son état, saurait opérer une sorte de rachat social en se faisant reconnaître comme auteur-philosophe – ajoutons, par ses pairs masculins.

Or ce n'est pas d'une minorité de lecteurs-auteurs « qui aiment à voir si un auteur pense comme eux » (S. 11, 159) que viendrait ce rachat. Les pouvoirs factuels se laissent enfin entendre : le « résident de Paris », une sorte de lecteur correcteur, se fait l'écho des critiques du libraire rappelant à la narratrice « qu'on ne lisait plus comme jadis » et « qu'on ne trouvait pas le mot pour rire dans [s]es raisonnements ; que cela faisait bâiller ; que de pareils ouvrages le mettraient sur le chemin de l'hôpital ; et qu'il [lui] conseillait cordialement de, etc. » (S. 11 : 162). La Spectatrice doit donc rectifier son penchant en subsumant dans les points de suspension une « spéculation élevée » la menant loin du « goût de la plupart des lecteurs » (S. 11, 161) qu'elle souhaite pourtant combler. C'est bien le nombre de lecteurs qui décident de la continuité du périodique ainsi que de son succès. Et si comme la Spectatrice le pense, « il n'est point d'auteur sans ouvrage » (S. 11, 163), il n'est pas moins vrai que seul le lecteur qui adresse son avis dans une lettre à « *Madame la Spectatrice* » la couronne comme « femme auteur » (S. 11, 163).

En fin de parcours, le lecteur est souverain…
… Nulle trace des lectrices.

Références bibliographiques

ANONYME : *Recueil de toutes les feuilles de la Spectatrice qui ont paru et de celles qui n'ont point paru*. Paris : Pissot 1730.

ADDISON, Joseph/Richard Steele: *The Spectator*. Éd. Donald F. Bond. Oxford: Clarendon Press 1987, 5 vols.

BOULARD-JOUSLIN, Claire : « De l'Hermaphrodite à la coquette : histoire des *Spectatrices* française et anglaise au XVIIIe siècle ». In : *La Spectatrice*. Éd. Alexis Lévrier. Reims : EPURE 2013, 283–310.

BRÉTÉCHÉ, Marion : « Faire profession de témoignage : les pratiques d'écriture d'Anne-Marguerite Dunoyer (1707–1719) ». *Épistémè* : *Les femmes témoins de l'histoire*, *Études* 19 (2011), 66–85. <https://journals.openedition.org/episteme/629>.

BRÉTÉCHÉ, Marion : « Marie-Jeanne L'Héritier, Anne-Marguerite Dunoyer et La Spectatrice : généalogie d'une prise de parole féminine dans la presse francophone (France-Provinces-Unies, 1703–1729) ». In : *La Spectatrice*. Éd. Alexis Lévrier. Reims : EPURE 2013, 247–263.

DESFONTAINES, Pierre-François Guyot, abbé, et al. : *Le Pour et le contre. Ouvrage périodique d'un goût nouveau*. Vol. 2. Paris : Didot 1733, 337–360.

DIDEROT, Denis : « Éloge de Richardson ». In : *Diderot. Œuvres esthétiques*. Éd. Paul Vernière. Paris : Garnier 1959, 29–48.

Mercure de France. Paris : Cavelier, Veuve Pissot et Jean de Nully, juin 1728, vol. 1, 1204–1208.

ERTLER, Klaus-Dieter : « Le système narratif des 'spectateurs' et leur réception en Espagne : quelques vecteurs discursifs dans le *Pensador* de José Clavijo y Fajardo ». *El Argonauta español* : *Pratiques journalistiques aux premiers temps de la presse espagnole (XVIIIe–début du XIXe siècle)* 11 (2014). <https://journals.openedition.org/argonauta/ 2002>.

HAMON, Philippe : *Le Personnel du roman. Le système des personnages dans* Les Rougont-Macquart *d'Émile Zola*. Genève : Droz 1983.

JUNQUA, Amélie : « Du *Spectator* à *La Spectatrice* : les fascinants dédoublements du modèle spectatorial ». In : *La Spectatrice*. Éd. Alexis Lévrier. Reims : EPURE 2013, 265–281.

LÉVRIER, Alexis : *Les Journaux de Marivaux et le monde des « spectateurs »*. Paris : Presses de l'Université Paris-Sorbonne 2007.

LÉVRIER, Alexis (éd.) : *La Spectatrice*. Reims : EPURE 2013.

MOUREAU, François : *La Plume et le plomb. Espaces de l'imprimé et du manuscrit au siècle des Lumières*. Paris : Presses de l'Université de Paris-Sorbonne 2006.

REVON-RIVIÈRE, Élise : « De la Spectatrice à Javotte : enquête sur d'improbables promeneuses (avec quelques détours par Jean-Jacques Rousseau) ». In : *La Spectatrice*. Alexis Lévrier (ed.). Reims : EPURE 2013, 311–331.

SGARD, Jean : *Dictionnaire des journaux 1600–1789*. <http://c18.net/dp/>.

Claire Boulard-Jouslin

(University Paris 3–Sorbonne Nouvelle)

Joseph Addison in Lausanne: Reading Addison's works at the Société du Comte de la Lippe

In 1737, Simon Auguste de la Lippe (1727–1782), the German protestant Count of Lippe-Detmold, was sent to Lausanne, where he stayed until 1747. Lausanne was then a small French-speaking town in the canton of Vaud where academies and salons attracted foreigners on the Grand Tour. Simon Auguste de la Lippe went there to be educated and to learn how to manage the state of Lippe-Detmold, which he had inherited upon his father's death in 1734. He was instructed by a governor, Charles de la Pottrie, and a Calvinist divine, Daniel Pavillard, who was to become Edward Gibbon's teacher when Gibbon later resided in Switzerland (François Rosset 2013, 3).

When the young Count was 15, his governor decided to organise weekly meetings at the Count's house in Lausanne, in order to complete his training as a future head of state. Every Saturday between 1742 and 1747, Simon Auguste de la Lippe attended two-hour conferences held by an assembly of learned men who gave themselves the name of the Société du Comte de la Lippe. The debates of these 80 sessions were recorded in 2 volumes by Daniel Pavillard, who became the amanuensis of the small society.

Like many learned societies and clubs, the Société du Comte de la Lippe had rules: the Société could not have more than 12 members (except when there were visiting guests)—women were excluded, and it had a quorum of 6. The regular members were all part of Lausanne's intellectual elite. Among them were George Polier de Bottens, professor of Greek and Hebrew and rector of Lausanne's Academy, Loys de Cheseaux, an academician and a well-known astronomer (Huguenin 2013, 10), and Gabriel Seigneux de Correvon, a member of several foreign academies (notably that of Marseilles) and the future translator of Joseph Addison's *Evidence of Christian Religion* (*De la Religion Chrétienne*, 2 vols., 1757).

Each session was framed by the following ritual: a week in advance the Count would choose a topic for discussion or would select an extract from a book. On the following Saturday, after drinking coffee, one member would develop the points or would read an extract aloud to the assembly; each member would then draw lots to know who was to start the discussion. Each would then comment upon the text or the chosen topic in turn. In the next conference, the young Count would sum up both the text and the debates it had generated, so as to show what conclusions and instruction he had derived from the lectures. Finally, they would all listen to a new text or a new topic, on which they would again begin to comment.

The aim of these regular gatherings was clearly didactic, as revealed by the general choice of topics:

> Toutes les questions au choix de Monsieur le Comte, ne rouleront que sur quelque point de Religion, de Morale, de politique, de Droit naturel & civil, d'Histoire & de Litterature, qu'il lui importera de connoitre, pour remplir les différens devoirs auxquels il est apellé comme homme, comme Chrêtien & comme Souverain. Pour diversifier les entretiens, l'on poura de tems en tems, si l'on veut de 15 en 15 jours faire quelque lecture d'ouvrages qui tendent au même but.[1]

Comments on books were, therefore, slightly less frequent than lectures (36 out of the 80 sessions were devoted to them). As they were faithfully recorded in the Societé's books by Pavillard, the minutes constitute "a manual of princely education" (Huguenin, 2013, 11), which the Count later used to rule his own conduct and also to bring up his own son.

Among the texts studied, no fewer than nine conferences (out of thirty-six focusing on texts) were devoted to the examination of Steele's and Addison's periodicals. Indeed, eight *Spectator* essays were examined during seven meetings, while two *Guardian* essays were the subject of two other conferences. This is intriguing for several reasons.

Firstly, it suggests that the *Spectator* attracted the attention of the assembly far more than any other periodical. It came well before any other book dealing with social issues and before any other English book.[2] For instance, Mandeville's *Fable of the Bees* (1714) and *Essay on Charity and Charity Schools* (1723) were

---

1 Société du Comte de la Lippe, Assemblée 1, in *Extrait des conférences de la Société de Monsieur le comte de la Lippe*, Lausanne, 17 octobre 1742, vol. 1, 1–5 (3). Selon la transcription établie par Lumières. Lausanne (Université de Lausanne). URL: <http://lumieres.unil.ch/fiches/trans/390/>. All quotes from the records of the Société du Comte de la Lippe are taken from this web site. They will be signaled SCL, with the Assemblée number, the date of the meeting, the volume record and with the URL.

2 Among the English books studied in translation were Gordon's *Lettre sur le régicide*, Dr. Stephens's *La Religion des Dames*, and Ramsay's *Discourse sur la Franc maçonnerie*.

the topic of one conference each[3]; Alexander Pope's "To a Lady, On the *Caracters of Women*" was studied in one conference as well.[4] One might conclude that the variety of topics in the two periodicals may explain this interest in them. Yet, the assembly read only one essay from the *Bibliothèque britannique*, another periodical that could have provided them with many different subjects for deliberation.

Secondly, the recurrent study of Steele's and Addison's periodicals is all the more intriguing as the general tone of the debates and of the other books examined was definitely learned and serious. Six meetings were devoted to pondering the German philosopher Johan Schmauss's political conferences on natural law and human reason, another four were devoted to Abbé de Saint Pierre's *Ouvrages de morale et de politique* (1733–1740), and the Société also focused, for instance, on Abbé Duguet's *L'Institution d'un prince* (1739), Charles Rollin's *Traité des Études*, and Frederick II's *l'Anti-Machiavel*, published by Voltaire in 1740. Incidentally, all these authors dealt with the nature of political rule and its links with education and knowledge. And they have in common that they offer reformed conceptions of absolute monarchy. While the didactic purposes of the *Spectator* and *Guardian* may have been in line with the pedagogic aim of the Société, their other purpose, namely to entertain readers with light and humorous essays, seems to jar with such texts. How did the essays then fit in the whole project of educating a young prince in an enlightened way?

The aim of this chapter is to study the records of the nine meetings during which the Société du Comte de la Lippe read the two journals and to examine what material they selected in the two periodicals. I will analyse how the selection was used and endeavour to determine what it reveals about the way the journals were perceived. Finally, I will examine what these records tell us about Joseph Addison's reputation in Switzerland.

The selection

All the foreign texts studied by the Société were translated into French. The members, therefore, discussed the French translations of the *Spectator* and of the *Guardian*, namely *Le Spectateur ou le Socrate moderne* (6 vols., 1714–1726) and Van Effen's 1727 translation: *Le Mentor moderne*. There is one obvious explanation for this: although many of the Société's members read English, Auguste

3 Respectively SCL 36, 18 Jan. 1744, vol. 2, 41–54 <http://lumieres.unil.ch/fiches/trans/472/ and SCL 39, 08 Feb. 1744, vol. 2, 75–89. <http://lumieres.unil.ch/ fiches/trans/ 481/>.

4 SCL 11, 26 Jan. 1743, vol. 1, 131–135. <http://lumieres.unil.ch/fiches/trans/502/>.

Simon de la Lippe did not and did not learn it either. This means that, from the outset, neither the *Spectator* nor the *Guardian* were seen as literary masterpieces to be studied for their prose style.

Yet, when recording the lectures, Pavillard added comments of his own in the margins indicating that these works in French were very popular readings ("fort commun (s)").[5] They were in fact so well-known in Switzerland that he thought it a waste of time to report their content extensively: "Comme ce Livre (le *Mentor*) est aussi connu que le *Spectateur* je n'en ferai pas un Extrait étendu".[6] In 1744, the two periodicals seemed therefore to be self-selecting works that members of the elite were expected to have read. The records also reveal that, even if the *Spectateur* was more popular than the *Mentor*, the *Mentor* was somehow perceived on the continent as a sort of sequel to the *Spectateur*. So what did the members of the société choose in those two periodicals that was of interest to them?

Obviously, the Société read neither the *Spectateur* nor the *Mentor* to enlighten the prince with philosophy. It only examined one such essay of the *Spectateur*, one that dealt with the question of "the nature of the soul when dreaming" ("la nature de l'âme à l'occasion des rêves").[7] It is also to be noted that, when the members of the Société debated about imagination, they alluded to Locke's theories and ignored Joseph Addison's famous series on the pleasures of the imagination. The only significant article dealing with political philosophy was an essay on justice. Addison stated that justice was the highest divine virtue that a ruler should endeavour to possess. He eulogised the clause of the 1701 Act of Settlement, which provided that judges should be paid salaries, and which prevented justices from being dismissed unless by due course of law. Finally, he celebrated the integrity of justices who were able to render judgment without passion and without consideration of their interests. They, he stated, were the foundation of the kingdom's prosperity and stability.[8]

Although in the English context of 1713, this essay was written to defend the anti-High Church policy of some Whig judges and was therefore a highly partisan piece,[9] it defended the enlightened principle of the independence of justice.

---

5 SCL 50, 25 Apr. 1744, vol. 2, 204–10. <http://lumieres.unil.ch/fiches/trans/547/>.

6 SCL 60, 18 Jul. 1744, vol. 2, 291–295. http://lumieres.unil.ch/fiches/trans/512/>. ("Since this book is as well-known as the *Spectator*, I will not report its content").

7 SCL 54, 23 May 1744, vol. 2, 233–240. <http://lumieres.unil.ch/fiches/trans/496/>. It was *Spectator* 487 translated as discourse 26 from the *Spectateur* vol. 4, 149.

8 *Mentor Moderne*, vol. 4, discours 81, 598–599.

9 See John Calhoun Stephens's note on *Guardian* 99, 689.

This lesson, it seems, was well understood by Simon Auguste de la Lippe who accurately summed up the essay thus:

> *Le Mentor* dans le Discours que vous lutes, il y a huit jours parle de la Justice, et après avoir montré que la Justice de Dieu est sa Vertu par excellence, il dit que la Justice qui approche de cette Perfection autant que la foiblesse humaine le permet, est la plus grande qualité de l'Homme, celle qui l'approche le plus de la Divinité; Qu'un Souverain qui aime la Justice, est la plus noble image du Créateur, que par l'exactitude avec laquelle il punit les coupables, il déracine le crime, et détourne de dessus une Nation, les jugemens de Dieu.
> Dès qu'une Nation ne respecte plus la Justice, dès qu'elle tache d'intimider ceux qui la doivent exercer, dès que les Juges dans leurs décisions sont sensibles à d'autres motifs qu'à ceux de la Justice; qu'ils s'écartent des Loix; on peut dire que cette Nation est près de sa ruine. Rien ne doit faire plus de plaisir que de voir sur le trone un homme intègre, qui résiste à la haine, aux sollicitations, à la pitié même, quand il s'agit de juger, il s'attire le respect et la confiance de tous ceux qui lui sont soumis.[10]

And he added:

> Vous m'avez montré, Monsieur D'Apples, que la Puissance, la Sagesse et les Connoissances sont le fondement d'une bonne et exacte Justice. Les Princes donc qui sont appellés à exercer la Justice doivent s'appliquer avec soin à aquerir toutes les connoissances qui leur sont nécessaires.

On the whole, it was morality rather than philosophy that interested the Société. To incite the young prince to gain sound moral principles seems to have been the common point between all the periodical essays selected by the Société. As one may guess, the selection shunned the lighter moral essays castigating fashions or the peccadillos of daily life which turned the periodicals into guides of etiquette. Unlike the *Journal Helvétique*, which quoted long extracts from the *Spectateur* condemning political patching or pernicious readings, the Société du Comte de la Lippe concentrated on subjects liable to furnish rules of conduct[11] for the prince.

The main aim was to show Simon Auguste de la Lippe that, in order to be a good ruler, a prince had to be guided by strict religious principles that guaranteed his private virtues, and triggered his sense of work, justice, charity and

10 SCL 57, 13 Jun. 1744, vol. 2, 270–271. <http://lumieres.unil.ch/fiches/trans/499>.

11 In Assemblée 57, Professor Polier explicitly described the journals as books on good conduct: "Monsieur De Cheseaux vous a lu un Discours de sa façon sur l'art d'être toujours content, et Mr Pavilliard un autre du *Spectateur Anglois* sur la bonne Humeur considérée comme un Devoir qui en est l'effet. Chacun de ses Discours vous a proposé des régles excellentes de conduite", 272.

good-humour. The Count was, therefore, invited to ponder over cheerfulness, over being good-natured and over the complaisance of great men.[12] The stress was also put on the relationship a ruler might entertain with God, a theme that was central to the Société, since the topics of the first conferences centred on the profit one may derive from religious practice ('*des avantages de la religion*' (SCL 2); '*des avantages de la religion pour un prince*' (SCL 4); *des avantages de la religion pour la société*' (SCL 5). Pondering over religion was encouraged again with the study of the famous vision of Mirza on human frailty.[13] Another essay titled the "effets de la coutume à l'égard de la vertu et du vice" was one of the famous Saturday 'sermons' of the *Spectator.*[14] In this essay, Mr. Spectator encouraged readers to save money for charitable action and presented people who were models of charitable behaviour. After describing the character of Eugenius, a benevolent lay man, he quoted an extract from the book of Job in which Job agrees that a lack of charity deserves divine punishment. In so doing, the essay not only presents Job as another model to follow, but it also recalls the central role of the Bible in guiding readers in their private behaviour. So in this case, the essay was selected both because it focused on an essential point of morality—how a ruler should take care of the poorest—and because it emphasized the Protestant centrality of the Bible.

It seems, therefore, that the *Spectateur* and the *Mentor* were chosen by the Société because they backed a moderately enlightened view of what an absolute ruler should be, namely a man who was willing to exercise power in order to promote the welfare of his people, under the supreme control of natural religion, whose main function was to check the sovereign's actions. Such views echoed those of l'Abbé Duguet and l'Abbé St Pierre, two authors whose conception of the power of a prince were considered provoking enough for their authors to be persecuted in France (Dornier 2011; Bois 2017).

But as the *Spectator* and *Guardian* were not primarily written for the education of princes, their maxims being rather intended for commoners and middle-class

12 The essay on the complaisance of noblemen is *Guardian* 162, translated as *Mentor Moderne* 134 vol. 4, 902 (SCL 60); that on Justice is *Guardian* 99, translated as *Mentor Moderne* 81 (SCL 57). They also examined one essay on cheerfulness (*Spectator* 381, *Spectateur* 22, vol. 4; SCL 50), two essays on good nature (*Spectators* 169 and 177, *Spectateur* 42 and 48, SCL 63) and one on the usefulness of travel. (*Spectator* 364, *Spectateur* 14, vol. 4; SCL 53).

13 SCL 59, 11 Jul 1744, vol. 2, 287–291. <http://lumieres.unil.ch/fiches/trans/511/>.

14 SCL 51, 02 May 1744, vol. 2, 210–216. <http://lumieres.unil.ch/fiches/trans/548/>; *Spectator* 447; *Spectateur* 72, vol. 4.

people, one may wonder whether this selection was well suited to the project of morally educating a sovereign.

Inserting the selection into a princely pedagogical project

Given the club-like arrangements, it is reasonable that the two periodicals were selected for an educational project that was based on sociability and conversation. In spite of this, the members of the Société found themselves adapting their comments in an effort to make them relevant to their aristocratic pupil. When the Société discussed the *Spectateur* essay on 'the usefulness of bodily exercise for pleasure but also for work', they highlighted the *Spectateur*'s ideas that moderate physical exercise was valuable to people from all social ranks. Addison's original anti-Tory satire of Sir Roger de Coverley's passion for hunting, which he mockingly described as useful work, was thus turned into a piece of advice advocating princely moderation and a plea against aristocratic idleness. The Baron de Caussade somewhat flatly explained Addison's satire in the following manner:

> que le travail est utile pour la santé; mais il est difficile que les jeunes Gens n'en abusent; c'est ainsi que les exercices de la Paume, de la Chasse entrainent, pour l'ordinaire ceux qui s'y attachent. J'ai ouï dire, a-t-il ajouté, qu'il y a des Princes qui passent leur vie dans les bois; ce n'est plus alors un amusement, ni une récréation utile, et agréable; ils y aquiérent de la férocité, et le temps qu'ils y emploient est en partie un tems qu'ils dérobent aux affaires. Il faut donc accoutumer les Grands à ne s'y pas donner avec trop de passion, mais à mêler l'exercice du corps avec celui de l'esprit, parce que l'exercice du corps poussé trop loin, quelquefois détruit la santé, et fait même perdre la vie quelquefois.[15]

Le Boursier Seigneux sternly recalled the duties of the monarch pointing out the *Spectator*'s point of view that even the nobility who had leisure had a duty to work:

> Personne au contraire n'y est autant obligé que les Princes. L'homme a été condanné au travail dès le commencement du monde, […] il faut donc que chacun en ait sa portion. Les Princes et les Monarques même. C'est donc une idée fausse que celle de ceux qui ne font consister leur grandeur qu'à n'être obligés à aucun travail.[16]

Seigneux, thus, repeated views that had been previously stressed by the assembly when reading Abbé Duguet's *Institution d'un prince* (1739)[17]: a prince should

15 SCL 56, 6 Jun. 1744, vol. 2, 260–265. <http://lumieres.unil.ch/fiches/trans/498/>.

16 *Ibid.* Seigneux comments on the following passage from the *Spectateur*: "ceux qui ne sont pas obligés de travailler, par l'état où leur naissance les a mis, seroient plus malheureux que les autres hommes s'ils ne s'appliquoient au travail volontaire, qui porte le nom d'exercice" (Discours 20, vol. 2, 125).

17 SCL 17, 16 March 1743, vol. 1, 186–195. <http://lumieres.unil.ch/fiches/trans/532/>.

consider wisdom as a moral virtue superior to strength and sovereigns have duties towards their people rather than rights. He also pointed out the convergence of ideas between the *Spectateur* and Abbé Duguet's book, which renewed the definition of the ideal prince (Alimento, 2003; Chopelin-Blanc, 2011).

Commenting on this essay, Professor d'Apples also deflected the irony of M. *Spectateur*'s ludicrous advice to ring silent bells so as to give recreation to the body and divert the soul. He invited his illustrious pupil to indulge in activities more useful to the community and more worthy of a prince:

> Je crois que les exercices dont le Spectateur parle, ne sont pris pour exemple que d'une manière ironique. Je suis au reste dans l'idée que les Princes peuvent prendre des exercices de plaisir, mais modérément, tels la chasse etc. […] Les Gens d'étude doivent avoir de l'exercice; mais ils ne doivent pas recourir pour cela à des Cloches, ou à d'autres exercices aussi inutiles; ils pourroient aller voir les malades, surtout ceux qui seroient dans des lieux éloignés; s'attacher à la connoissance des plantes, dans tout cela, ils exerceroient leur corps par la promenade et leur esprit par la réflexion.[18]

In the next meeting, the Count summed up the *Spectateur*'s arguments:

> Le Discours du *Spectateur* que vous lutes en dernier lieu traite de l'utilité de l'exercice corporel […] L'Auteur ne regarde pas seulement l'exercice comme utile; mais il l'envisage de plus comme un Devoir, et il pense que l'Homme est obligé d'entretenir son Corps en Santé par le travail, comme il est obligé de perfectionner son Ame par l'étude et la méditation.[19]

He then reported the various comments of the assembly, expressing thus the quintessential points he as a prince should remember about bodily exercise:

> Vous m'avez dit Monsieur le Boursier que c'étoit avoir une idée bien fausse de la Grandeur que de croire qu'elle dispense du travail; Personne au contraire n'y est autant obligé que les Princes. Le travail a été imposé à tous les hommes dès le commencement du Monde, et c'est avec beaucoup de raison que le *Spectateur* tourne en ridicule ceux qui ne s'occupent que de jeu, de chasse ou de plaisirs. […] Les Princes, au lieu des exercices fatigans auxquels ils s'attachent, devroient voiager dans leurs Provinces, pour aprendre à connoitre leurs Sujets ce seroit là un exercice dont ils retireroient bien de la Satisfaction. C'est ce que vous m'avez dit sur ce sujet Monsieur D'Apples.[20]

Such conclusions show that the *Spectateur* could easily be adapted to fit the pedagogical aim of the assembly and was, therefore, considered by this learned

---

18 *Ibid.*
19 SCL 57, 13 June 1744, vol. 2, 265–270. <http://lumieres.unil.ch/fiches/trans/499/>.
20 *Ibid.*

assembly as a pedagogical authority, alongside such an educational expert as Charles Rollin, who was also studied by the Société.

Moreover, the members of the Société found the two journals useful pedagogical tools paradoxically because they were occasionally flawed. They could, therefore, serve as warnings while helping train the young Count to exercise his critical faculties. For instance, when they discussed the essay on justice published by the *Mentor moderne*, some members pointed out the gaps in the periodical's reasoning:

> Voici les réflexions de Monsieur le Professeur D'Apples:
> L'Auteur auroit pu ajouter que la Justice est fondée en Dieu sur la Sagesse, et sur une connoissance exacte du prix et de la valeur de chaque objet. En appliquant ces idées aux Princes, aux Souverains & aux Magistrats, il auroit du montrer l'obligation ou ils sont d'aquerir des connoissances pour être en état de prononcer sur les différens cas ou ils sont appelés à le faire. La connoissance; l'Autorité et la Sagesse sont le fondement d'une bonne Justice. [...] L'Auteur pour rendre son Discours plus intéressant auroit du parler de la Justice des Particuliers. Tous les jours des Magistrats ne sont pas apellés à rendre la Justice, mais les Particuliers le sont continuellement. S'ils connoissent donc la Justice, qu'ils soient désintéressés, ils se conduiront les uns à l'égard des autres avec droiture, et ils se rendront aisément Justice.[21]

Significantly, the members of the société also criticized the didactic method used by the *Spectateur*. Addison claimed that the most efficient method to moralise an audience was to mix wit and morality so as to instruct the reader under cover of entertainment: "I shall endeavour to enliven morality with wit and temper wit with morality",[22] he famously wrote in *Spectator* 10. Entertainment took the shape of fiction and portraits that were often allegorical. Some members of this Calvinist Société du Comte de la Lippe seemed to condemn specifically the allegory, a genre in which Addison excelled and which was at the heart of the *Spectator*'s reformist project. This came to light when they were asked to comment upon the famous 'Vision of Mirza'. On this occasion, George Polier de Botens, the rector of the Academy of Lausanne expressed his iconoclasm and his mixed feelings towards such visual teaching.

> "Il est surprenant que les Hommes aient besoin de ces images pour se rappeler ces idées, ils n'auroient qu'à considérer les événemens qui se passent sous leurs yeux. [...] Je remarque que les images ont toujours quelque chose de faux, ce qui fait que je ne les goute pas".[23]

---

21 *Ibid.*

22 *Spectator* no. 10, Monday, March 12, 1711.

23 SCL 59, 11 July 1744, vol. 2, 287–291. <http://lumieres.unil.ch/fiches/trans/511/>.

He, nevertheless, toned down his criticism explaining that such forms of teaching, though unworthy of serious men, were necessary evils likely to instruct other intellectually weak groups.

> Quoique les images ne soient pas toujours fort justes, cependant elles conviennent aux femmes et aux enfans, parce qu'elles frappent leur imagination; elles les ont amusé, on peut les rappeler aisément, et elles inspirent des Sentiments de Vertu. Que l'Histoire soit vraie ou fausse, l'instruction est la même; une leçon suivie ennuieroit les enfans qui sont legers; il faut amener les Gens par diverses voies: ceux qui sont formés, il faut les enseigner d'une manière directe; mais le nombre des personnes légères est le plus grand, il faut donc des images.[24]

No doubt this was intended to warn the future sovereign against the power of images. For this strict—and misogynistic—Calvinist, the allegorical device of turning words into images was a problem because it appealed to the imagination—a force he denounced in another lecture as unreliable and the potential mother of vice[25]—and it revealed human levity. As Mr. De Lignon explained when dealing with Mandeville's *Fable of the Bees*, the lack of clarity of an allegory could lead readers into misunderstanding the true meaning of the text.[26]

A certain condescension towards such a playful method can be detected in his statement. To his mind, this indirect form of instruction made some inferior reading not worthy of such an assembly and of a thoroughly educated prince. This opinion was probably shared by some of the members of the Societé, for on that day attendance was low. There were 6 men present out of 12 and only 3 of them were willing to comment. One left the session before the Vision of Mirza was read and the two others, the Baron de Caussade and Jacques Bibaud de Lignon (the founder of the learned journal la *Bibliothèque italique*), simply declined to discuss the text. A week later, the summary the Count made was therefore exceptionally short, and yet it showed that he had understood the dual lesson that the content of the allegory and the comments on the allegory had taught him. He highlighted the drawbacks for a ruler to instruct by means of allegories. And he signaled the essential point of Addison's lesson: that even for a prince, life was full of traps and pitfalls, especially for the ungodly:

24 *Ibid.*

25 SCL 65, 26 September 1744, vol. 2, 313–328. <http://lumieres.unil.ch/fiches/trans/521/>, imagination is both a source of error.

26 SCL 36, 18 January 1744, vol. 2, 41–54. <http://lumieres.unil.ch/fiches/trans/472/>.

> Vous avez observé, Messieurs, que cette méthode de représenter des vérités sous des images, quoiqu'elle n'ait pas toujours bien de la justesse, est cependant utile pour attirer l'attention des personnes qui ont l'esprit leger, et que les vérités que renferme l'Allégorie de notre Auteur sont du nombre de celles qu'on ne devroit jamais perdre de vue.[27]

Thus, we may observe that this particular essay, which was greatly admired in England and which helped Joseph Addison gain his reputation as a great writer, was merely viewed by this learned circle as a pleasant and facile moral text. It also reveals that on the continent, despite the esteem the members of this club held for the two periodicals and their authors, the *Spectateur* was far from considered a canonical text whose maxims should be revered.[28] Paradoxically, educating through visual and fictional entertainment, a pedagogical method that was central to Addison's periodical venture, was disregarded and replaced by a narrower and strictly verbal form of instruction. Did this mean that Addison's project was misunderstood?

This consideration leads us, therefore, to raise a final question. What does the use and interpretation of the periodicals reveal about the way Addison was perceived by the members of the Société du Comte de la Lippe?

Addison's standing in Lausanne

Firstly, it seems to confirm that such moral and didactic use of the *Spectator* and *Guardian* became increasingly connected with Addison as the eighteenth century drew to a close. It is striking that out of the ten essays chosen by la Société du Comte de la Lippe, nine were by Addison.

Indeed, an anecdote reveals that, for the Société, it was Addison and not Steele who was believed to be the author of the more serious and profound *Spectator* essays.[29] On May 16, 1744, the assembly commented upon an essay on the

27 SCL 60, 18 July 1744, vol. 2, 291–295. <http://lumieres.unil.ch/fiches/trans/512/>.

28 This is echoed by la *Réduction du Spectateur anglois*, an abridged translation of the *Spectator* published in Paris in 1753. The translator wrote: "D'ailleurs j'avoue ingénument que malgré toute la vénération que j'ai pour le Spectateur, je ne l'envisage pas tout à fait sur le pied de l'Apocalypse dont il n'est pas permis de retrancher une syllabe & et je m'assure que les gens sensés de sa Nation seront de mon avis", xvij.

29 In fact, it is quite striking that the members of the Société hardly named the authors of the essays they read. They either mentioned the *Spectateur* or 'the Author'. Of course they must have known that Addison and Steele were the main contributors, since they read the 1731 edition of the *Spectateur ou Socrate moderne*. In the preface of the *Spectateur*, the translator revealed the identity of both writers and indicated that Addison had signed his essays with one of the letters forming the name CLIO. As for the *Mentor*, Van Effen revealed the identity of the authors on the title page of the book.

benefits of travelling for young people and some members attributed the authorship of the text to Addison, arguing that the essay was the fruit of experience.

> On peut tirer parti du Discours de Mr Addisson sur les Voiages; a dit Monsieur le Lieutenant Baillival DeBochat, parce qu'il a voiagé. […] Ce que dit Mr Addisson qu'il faut examiner les lieux dont parle l'Histoire, que cette vue anime, et porte à faire des efforts pour ressembler aux personnes qui se sont rendues illustres dans ces divers endroits, cela est certain ; mais il faut avoir ces endroits des Historiens bien présens à l'esprit. Mr Addisson a voiagé dans ce gout.[30]

The Baron de Caussade, who also debated on this topic, was to approve this argument as well as the identification. Yet, as the 1731 edition of the *Spectateur* signals, the essay was signed with a capital T, which shows that it was Richard Steele who had written it, an authorship confirmed by D. F. Bond in his seminal edition of the *Spectator.* Obviously, the members of the Société du Comte de la Lippe had neglected this detail and had been misled by the content of the essay, as well as by their knowledge of the life of Addison.

For we may infer from de Bochat's statement that these learned men had read Addison's *Remarks on Several Parts of Italy*, either in English or in the French translation—the travel book had been released in 1705 and translated into French in 1722. They, therefore, knew that Addison had undertaken the Grand Tour when he was 27 and had stayed one night in Lausanne in 1703, while he was on his way to Geneva (Addison 1705, 465–466). They knew that he had applied to himself the remarks made in the *Spectator*, according to which travelling was more intellectually valuable and rewarding when done at a mature age—when one could meditate on Ancient Ruins and the classical texts one had read—than when one is young and ignorant. This anecdote thus reveals how famous Addison was as a travel writer and a grand tourist, while also showing how naturally his name was associated with the more thoughtful essays.

Indeed, by identifying Addison as the author of the essays, and by selecting essays that were predominantly moral essays, the Société indirectly featured Addison first and foremost as a wise and experienced man, a moralist and a virtuous pedagogue, a characterisation that was to grow increasingly popular in England and in Europe in the eighteenth century. A book like *Recueil choisi des Traits historiques et de contes moraux* (1799) is a good example of this image of Addison. Offering young readers the didactic examples of various historical figures, it included a significant anecdote about Addison, then on his deathbed, delivering a last lesson to his dissolute step-son the Duke of Wharton

30 SLC 53, 230–231.

by declaring: "Voyez avec quel calme, avec quelle résignation un chrétien peut mourir"[31] (34).

However, what is more unusual here is that beyond the moralist it was paradoxically Addison the politician they had in mind when they associated his writings with such a unique educational venture. Unlike the various reviewers of the French translations of the *Spectator*, who only saw in the periodical a new and pleasant way of teaching morality,[32] they indirectly recalled the highly political nature of Addison's periodicals, making the link between his discourses about Christian morality and the defence of an enlightened political regime.

As Ran Halévy has noted, the fact that the young Count's political training was supervised by a group of intellectuals and not by one single politician already showed how much his political upbringing differed from educational manuals produced for absolutist princes—for instance, Louis XIV's *Mémoires* or even Duguet's (Halévy 2013, 9). Moreover, that the periodical essays should be used as starting points for moral, religious, social or political discussions shows how sensitive continental readers were to the conversational nature of these periodicals and how much they were aware of the political nature of conversation. Besides, by transferring to a prince moral lessons primarily intended for a large middle-class audience, they tacitly acknowledged the centrality of Addison's (Whig) conception of polite education in political and governmental matters. Although the Société's use of the two periodicals seems to restrict the reading of Addison's prose to a very limited and exclusive group of men—and therefore seems to contradict Addison's will to "bring philosophy out of closets and Libraries, Schools and Colleges",[33] it actually does just the reverse. By placing the periodical essays in the hands of a prince, along with other political texts, even in an abridged version, the members of the Société on the contrary made it possible to implement Addison's principles about public opinion, religion or political rule or see them implemented through the will of the future ruler. So one should see in this transformation of the *Spectator* and the *Guardian* into an exclusive princely educational book the ultimate sign of the success of the moderate enlightened principles of conversation defended in the two journals.

---

31 "See in what peace a Christian can die". This anecdote was also reported by Edward Young in *Conjectures on Original Composition, in a Letter to the Author of Sir Charles Grandison*, London 1759, 103-104.

32 Read, for instance, Jean Leclerc's review of the first volume of *Le Spectateur ou le Socrate moderne* in *La Bibliothèque ancienne et moderne*, vol. 1, 1714, 383.

33 *The Spectator* no. 10., vol. 1, 44.

Finally, it is amusing to note that although the evidence of the success of the *Spectator* and *Guardian* was the exact opposite to the signs of success of Fénelon's *Telemachus*, another best-seller—published in 1699—originally written for the exclusive instruction of King Louis XIV's grandson, they shared the same conception of education. Like Addison, Fénelon considered the spiritual and moral training of a prince to be the foundation of the political community maxims that were acknowledged to be universal. This indeed may not have escaped the members of the Société du Comte du la Lippe, for they endeavoured to turn the Comte de la Lippe into a new Telemachus who worked under the guidance of a new Mentor moderne featuring Joseph Addison.

References

"Extrait des conférences de la Société de Monsieur le comte de la Lippe, 1742–1745". In: Béla Kapossy/Danièle Tosato-Rigo/François Rosset (eds.). Lausanne: Lumières. Projet "Société du comte de la Lippe (1742–1747)". Université de Lausanne. <http://lumieres.unil.ch/projets/>

ADDISON, Joseph: *Remarks on several Parts of Italy &c, in the Years 1701, 1702, 1703*. London: Jacob Tonson 1705.

ALIMENTO, Antonella: "L'Institution d'un prince de l'abbé Duguet". In: *L'Institution du Prince au XVIIIe siècle*. Actes du 8ème colloque franco-Italien organisé par Catherine Vohlpilhac en 1999. Centre international d'études du XVIIIe siècle: Ferney Voltaire 2003, 104–114.

ANON: *La Bibliothèque ancienne et moderne*. La Haye: Husson 1714, Vol. 1.

ANON: *Recueil choisi de Traits historiques et de contes moraux*. London: J. Johnson 1799.

BOIS, Jean-Pierre: *L'Abbé de St Pierre: Entre Classicisme et Lumières*. Ceizérieu: ChampVallon 2017.

BOND, Donald F. (ed.): *The Spectator*. Oxford: Clarendon Press 1987 [1965], 5 vols.

CHOPELIN-BLANC, Caroline: "*L'Institution d'un Prince* de Duguet, un traité d'éducation à la charnière des XVIIe et XVIIIe siècles: Entre programme de formation et idéal de cité chrétienne". In: *Chrétiens et sociétés.* [En ligne], 18 (2011). https://journals.openedition.org/chretienssocietes/2972>.

DORNIER, Carole (ed.): *Les Projets de l'abbé Castel de Saint Pierre (1658–1743). Pour le plus grand bonheur du plus grand nombre*. Caen: Presses Universitaires de Caen 2011.

DUGUET, Jacques-Joseph: *Institution d'un Prince ou traité des qualitez, des vertus et des devoirs et des devoirs d'un souverain (1739)*. Londres: Jean Nourse 1743.

HALÉVY, Ran: "L'Education du prince absolu". In: Béla Kapossy/Daniele Tosato-Rigo/François Rosset (eds.): *L'Europe en province: la Société du comte de la Lippe (1743–1747). Actes du colloque organisé à l'Université de Lausanne du 25 au 26 juin 2009*. Lausanne: Lumières 2013. <http://lumieres.unil.ch/fiches/biblio/5738/>

HUGUENIN, Séverine: "La Société du Comte de la Lippe entre éducation et société savante". In: Béla Kapossy/Danièle Tosato-Rigo/François Rosset (eds.): *L'Europe en province: la Société du comte de la Lippe (1743–1747). Actes du colloque organisé à l'Université de Lausanne du 25 au 26 juin 2009*. Lausanne: Lumières 2013. < *in 2009*. Lausanne: Lumières 2013. http://lumieres.unil.ch/fiches/biblio/5608/>

Le Mentor Moderne ou Discours sur les moeurs de ce siècle traduit de l'anglois du Guardian. Amsterdam: Pierre Humbert 1727.

Le Spectateur ou le Socrate moderne. Amsterdam: David Mortier: 1714–26, 6 vols.

ROSSET, François: "La littérature: tache aveugle dans les conférences du comte de la Lippe". In: Béla Kapossy/Danièle Tosato-Rigo/François Rosset (eds.): *L'Europe en province: la Société du comte de la Lippe (1743–1747). Actes du colloque organisé à l'Université de Lausanne du 25 au 26 juin 2009*. Lausanne: Lumières 2013. http://lumieres.unil.ch/fiches/biblio/5685/ >.

STEPHENS, John Calhoun (ed.): *The Guardian*. Kentucky: The University Press of Kentucky 1985.

YOUNG, Edward: *Conjectures on Original Composition, in a Letter to the Author of Sir Charles Grandison*. London: A. Miller 1759.

Die Aufklärung in der Romania
Lumières - Ilustración - Illuminismo

Herausgegeben von Klaus-Dieter Ertler

Band 1 Klaus-Dieter Ertler / Jessica Köhldorfer: Die *Spectators* in Spanien. *El Duende Especulativo sobre la Vida Civil* von Juan Antonio Mercadàl. 2010.

Band 2 Juan Antonio Mercadàl: *El Duende Especulativo sobre la Vida Civil. Editado por Klaus-Dieter Ertler.* 2011.

Band 3 Klaus-Dieter Ertler (Hrsg.): Die *Spectators* in der Romania - eine transkulturelle Gattung? 2011.

Band 4 Klaus-Dieter Ertler / Elisabeth Hobisch / Andrea Maria Humpl: Die spanischen *Spectators* im Überblick. 2012.

Band 5 Klaus-Dieter Ertler / Alexis Lévrier / Michaela Fischer (éds.): Regards sur les "spectateurs". Periodical Essay - Feuilles volantes - Moralische Wochenschriften - Fogli moralistici - Prensa moral. 2012.

Band 6 Klaus-Dieter Ertler / Elisabeth Hobisch: Die *Spectators* in Spanien. Die kleinen Schriften der 1760er Jahre. *El Murmurador imparcial. El Amigo y Corresponsal del Pensador. El Escritor sin Título. El Belianís literario.* 2014.

Band 7 Klaus-Dieter Ertler / Elisabeth Hobisch / Andrea Maria Humpl: Die *Spectators* in Spanien. Die kleinen Schriften der 1780er Jahre. *La Pensatriz salmantina. El Curioso Entretenido. El Apologista Universal. El Corresponsal del Apologista. El Teniente del Apologista Universal. El Duende de Madrid. El Observador. El Argonauta Español.* 2014.

Band 8 Michaela Fischer: Die Figur des Lesers im Kommunikationssystem der Spectateurs. 2014.

Band 9 Alexandra Fuchs: Spuren der Moralischen Presse im Erzählwerk von Antonio Piazza. 2016.

Band 10 Elisabeth Hobisch: La forma epistolar en los espectadores españoles. Características y tipología de las cartas. 2017.

Band 11 Michaela Fischer-Pernkopf / Veronika Mussner / Klaus-Dieter Ertler: Die Spectators in Frankreich. 2018.

Band 12 Hans Fernández / Pascal Striedner: Bento Morganti. Collecçam dos Papeis Anonymos. 2019.

Band 13 Klaus-Dieter Ertler / Yvonne Völkl / Elisabeth Hobisch / Alexandra Fuchs / Hans Fernández (eds.): Storytelling in the Spectators / Storytelling dans les spectateurs. 2020.

Band 14 Klaus-Dieter Ertler / Elisabeth Hobisch / Ellen Krefting (eds.): La Spectatrice danoise de La Beaumelle. 2020.

Band 15 Claire Boulard Jouslin / Klaus-Dieter Ertler (eds.): Addison and Europe / Addison et l'Europe. 2020.

www.peterlang.com

www.ingramcontent.com/pod-product-compliance
Lightning Source LLC
Chambersburg PA
CBHW060611310726
48982CB00003B/526
* 9 7 8 3 6 3 1 8 1 3 5 9 1 *